Juveniles' Waiver of Rights

LEGAL AND PSYCHOLOGICAL COMPETENCE

Perspectives in Law & Psychology

Series Editor: **BRUCE DENNIS SALES,** *University of Nebraska, Lincoln*

Volume 1	**THE CRIMINAL JUSTICE SYSTEM** Edited by Bruce Dennis Sales
Volume 2	**THE TRIAL PROCESS** Edited by Bruce Dennis Sales
Volume 3	**JUVENILES' WAIVER OF RIGHTS** **Legal and Psychological Competence** Thomas Grisso
Volume 4	**MENTAL HEALTH LAW: Major Issues** David B. Wexler

Juveniles' Waiver of Rights

LEGAL AND PSYCHOLOGICAL COMPETENCE

Thomas Grisso

St. Louis University
St. Louis, Missouri

PLENUM PRESS · NEW YORK AND LONDON

Library of Congress Cataloging in Publication Data

Grisso, Thomas.
Juveniles' waiver of rights.

(Perspectives in law and psychology; v. 3)
Bibliography: p.
Includes index.
1. Right to counsel–United States. 2. Confession (Law)–United States. 3. Juvenile justice, Administration of–United States. 4. Criminal psychology. I. Title. II. Series.
KF9813.G74 345.73'087 80-20488
ISBN 978-1-4684-3817-8 ISBN 978-1-4684-3815-4 (eBook)
DOI 10.1007/978-1-4684-3815-4

Softcover reprint of the hardcover 1st edition 1981
A Division of Plenum Publishing Corporation
227 West 17th Street, New York, N.Y. 10011

To my Parents

To my Parents

Preface

The research studies reported in this book were completed between June, 1976 and November, 1979, with a USPHS research grant (MH-27849) from the Center for Studies of Crime and Delinquency, National Institute of Mental Health. Every phase of the project was an exercise in combining the research methods of psychology with the concerns of law, legal systems, and legal process.

Research psychologists will be especially interested in our efforts to apply psychological constructs and research methods to a difficult decision-making problem in law. This report describes in some detail the project's development of experimental measures of psychological conditions related to legal standards and demonstrates the ways in which research design was influenced by concerns of law and the juvenile justice system.

Lawyers, judges, and youth advocate groups have already expressed considerable interest in the implications of the project's results for the formation and modification of juvenile law and procedure. In each chapter, I have attempted to describe carefully the ways in which the empirical research results are applicable to these concerns, and I have tried to specify the limits which must be acknowledged in interpreting the results for application in the legal process.

Writing a book to be read and used by both lawyers and psychologists has been a difficult task. The very different needs, interests, and perspectives of lawyers and social scientists frequently required compromises between that which would have been written for either audience alone. If I have succeeded at all in communicating adequately to both professions, it is in large part because of the insight and conceptual skills of Bruce Dennis Sales, the editor of this series. His tireless guidance, direct yet always sensitive, often provided the alternative organization, thought, or wording which was needed. I am indebted to several other lawyers and psychologists for their reviews and comments on the initial drafts of one or more of the chapters: Jeanette Ganousis, Jesse Goldner, David Howard, Eugene Kissling, and David Munz.

Concerning the research project itself, my acknowledgments must be extensive because of the large number of people, agencies, and organizations who contributed directly to the work.

The interest and open-mindedness of administrators at the St. Louis County Juvenile Court were crucial for the completion of the project. Throughout two years of nearly daily contact with court staff and detention center personnel, the research staff experienced congenial support in the process of data collection. This was manifested in material ways such as the provision of a private research office in the court building, and in more personal ways through the exchange of ideas and perspectives. Access to adult ex-offenders was possible through the cooperation of the Magdala Foundation, a system of halfway houses for ex-offenders. Psychologist Warren Cass and the house directors of Magdala contributed greatly to our ability to obtain an adult sample with which to compare the abilities of juveniles in the study. I must acknowledge anonymously the helpfulness of the administrators and parent associations of a middle school and a high school, and the administrators and staffs of a school for delinquent youths and a boys town.

Among the project personnel, Eugene Kissling, my colleague and co-investigator for two of the project years, played a critical role in establishing and maintaining the project's relationships with the juvenile court. It was also through him that the topic of juveniles' competence to waive rights was identified as deserving of experimental study. A doctoral dissertation by Sam Manoogian provided the background and pilot studies for the project. For two years, Carolyn Pomicter, in her role as research associate, expertly managed the administrative details of data collection at the juvenile court. Eleven research assistants in psychology graduate studies at St. Louis University served the project at different times during its three years: Patricia Anderten, Lindsey Breeden, Pamela Casey, Thomas Lovinguth, John MacDonnell, Robert Neems, Ronald Peal, Melissa Ring, Valerie Staulcup, Rachel Tomkins, and Linda Vierling. Their degree of involvement in all phases of the research made the project as much theirs as mine.

Lawyers at the National Juvenile Law Center—especially Jeanette Ganousis, David Howard, Paul Piersma, and Harry Swanger—and the legal consultation of Jesse Goldner and Corinne Goodman contributed to the project at every stage from initial conceptualization to interpretation of the results. Important consultation on research methodology was received from David Munz.

Any work of this type owes much to the less tangible support and encouragement of friends, among whom the most important to me has been my wife, Donna. Finally, I thank my colleagues in St. Louis University's Psychology Department for providing a sense of community and cooperative achievement, a most fortunate milieu within which to work.

THOMAS GRISSO

St. Louis, Missouri

Contents

1

Introduction

Apart from the conditions which led to the formation of the juvenile justice system early in this century, there is no single event which has had as much impact on its present form as Justice Fortas's opinion for the majority in *In re Gault,* 387 U.S. 1 (1967). Juveniles deserve more, he said, than a "kangaroo court." "Neither the Fourteenth Amendment nor the Bill of Rights is for adults alone" (at 13); the Court decided that juveniles should have the same general due process protections in court proceedings as do adults.

Two of the due process issues which were at the heart of this case were the Constitutional rights to counsel and against self-incrimination. Gerald Gault, a 15-year-old, was facing the prospect of six years of incarceration because an Arizona court had determined that he had made obscene phone calls. The Supreme Court ruled that his confession was improperly used as evidence at his trial hearing, in that he had not been warned that he was not required to answer questions posed to him by legal authorities or that he had a right to legal counsel at critical stages of the legal process.

To understand the enormous impact of this decision on the juvenile justice system, at least three broad observations must be made. First, the ruling drew widespread disapproval from juvenile courts because of apparent incongruities between rigid due process protections and the prevailing philosophy and form of a more than 60-year tradition of juvenile justice. Second, the decision led the way for subsequent rulings on other due process protections in juvenile cases, several of which established an increasing number of procedural restrictions. Third, many post-*Gault* courts of appeal were persuaded that because of the relative immaturity of juveniles, due process protection of juveniles' "new" rights required special considerations which had not been typical in adult criminal procedures. Ways of assuring due process could not merely be borrowed from criminal court procedure, but must be modified to take into consideration the inherent social, emotional, and psychological characteristics of juveniles.

The last of these three results is central to this book. Specifically, adults' capacities to decide regarding these important rights have generally been presumed; but since *Gault* this presumption has been challenged continuously in juvenile cases. Later in this chapter we will develop this problem more completely, since it defines the area of law to which the research results reported in this book are related. But to understand the problem, we must first briefly review the history of the juvenile justice system, as well as the major court rulings which challenged its traditional philosophy and precipitated the legal questions whnih we determined to address through empirical research methods.

THE BEGINNING OF THE JUVENILE COURT

The decision in the late nineteenth century to establish a separate justice system for errant juveniles was a product of three developments spanning several prior centuries: (1) changing conceptualizations of childhood; (2) new explanations for the deviant behavior of children; and (3) definitions of the relationship between the state, the family, and the child.[1]

Western societies' views of what a child is—socially, emotionally, and intellectually—underwent considerable change from the seventeenth to the late nineteenth centuries. Earlier conceptualizations made very few distinctions between younger and older children, except that children past the age of seven were viewed as capable of discerning right from wrong. The modern view of childhood as a process of development—a time when a person is prepared for adulthood—emerged early in this period (Aries, 1962). Yet it was not until the ideas of G. Stanley Hall in the late nineteenth century that the period of

[1]The observations in this section have been reiterated and examined in greater detail by many authors. Since these historical matters are so generally accepted and described, they are not cited in the text. Material for this section was drawn from the following sources, any of which will provide the reader with greater depth in the historical and philosophical underpinnings of the juvenile justice system: Cicourel, 1968; Empey, 1976; Platt, 1969; Schlossman, 1977; Stapleton and Teitelbaum, 1972.

adolescence was set aside as a developmental stage distinct from both adulthood and early childhood (Ross, 1974).

Our view of children's deviant behavior has also changed. Interpreting children's misbehavior as a consequence of their naturally sinful nature, Puritan colonists responded with harsh punishments and preventive measures including education steeped in moralism and the message of control by authority. In successive centuries, through the nineteenth, children above the age of seven who committed crimes were dealt with by the courts in the same manner as were adults, except that the matter of criminal responsibility was rebuttably presumed between ages seven and fourteen. Our views of the causes of crime, however, were gradually transformed, so that explanations based on sin gave way to deterministic positivism. That is, crime came to be viewed as the consequence of social conditions or as the developmental consequence of inadequate child-rearing, poverty and deprivation, or other social misfortunes. As a consequence, the nineteenth century saw the development of rehabilitation and social reform in dealing with crime and criminals, efforts which had not logically followed from the earlier identification of crime with a condition of the soul.

A third factor contributing to the development of juvenile courts was the nineteenth century interpretation of the doctrine of *parens patriae*. This concept originated in medieval English law. It served to justify the intervention of the state as a superior parent, when the economic value of a child to a feudal landowner was threatened by the inability of the child's parents to raise the child properly. Nineteenth-century American courts borrowed the *parens patriae* doctrine, empowering the courts to separate parent and child when this was justified for the welfare of the child and the state. Under this doctrine, the courts placed wayward and criminal children in the reformatories and other institutions which developed during the nineteenth century, in response to the enlightened developmental and positivistic views of children and their deviant behavior. This growing "humanitarian" concern also contributed to statutes providing for the apprehension of children who had committed no crimes, but whose general conduct or lack of parental guidance could be construed (however vaguely) as precursors to potential disobedience.

By the late 1800s, then, society and the law had identified children and adolescents as persons in need of special attention because of characteristics specific to their developmental stages. Criminal behavior by juveniles was thought to be the consequence of unfortunate upbringing or social conditions, not merely malevolent intent, and the formative nature of children offered the potential for rehabilitation. It was felt that the State itself should provide this rehabilitation, acting as the benevolent and guiding parent in place of the natural parent under whose custody the juvenile had gone astray.

These ideas were the basis for the development of juvenile courts and a separate legal system for juveniles, most of which took form between 1899 and 1925. In philosophy, the new courts were an extreme departure from the criminal justice system within which criminal cases involving juveniles had formerly been tried. Juvenile courts were to be relatively unconcerned with the crime itself, and were designed to protect juveniles from the adversarial and harsh nature of sentencing and punishment. The approach of the juvenile court was clinical, involving the determination of those factors which had produced difficulty in a juvenile's life, with emphasis being placed on the provision of treatment or other modifying circumstances which would set the juvenile on a productive course toward adulthood.

In exchange for this benevolence, juveniles were to be deprived of the due process which is provided in criminal cases. It was reasoned that lawbreaking by juveniles was now to be treated as a matter of civil rather than criminal law; this, in conjunction with the parental stance of the juvenile court in providing for the child's needs (instead of merely punishing), provided the legal justification for withholding of due process protections. There was no need for defense attorneys or formal hearings in a system given to nurturance of the child. Such matters, more typical of adversial systems, would only hinder the court in its benevolent relationship to the child and hinder the child in accepting the treatment to be provided.

THE IMPACT OF *GAULT*

It was this trade-off—the foregoing of due process in juvenile courts in return for benevolent treatment—with which the Supreme Court took issue in *Kent* v. *United States*, 383 U.S. 541 (1966) and *In re Gault*, 387 U.S. 1 (1967). In the former case, the court had ruled that hearings on the issue of a juvenile's transfer to an adult criminal court for trial "must measure up to the essentials of due process and fair treatment" (at 562). This case established that the Fourteenth Amendment to the United States Constitution could be applied to the juvenile court. The ruling, however, was confined to a specific and relatively infrequent type of hearing, so it did not have the impact of *Gault*. But the basis for the majority opinions was the same in both cases. Juvenile courts had failed to deliver on their promise of treatment, and instead were merely providing punishment in the form of training schools or other types of incarceration. Whenever juvenile proceedings could lead to confinement, the Court said in *Gault*, "it would be extraordinary if our Constitution did not require the procedural regularity and exercise of care implied in the phrase 'due process'" (at 27–28). Therefore, the Court found that juveniles in adjudicatory hearings have a valid claim to adequate notice, to legal counsel, to the privilege against self-incrimination, and to confront and cross-examine opposing witnesses.

Justice Fortas's opinion for the majority in *Gault* was strong in its pronouncement of the failure of juvenile courts to provide treatment, the consequent burden of juvenile courts to prove the necessity of their jurisdiction over juveniles, and the importance of the opportunity for juveniles to have a strong legal defense in the hands of counsel. But it is important to note that the decision in *Gault* was not a denunciation of the juvenile justice system as a whole, nor of the need for a special legal system for juveniles. Justice Fortas specifically stated that the Court was not considering "the impact of these Constitutional provisions upon the totality of the relationship between the juvenile and the state" (at 13). Nor did the Court intend that juvenile proceedings be patterned after criminal proceedings; Justice Fortas repeated the Court's earlier message in *Kent*, that "We do not mean . . . to indicate that the hearing to be held must conform with all of the requirements of a criminal trial or even the usual administrative hearing" (at 30).

Thus, juvenile courts were still to operate in the best interests of juveniles and with consideration for the special needs and characteristics of youthful offenders, as the nineteenth-century founders had proposed. But if it could provide nothing more than confinement, its role as *parens patriae* must be restricted by the formal protections of due process. Both *Kent* and *Gault* denied that due process would hinder the provision of rehabilitation and treatment when it was available.

There have been two major difficulties in applying *Gault* to juvenile court proceedings. First, while most juvenile courts complied with the Constitutional requirements provided through *Gault*, they tend not to have complied in a manner consistent with the intent of those requirements (Nejelski, 1976). For example, public defenders are generally far more available to juveniles now than in pre-*Gault* years. But the public defender in many juvenile courts functions in cooperation with court personnel and as an adjunct court staff member (Emerson, 1969; Stapleton & Teitelbaum, 1972). Similarly, although juveniles usually are warned of the right to silence in police interrogations, such warnings generally are not required in pretrial interviews with probation officers

(Piersma, Ganousis, Volenik, Swanger, & Connell, 1977), even though the probation officer frequently provides testimony in court hearings based on his or her contact with the juvenile. Both of these situations prevail because of the juvenile court's continued philosophical commitment to do what is in the best interests of children. Thus, the adversarial position of the defense lawyer has been a difficult role for most public defenders to maintain (Emerson, 1969) and juvenile court judges have tended to look aside when rigid interpretations of the right to silence could be construed as running counter to the counseling and welfare function of probation officers. Furthermore, ambiguity regarding the application of due process to juvenile proceedings was increased by subsequent Supreme Court decisions. For example, while *Gault* had suggested the need for adversarial-like vigor in the defense of juveniles, the Court in *McKeiver* v. *Pennsylvania,* 403 U.S. 538 (1971) withheld the right to jury trials from juveniles, stating in the opinion that the informal, nonadversarial quality of juvenile hearings was as asset of the juvenile justice system.

A second difficulty has been that of deciding how to render due process in a manner which is sensitive to the special cognitive, emotional, and social characteristics of children. In *Gault,* the court recognized that the Constitutional rights of juveniles might need to be protected by different procedures than those employed with adult defendants in the criminal justice system. Justice Fortas, justifying the need to extend to juveniles the rights to counsel and against self-incrimination, commented on their greater vulnerability in relation to the question of voluntariness of a confession. Never discussed, however, was the rationale for believing that juveniles would be less vulnerable merely because juvenile courts were required to inform them of these rights. For example, there was no inquiry into possible differences between juveniles and adults in their abilities to make free and informed choices regarding the rights to silence and counsel. *Gault* left these questions unanswered.

Moreover, it is not surprising that the issue of how the rights to silence and counsel would be applied in juvenile courts became a center of controversy and resulted in a large volume of court appeals in the years following *Gault.* At what stages of the court process were juveniles to have these rights or to be informed of them? Under what circumstances would a juvenile's waiver of these rights be viewed as free and informed? Were there juveniles who were not competent to waive their rights? What special procedures might be necessary to assure that a juvenile's waiver met the standards for a valid waiver? Let us examine the leading cases which addressed these questions.

MIRANDA TO *WEST*[2]

One year prior to *Gault*, the Supreme Court had held in *Miranda* v. *Arizona*, 384 U.S. 436 (1966) that suspects must be provided certain warnings prior to any interrogation. These warnings informed suspects of the right to silence, the potential for use of their statements in later court proceedings, the right to legal counsel prior to interrogation, and the availability of free legal counsel. Confessions could be validly admitted as evidence in later court proceedings only if the suspect had been so warned and if the suspect had waived these rights "voluntarily, knowingly, and intelligently." *Miranda* was an adult case, and the ruling applied to police interrogations and other important stages of the accusatory process.

The Court in *Gault*, although approving the use of *Miranda* warnings, confined itself to a consideration of due process at the stage of adjudication—the formal delinquency hearing. But almost all post-*Gault* courts addressing the issue concluded that the rights to silence and counsel applied at preadjudicatory stages for juveniles just as for adults (see Piersma *et al.*, 1977). Thus, a juvenile's confession to police could not be used in an adjudication hearing unless the rights had been waived prior to police interrogation.

But are juveniles capable of waiving rights in accordance with the voluntary, knowing, and intelligent standard? The leading case addressing this question came in the same year as *Gault*. In *People* v. *Lara*, 432 P.2d 202 (1967), the California Supreme Court ruled that the mere fact of being a juvenile did not invalidate a waiver of rights. The *Lara* Court recognized that some juveniles might not have the intellectual or emotional characteristics required to satisfy the standard for valid waiver set forth in *Miranda*. But the validity of a juvenile's waiver was not to be determined on the basis of any single factor alone—for example, age or intelligence. Instead, each case would have to be decided in light of the "totality of circumstances" in the case. The vast majority of subsequent cases testing the validity of juveniles' waiver of rights have adopted the "totality of circumstances" approach.

This approach was consistent with the traditional concern in juvenile court philosophy to treat each juvenile according to his or her own particular characteristics and needs. On the other hand, juvenile

[2]This section is a general overview of only the major cases relevant to juveniles' waiver of *Miranda* rights. The issues raised here are discussed in greater detail in subsequent chapters, and comprehensive legal reviews relevant to each of these issues are provided in those later chapters.

court judges were entirely without any guidelines concerning the relevant circumstances to be weighed. Police officers, already beset with the difficulties of instigating new procedures required for juvenile interrogations, had no way to decide whether a given juvenile in their custody might present "circumstances" which would lead to the later exclusion of a confession.

A federal court in *West* v. *United States,* 399 F.2d 467 (1968) attempted to remedy this situation by providing a list of considerations to be weighed when applying the "totality of circumstances" test. Among the nine considerations were some pertaining to characteristics of juveniles themselves (e.g., age and education), and others focusing on the situation of interrogation (e.g., whether the juvenile had been allowed to consult with relatives, friends, or an attorney). The list in *West* at least provided a place for juvenile court judges to start in their deliberations, and thus, *West* was cited in many subsequent cases.

The Court in *West,* however, had purposely left open certain questions about how the variables in this list were to be used. In keeping with *Lara,* no single age and no given combination of any specific factors was to be construed as suggesting an invalid waiver. Juvenile court judges since *West* have had to use the variables in whatever way they could, without empirical knowledge of the ways in which the various characteristics of juveniles or interrogation situations might influence a juvenile's ability to provide a voluntary, knowing, and intelligent waiver. We will see in a subsequent chapter that many judges turned to intelligence test scores and the courtroom testimony of mental health professionals in order better to address the question of juveniles' capacities to understand the *Miranda* warnings. But the relationship, if any, between a valid waiver of rights and an intelligence test score or mental condition has been largely a matter of speculation.

THE RESEARCH PROJECT AND OUTLINE OF THE BOOK

The issues addressed in *Lara* and *West* set the stage for many of our studies which are reported in the following chapters. The research aim was to provide empirical information with which police, lawyers, judges, and legislative lawmakers could address the question of juveniles' competence to waive *Miranda* rights. In general terms, the research sought to establish relationships of various demographic and intellectual characteristics of juveniles with measures of their understanding of the meaning and significance of the rights to silence and counsel.

The research was viewed as both descriptive and hypothesis testing. Descriptively, the relationships could provide decision makers in the juvenile justice system with more specific guidelines to be used in the process of determining which juveniles could meet the legal standard for valid waiver. To state here what will be said often in subsequent chapters, it was not assumed that this research would produce a "formula" for decision making or could replace the need for judicial discretion. Instead, the intent was to provide an empirical base concerning juveniles' capacities, which could be applied by decision makers who must weigh those factors in combination with social and philosophical considerations which are beyond the purview of empirical research methods.

But the studies were also hypothesis-testing in nature. Across twelve years of relevant appellate cases since *Gault*, a very large number of judges have expressed in case opinions the reasons for their decisions to accept or invalidate juveniles' waivers of their rights. Their reasoning has often revealed their assumptions about the ways in which various characteristics of juveniles are related to their competence to waive rights. Viewed collectively, these assumptions can be conceptualized as hypothetical relationships. Therefore, after describing relationships between juveniles' waiver competencies and their demographic characteristics, our research results could be compared to judicial assumptions—essentially, to test the hypotheses derived from past judicial opinions.

As an applied research effort, it was essential that the research be conceptualized in terms which were relevant to the existing law, legal system, and legal process. Chapters 2 and 3 reflect that objective. Chapter 2 reviews existing literature concerning the role of interrogation in police and court practice in juvenile cases, and describes a study of the circumstances of juvenile interrogation and waiver of rights in one large juvenile court jurisdiction. Chapter 3 describes the process by which legal standards for competence to waive rights were translated into behaviors which could be studied with behavioral science research methods. This chapter also describes the construction of the experimental measures which were used in subsequent studies to assess juveniles' understanding and perceptions relevant to rights waiver.

Chapters 4 and 5 are central to the book, reporting results of experimental studies which measure juveniles' (Chap. 4) and adults' (Chap. 5) abilities to understand the standard *Miranda* warnings. Chapter 5 also includes a comparison of juveniles' and adults' abilities to comprehend the warnings. A comprehensive legal review of relevant appellate cases is provided in Chapter 4, from which a summary of judicial assumptions about juveniles' *Miranda* comprehension is derived.

Chapters 6 and 7 report our studies of juveniles' perceptions of *Miranda* rights in the context of the legal system and legal process. The study in Chapter 6 focuses on juveniles' understanding of the function and significance of the rights in light of their perceptions of the roles of police, defense attorneys, and judges. In Chapter 7, an exploratory study is directed toward understanding the reasoning which juveniles employ when considering whether or not to waive their rights to silence and counsel. Special attention is given to the consequences which they expect will follow the various choices they might make in response to the *Miranda* warnings.

Chapter 8 addresses the question of parents' capacities to provide meaningful advice and protection to their children by their presence at the interrogation. This has been a very active issue in legal cases concerning the validity of juvenile waiver. Those cases are reviewed, followed by the results of two relevant studies. In the first, we examine the attitudes of parents toward the rights of juveniles. The second study documents the communications between parents and their children during the waiver decision prior to actual police interrogations.

Chapter 9 synthesizes the results of the foregoing studies and directs them toward policy issues. Existing procedures for protecting juveniles' rights in pretrial interrogation are examined for their adequacy in light of the research findings, and the results are applied to recommendations and proposals which might satisfy the intent of *Gault* as well as the welfare mission of the juvenile court.

2

The Role of Interrogation in Juvenile Justice

The popular image of the interrogation of a criminal suspect probably derives in large part from television dramas. It begins with a police officer frisking a suspect who is leaning forward against an auto with his arms and legs spread wide, while another officer mechanically reads aloud the *Miranda* warnings: "You do not have to make a statement and have the right to remain silent. Anything you say can and will be used against you in a court of law. You are entitled to consult with an attorney before interrogation and to have an attorney present during the interrogation. If you cannot afford an attorney, one will be appointed for you."[1]

One imagines that after a ride to the police station, the arrested suspect is taken to an austere room where, with a bright light shining in his eyes, he bears the discomforts of an officer who endeavors to extract a confession. The purpose of this ritual, one assumes, is to assure that justice is done by obtaining evidence which will secure a guilty verdict when the case is heard by judge and jury. The image may include considerable verbal insistence by the police officer, and one's imagination will often add to the picture some physical abuse, or threat of it, by the police.

With regard to the interrogation of most juveniles, this perspective

[1]The U.S. Supreme Court in *Miranda* required that suspects be informed of each of these elements. The wording, however, may vary slightly in different jurisdictions.

is inaccurate in many respects. But most importantly, it is simply far too simplistic to provide a necessary understanding of the extraordinary significance which questioning and confessions can have in the investigation and processing of juvenile cases. Juveniles can be (and often are) questioned about their alleged illegal involvements at nearly every stage of the legal process, from the police encounter to the adjudication hearing at which a judge decides whether to find a juvenile to be delinquent.

In their passage through this legal process, juveniles may find among their questioners not only their parents and the police, but also detention workers, intake or social workers, probation officers, public defenders, court (prosecuting) attorneys, psychologists or psychiatrists, and, of course, the juvenile court judge (Veillard-Cybulska, 1976). The law does not always prescribe the conditions under which confessions to any of these authorities can be admitted as evidence in judicial hearings for deciding the question of delinquency. But what must be understood about juveniles' statements is that both the questioning and the juveniles' responses serve a wide range of functions and purposes in the juvenile justice system, only one of which is the use of a confession at the stage of delinquency adjudication. In fact, the vast majority of juveniles' confessions probably play no role in determining their adjudication as delinquent, even though the confession may significantly alter the outcome of their encounter with the juvenile justice system in other ways.

To understand why this is so, it is important to recognize the importance of discretionary diversion as a police and juvenile court practice. Diversion refers to the practice of offering juveniles certain rehabilitation alternatives in institutions, treatment programs or other community resources at a point early enough in the legal processing of cases to avoid the formal adjudicatory hearing which juveniles would otherwise have received [2] In this way, police and court officers attempt to provide (and to persuade juveniles to accept) hopefully beneficial treatment without the need for a formal hearing. Thus, Nejelski (1976) has noted that for every 200 police contacts with juveniles, only 100 juveniles are arrested and only about 20 of the 100 finally appear before a judge. Many of the remaining 80 who are arrested are offered the alternative to accept treatment services or other rehabilitation programs in lieu of the case being pressed forward to the stage of a formal judicial hearing.

Modern diversion practices, now routine in most juvenile court

[2]For reviews of such diversion programs, see Cressey and McDermott (1973), Lemert (1971), Verenberg and Verenberg (1973), and Zimring (1974).

jurisdictions and some police departments, received strong support from many sources in the 1960s. The President's Commission on Law Enforcement (1967), for example, supported diversion into treatment programs as a means to protect juveniles from the stigmatizing and often punitive dispositions which the Court in *Gault* had acknowledged as being the frequent outcome of formal delinquency hearings.

In spite of the potential positive impact of diversion programs, however, they have become controversial because of their discretionary nature. That is, some observers believe that diversion practices perpetuate the discretionary control over juveniles against which the due process requirements in *Gault* were intended to protect. For example, Nejelski (1976) observed:

> The juvenile justice system has demonstrated considerable adaptability in avoiding the impact of *Gault* and other pressures for increased formalization. After genuflecting to the formalities [required] of the adjudicatory and dispositional hearings, it has delegated decisions to its extremities—police and intake at the beginning, correctional institutions and aftercare agencies at the end. (p. 108)

It is in this context that the role of juvenile interrogation and juveniles' responses to interrogation must be examined. Although juveniles' confessions are valuable for providing evidence for formal adjudication hearings, given present discretionary diversion practices one must examine other effects of juveniles' confessions on their lives—for example, on the decisions of police or court officers to propose diversion alternatives to them, and on juveniles' decisions to accept those alternatives.

The following section examines more specifically what has been written by others about interrogation and interviewing of juveniles by police and court personnel. Many observers of this area of juvenile law have tended to stress the potential for abuse of juveniles' freedoms. Unfortunately, very few have attempted to objectively document the range of relevant police and court practices or to provide data with which to evaluate the extent to which their concerns are grounded in fact.

Following this review, we will present the results of our empirical study of procedures, safeguards, and waiver of *Miranda* rights by juveniles in one juvenile court jurisdiction. Since this juvenile court (St. Louis County) was the site for many of the studies in our project, we will also take the opportunity in this chapter to describe the court itself in terms of its organization, physical properties, types of juvenile cases, and the metropolitan area which it serves.

LAW AND PRACTICE IN THE INTERROGATION OF JUVENILES: AN OVERVIEW

This section is intended for the reader who is relatively unfamiliar with police and juvenile court procedure, for which reason many finer points of law and practice have been omitted. References are provided to more comprehensive works examining police procedures and juvenile court law and practice.

Precustody Questioning

For many juveniles who later find themselves to be the focus of court proceedings, the first attempts by authorities to obtain information from them about their behavior will occur before they have been arrested, or in the terminology of juvenile law, before they are "in custody." Sometimes a police officer's decision to approach a juvenile will be in response to citizen requests to investigate a potential danger. Often, however, street questioning will occur when a police officer on patrol sees a juvenile who is engaging in potentially dangerous behavior or who appears to be behaving in an "improper" way. Certain types of juveniles—blacks, lower-income persons, or juveniles dressed in a manner which police associate with antisocial behavior—are more likely to be noticed and approached for informal questioning by police, because the police believe that these juveniles contribute to a disproportionately high number of crimes (Wilson, 1969).

Depending on local or individual police practice and on the situation, police officers approach this informal questioning by stopping for a few words of casual conversation (sports, cars), requesting personal identification, inquiring where the juvenile has been earlier in the evening and about the juvenile's plans for the remainder of the evening, or checking out neighborhood events. Occasionally they proceed to stronger forms of investigation, such as frisking or radioing the person's identification to the police station to obtain a file check (Kenney & Pursuit, 1970).

The law has allowed considerable discretion to the police as to who they will informally investigate, under what conditions, and with what questions. The Supreme Court in *Terry* v. *Ohio,* 392 U.S. 1 (1968) held that police may stop and informally question at any time their suspicion is aroused, even though existing evidence is insufficient to establish the degree of probable cause which is required to justify arrest. Suspicion can be based merely on the observed demeanor of the suspect (Paulsen

& Whitebread, 1974) or on information obtained from informants.[3] Permissable police discretion in such matters is broadened even further when juveniles are involved; most states have statutory provisions for taking juveniles into custody (therefore permitting precustody questioning on suspicion) not only when they might have been involved in criminal behavior, but also when police officers believe that the juvenile might be leading an idle, dissolute, lewd, or immoral life.

Information offered by the juvenile in precustodial questioning is admissable as evidence in a later court hearing to determine delinquency, even though *Miranda* warnings were not given. The Court's ruling in *Miranda* applies only to custodial interrogations. Thus, in precustodial questioning, confessions are valid when they occur spontaneously or in response to questioning on suspicion, even though the suspect has not been informed of (may not be aware of) the incriminating potential of the information being provided to police officers.[4]

Exactly when police questioning is considered to be custodial (requiring prior *Miranda* warnings) and when it is not has been a difficult question for courts. Generally, courts have defined arrest or "custody" as that point beyond which the suspect was not free to leave the questioning (Piersma *et al.*, 1977). Of course, some suspects assume that they are not free to leave an on-the-scene encounter with police officers even when, in fact, police have made no gesture to prevent an exit. Thus, some courts have added that custodial interrogation may be defined by a suspect's "reasonable belief" that he or she was not free to leave.[5] But generally the question is addressed by weighing circumstances such as the time and place of questioning, the technique of interrogation used, and the demeanor of the interrogators and the suspect.[6] The potential jeopardy associated with the specific questions asked by police has apparently not been a major factor in deciding whether interrogation is custodial. For example, courts have decided that interrogations were not custodial, and therefore required no *Miranda* warnings, in cases where

[3] *Adams* v. *Williams*, 407 U.S. 143 (1972).

[4] *People* v. *Rodney, P.*, 21 N.Y.2d 1, 233 N.E.2d 255, 286 N.Y.S.2d 255 (1967); *In re T.*, 15 Cal. App.3d 886, 93 Cal. Rptr. 510 (1971). Nearly all courts addressing the issue of statements volunteered prior to custody and without *Miranda* warnings have held such statements to be admissable. See *Annot.*, 31 A.L.R.3d 565, 580, 677–696 (1970), for a review of court decisions on this question.

[5] *People* v. *Rodney, P.*, 21 N.Y.2d 1, 233 N.E.2d 255, 286 N.Y.S.2d 225 (1967); *People* v. *Helm*, 10 Ill. App.3d 643, 295 N.E.2d 78 (1973).

[6] For a review of circumstances weighed in determining whether interrogations have been custodial, see *Annot.*, 31 A.L.R.3d 565 (1970 & Supp. 1976).

police officers had approached suspects and asked them to specify the location of an illegal substance, their whereabouts at the time of a crime, the ownership of a vehicle, and whether or not a suspect had committed a crime under investigation (Piersma *et al.*, 1977).

Another major consequence of a juvenile's response to precustodial interrogation is its effect on a police officer's decision concerning whether or not to take the juvenile into custody. The content of the juvenile's response can provide the "probable cause" which is necessary to make an arrest. But even without an incriminating response, a juvenile's demeanor when responding to the questioning is known to influence the decision regarding custody (Bittner, 1970; Cicourel, 1968; Piliavin & Briar, 1964). Taking juveniles into custody has traditionally been viewed both as a protective function of the police and as an acceptable tool for instilling in juveniles a respect for law (Davis, 1974). Thus, probable cause has been given a broader meaning in juvenile cases (Paulsen & Whitebread, 1974), one which encompasses the demeanor of juveniles. The result has been a wide latitude for police discretion in the arrest of juveniles (Kobetz, 1971), although the degree of discretion permitted may vary considerably from one jurisdiction to another. Different states provide more or less latitude for taking juveniles into custody, employing standards ranging from "improper conduct" to "reasonable cause to believe the juvenile has committed a felony" (Davis, 1974).Different communities also employ different standards and practices, some being more "legalistic" and others more discretionary in their arrests, depending on administrative policy (Wilson, 1969). Wherever greater discretion is allowed, a juvenile's manner of response to precustodial questioning will be more important in determining police decisions about arrest.

Even with the decision to take a juvenile into custody, police officers have not necessarily made the decision to refer the case to the juvenile court. At this time there are yet many decision points at which the juvenile may be diverted from any involvement with the court, and many of these options may rest in part on the outcome of police officers' attempts to interrogate the juvenile after an arrest has been made.

Custodial Interrogation by Police

There is much variability between jurisdictions concerning what happens to a juvenile when police take custody. A number of states require by statute that the juvenile must be delivered to a probation officer, a detention or shelter care facility, or the juvenile court (usually a designated court officer) immediately after the arrest (Paulsen & Whitebread, 1974; Piersma *et al.*, 1977).[7] Many statutes provide that parents must be notified at the earliest opportunity, and some states require that the juvenile be reunited with parents (or that a sincere effort to do so must have been made) before any further police action is taken. Some statutes require both of these protections—delivery to a court officer and reuniting with parents—while others do not require delivery to a court officer if parents are available (Davis, 1974). Finally, some states make neither requirement by statute, in which case, local jurisdictions are allowed to develop their own discretionary procedures.

Any of the aforementioned provisions which apply in a particular jurisdiction, then, would generally be carried out prior to custodial interrogation.[8] Even where a juvenile must be delivered to a court officer or detention facility, the police in most of these jurisdictions have several options for handling the case after so doing; they could reprimand and release the juvenile, talk to the parents, make a formal referral of the case to the court, or try to obtain immediate treatment, among other things (Ferster & Courtless, 1969; Kobetz, 1971). In some cases, the police will have decided to refer the juvenile to the court, and the interrogation will be used as a source of information to support the referral. But Kobetz (1971) has noted that officers frequently will interrogate a juvenile even when they are fairly certain that they will not be making a referral to the court. According to Kobetz, interrogation in these cases is aimed at providing police with information which they need to decide what sort of informal action is appropriate. For example, Kobetz notes that if police are to successfully divert juveniles from the court process and toward community agencies, they must assess the juvenile's involvement in the alleged crime, the attitudes of the parents and the juvenile which might suggest whether they will be cooperative or unreliable in carrying out diversion plans, and the juvenile's treatment needs. Interrogation is a way to obtain information relevant to these informal decisions. But apparently no one has documented the frequency of these police practices nor their variations across jurisdictions.

As noted earlier in this subsection, jurisdictional rule increasingly

[7]Delivery of a juvenile to court representatives at this point does not constitute a formal referral of the case to the court. The legislative intent for such provisions is to protect juveniles from the rigors of adult interrogations.

[8]A reading of *Miranda* warnings is not specifically required at the time of arrest. But since any spontaneous admission which a suspect might make in custody (for example, in transit from the "scene" to a police station) is likely to be ruled inadmissable in court if not preceded by the warnings, most police officers apparently read the warnings as a matter of routine at the time of arrest, whether or not formal interrogation is planned. *Miranda* warnings would be issued again just prior to the interrogation in most instances.

has required custodial interrogations to occur only at police stations, a detention center, or a place identified with juvenile court functions. The four standard *Miranda* warnings will usually be given by a police officer. Alternatively, some statutes charge probation or court officers with the responsibility of informing juveniles of their rights prior to any police interrogation. Many jurisdictions require that parents be present and that they also be informed of the juvenile's rights. The juvenile is then asked to waive the rights to silence and counsel by signing a waiver form (parents frequently sign as well), after having acknowledged that he or she understood the *Miranda* warnings. Once rights have been waived, police officers are free to question the juvenile with or without the continued presence of parents or the probation officer. In some jurisdictions a juvenile can be questioned without the presence of parents, especially when they themselves refuse to respond to reasonable attempts by police to secure their involvement.[9]

It is often claimed (Davis, 1974; Paulsen & Whitebread, 1974; Piersma *et al.*, 1977) that police interrogations of juveniles are inherently coercive because of the authoritative position of police and the threatening aura of police stations, in contrast to the powerlessness and potential vulnerability of many juveniles. If this is so, the potential danger of coercion seems to reside more in subtle uses of this power difference by police than in physical abuse or overt threat. Earlier in this century the Wickersham Commission (Chafee, Pollak, & Stern, 1931) dwelt at length on the use of third-degree tactics, which were found to be widespread; but many contributors to the President's Commission on Law Enforcement report (1967) felt that such tactics were no longer a serious problem.

Consistent with the philosophy that police, as well as the court, are to work in the best interests of the child, most police manuals encourage a friendly and concerned type of questioning (Inbau & Reid, 1967; Kenney & Pursuit, 1970). Manuals generally point out that such questioning methods are not only more humane, but also more effective in obtaining a suspect's cooperation than are methods which may arouse defensiveness. Kenney and Pursuit (1970) suggest that police should begin by expressing to the juvenile their interest in his or her welfare, and then should encourage the juvenile to cooperate and to provide as many details as possible. The interrogation is approached as an opportunity to unburden oneself of guilt feelings so that treatment efforts can begin (Kobetz, 1971). Police are told that "a review of facts as you know them

[9]Statute and case law which provide various requirements to be met in order for a juvenile's waiver of rights to be valid (and confession admissable) are reviewed in considerable detail in subsequent chapters.

can help [the juvenile] to admit participation in the offense" (Kenney & Pursuit, 1970, p. 211). Juveniles are also urged to admit to any other offenses so that they "can continue with a clean slate" (p. 212).

Kobetz (1971) describes a procedure in which police are encouraged to question juveniles and their parents at a station house"quasi-judicial hearing." The object of staging a formal hearing, it is said, is "to magnify the apparent authority of the [police] officer and to solemnify the interview with the juvenile [to] increase the chances of obtaining an admission of guilt" (p. 116). One would expect that more rigorous restrictions in legislation during the past decade might have reduced the frequency of such practices. But many jurisdictions would not find such interrogations objectionable, especially since confessions thus obtained may be used primarily to further preadjudication adjustments of cases and therefore might not need to meet the test of scrutiny by a court in relation to due process.

There are no data to indicate the degree to which these textbook descriptions of police interrogation procedures are practiced by police, nor have the probable range of police interrogation styles been systematically observed and documented. Thus the potential benefits and hazards of such "friendly" interrogations, to whatever extent they occur in practice, cannot be objectively weighed. Certainly there are instances in which juveniles might benefit from the informal station house adjustments made possible by their confessions under such circumstances. But to the extent that juveniles' confessions result in adjudication and punitive disposition or the negative consequences of a lengthy police record, such tactics could damage juveniles' perceptions of the fairness of the system. Further, it is arguable that friendly tactics are a form of deceit and coercion which takes advantage of the fearfulness and general vulnerability of many juveniles. Thus, whether or not juveniles' confessions are likely to be reliable under these conditions is a question which has concerned some courts.[10] This is not to say that a juvenile is better off remaining silent. Bittner (1970) has noted that police interpret the assertion of the juvenile's right to silence (or the juvenile's denial of guilt when available evidence supports guilt) as impertinence which requires a stern response—that is, referral to the court.

Preadjudication Court Processes

As noted earlier, police may decide as a result of their investigation that they can settle a case informally or that a juvenile is in need of no

[10] *In re Gault*, 387 U.S. 1 (1967).

further attention at all. Alternatively, they may decide that the circumstances of the case require the intervention of the juvenile court. In this case, police will file a formal referral of the case to the juvenile court. This sets in motion a set of preadjudication court processes carried out by juvenile court personnel themselves.

The first step is the "intake" or "preliminary inquiry," a relatively informal process by the court's intake or probation workers to determine whether there is justification for the court's intervention. Such matters as age, residence, and the circumstances described by the police which led to the court referral will be taken into account. The inquiry may include interviews with the juvenile and parents, frequently conducted by a court probation officer (often a social worker). Some courts routinely include a review of circumstances by a court attorney ("prosecutor") in order to weigh the sufficiency of evidence to sustain the charges.[11] If the intake worker decides that the juvenile appears to be a proper subject of the court's concern or supervision, the worker is authorized to do either of two things: instigate *informal court adjustment* of the case, or file a petition for a formal *judicial (adjudication) hearing*.

Piersma *et al.* (1977) have suggested that juveniles are encouraged to make statements (confessions) during intake interviews which might be against their interests. There are no data to support this or to indicate its frequency. That intake confessions are common in some jurisdictions, however, is suggested by the fact that some states have explicitly provided that they are not admissable at adjudication hearings.

When a case is to be informally adjusted, many jurisdictions provide for an informal adjustment hearing, at which the juvenile, the parents, and the court establish the conditions of probation and court supervision.[12] Part of these conditions often will be referral to community treatment services or delinquency programs. Paulsen and Whitebread (1974) and Piersma *et al.* (1977) have observed that a confession to police or intake workers, because of the threat of adjudication which it symbolizes, will sometimes be used to pressure juveniles into accepting treatment even when the court might have been found not to have sufficient grounds to take control of the juvenile if the case had gone

[11]Silberman (1978) has noted that when prosecutors play an active role in intake, the rate at which cases are not carried forward to the adjudicatory stage rises sharply, apparently because of the more careful scrutiny of evidence and the increased likelihood that it will be seen as insufficient to support the change. There is a growing tendency to create prosecutors' offices in juvenile courts.

[12]An informal adjustment hearing is rarely presided over by a juvenile court judge. It is usually in the hands of a court officer who is appointed by the judge as a "hearing officer" or "commissioner."

forward to a formal hearing. There is no documentation of this occurrence or its frequency, so one cannot evaluate the strength of these observations.

All states provide that when juveniles meet certain minimal criteria of age (often age 14) and seriousness of offense, the court may have a hearing to determine whether the juvenile is "amenable to treatment" within the juvenile justice system or whether, instead, the juvenile should be certified (transferred) to stand trial as an adult in a criminal court. Since this is not a hearing to determine the facts of the allegation, neither a confession nor any other evidence concerning the alleged offense can be used in the certification hearing in most jurisdictions. If a juvenile is transferred, a prior confession made in a proper custodial interrogation by police is admissable at the juvenile's trial in an adult criminal court. Juveniles' confessions take on additional importance in this light, since they might place the juvenile in jeopardy of the more severe forms of punishment typical of adult criminal sentencing.

The Adjudication Hearing

Approximately half of the cases referred to juvenile courts for delinquency determinations are formally adjudicated, the remainder being dismissed at intake or informally adjusted (Corbett & Vereb, 1974).[13] Any statement of guilt or denial made by a juvenile at earlier interrogations, so long as it was properly obtained, is admissable as evidence at this hearing; and if there is a modicum of evidence corroborating the confession, it can contribute to a finding of delinquency.[14] It is the essentially punitive and harsh nature of dispositions which can flow from a finding of delinquency—for example, several years in a training school—which caused the Supreme Court in *Gault* to extend formal due process regarding confessions (and their use) to juveniles in delinquency proceedings.[15]

Some courts have conformed to these requirements, resulting in a complex and relatively formal hearing process which attends closely to due process and fairness, casting many judges and attorneys into roles which depart extremely from the welfare tradition of juvenile courts. In

[13]This figure may vary from 20% to 70% in various juvenile courts (Corbett & Vereb, 1974).

[14]Many states require that a finding of delinquency must rest on more than a juvenile's confession alone. But in most cases only some quantum of evidence is necessary which will give the confession an "aura of authenticity" (Piersma *et al.*, 1977).

[15]Accordingly, the privilege against self-incrimination does not always apply in cases where juveniles are charged with status offenses, or in other situations where incarceration is unlikely to follow from adjudication (Davis, 1974).

contrast, Paulsen and Whitebread (1974), in a textbook for juvenile court judges, have said:

> The main point for lawyers today... is not that *Gault* records a procedural nightmare but that *Gault* is probably still ignored in many juvenile courts.[16] (p. 151)

But there is no sound data on any representative sampling of juvenile courts which would provide conclusions regarding juveniles' rights to silence and counsel in actual practice in adjudication hearings.

This review of police interrogation and juvenile court processes has revealed many areas in which it is difficult to draw conclusions about the nature of interrogation of juveniles because of a lack of systematic observations and data. Therefore, we sought to document some basic aspects of juvenile interrogation in a metropolitan jurisdiction.

SITE OF THE RESEARCH

Juvenile courts differ considerably from one jurisdiction to another, as do the laws and procedures we have just reviewed. Thus, it is important to describe the juvenile court system and procedures in the jurisdiction in which our research project was performed.

St. Louis County, comprised of over 90 suburban municipalities, forms a crescent around the city of St. Louis with both ends meeting the Mississippi River. The expanding population of about one million was served by approximately 65 police departments during the years when our project was active (1976–1978). The area as a whole was racially and socioeconomically heterogeneous, several of the municipalities being populated predominantly by black residents, and income and housing conditions ranging from well below standard to very wealthy.

The St. Louis County Juvenile Court is located in the geographic center of the county in a large, modern building constructed in 1968. During the project years, regional (branch) court centers, located in the northern and southern parts of the county, provided probation and social services to those areas, and several probation officers were stationed at police departments throughout the county. All judicial hearings were held at the main Juvenile Court building, which also contained legal, probation, social service, and clinical service departments, as well as the detention center.

[16]This impression is confirmed by more recent observers as well (Piersma *et al.*, 1977; Silberman, 1978).

The juvenile court judge is appointed yearly from the Twenty-First Judicial Circuit, but the past two judges have served two-year (1974–1975) and three-year (1976–1978) terms. Judges have appointed several commissioners and hearing officers to deal with informal hearings. Court administration was the responsibility of a Director of Court Services, appointed by the judge; the Director regulated the activities of the large number of legal, social service, and probation and detention divisions within the court.

The divisions and functions of this juvenile court reflected its historic response to both the welfare tradition of juvenile justice and the national trend toward due process and the legalistic approach. On the one hand, the court had established a legal department, comprised of attorneys working under a Chief Legal Officer whose function was conceptualized as legal counsel for Deputy Juvenile Officers (probation officers). The legal department was active in reviewing cases at intake to determine the sufficiency of evidence in relation to legal requirements and it played a major role in bringing cases forward to formal hearings or dismissing referrals when they were not substantiated. But consistent with a welfare tradition, this court also took on the responsibility of providing a wide range of youth services, using its own budget and federal grants. In addition to a sizable staff of probation or supervision officers, the court maintained: a clinical services department, which provided psychological and psychiatric evaluations; four group homes; a prevocational career counseling project; a court community services program, which provided a community-wide network of special court personnel to staff diversion programs; a volunteer home program; a family treatment program; and a special diagnostic service to deal with learning disabilities. Approximately one-fifth of the court's nearly three-million dollar annual budget was spent on social and treatment services.

In recent years the juvenile court has received approximately 18,000 referrals per year. About 11,000 of these referrals were for alleged delinquent acts, the remainder being traffic violations and neglect cases. Of the alleged delinquency referrals, approximately 7,000 were for violations which would be crimes if committed by adults and 35–40% of these were for alleged felonies. The remaining 4,000 referrals for alleged delinquent acts were for juvenile status offenses (e.g., runaways and truancy). Adolescents accounted for a sizable percentage of total yearly arrests by police. For example, juveniles (under age 17, which defines the juvenile jurisdiction in Missouri) made up about 34% of the county population; it can be estimated that about half of the juveniles (17% of the population) were between 10 and 16 years of age, the ages during which almost all juvenile arrests would be made. This 17% of the population contributed about 30% of the total police arrests in the county.

The study which we will describe shortly was an investigation of interrogation events which occurred in this jurisdiction in 1974, 1975, and 1976. Policy and rules regarding interrogation procedures with juveniles were different for each of these years, as described below.

In Missouri in 1974, police were being "advised" to take juveniles directly to a court juvenile officer (usually at the detention center) when they were taken into custody (Gomolak, 1973) and to notify the parents or guardian as soon as possible. However, there was no uniform procedure regarding interrogation after a juvenile was in custody (Gomolak, 1973), apart from the required *Miranda* warnings and a voluntary waiver. In the local jurisdiction participating in this study, the presence of a court representative and/or a parent at the time of the rights waiver decision was considered advisable, but not essential in obtaining a valid confession during 1974.

Early in 1975, the St. Louis County Juvenile Court informed law enforcement officers in its jurisdiction, through communiques and workshops, that the presence of a court representative and parent, guardian, or attorney at the time of the waiver of rights by a juvenile would be essential in determining the admissability of confessions. A new state-wide manual for police officers (Gomolak, 1975) reinforced these requirements. Both actions appear to have been stimulated by the decision in *In re K.W.B.*, 500 S.W.2d 275 (Mo. App. 1973), in which the aforementioned requirements were set forth by a Missouri court, and by anticipation of new rules which were being drafted by a state planning committee. The requirement that a court representative (probation or detention officer) be present to offer *Miranda* warnings and to monitor the interrogation process forced the police to transport juveniles to the central court-detention facility for any custodial interrogation.

In December, 1975, the Missouri Supreme Court adopted new Rules of Practice and Procedure in Juvenile Courts (1976) which stated the aforementioned procedural safeguards as rule. The Rules were given wide distribution in a manual for local police prepared by the juvenile court in February, 1976. Also early in 1976, the juvenile court sought to assist the police in complying with the requirements by assigning a special unit of court juvenile officers to approve and monitor interrogations at many police stations. This was intended to reduce difficulties encountered in the transportation of juveniles and parents to the central court (detention) facility in this large geographic area.

In the study which follows, the differences in procedural requirements between these three years became a variable which was investigated in relation to possible changes in juveniles' responses to interrogation.

FREQUENCY OF INTERROGATION AND RIGHTS WAIVER

Until the present study,[17] law and social science literature on the interrogation of juveniles was silent concerning empirical information about the basic parameters of interrogation in juvenile cases. For example, there has been no observation of the frequency of custodial interrogation of juveniles by police, differential application of interrogation with various types of juveniles, or the frequency with which juveniles waive or assert their rights to silence and counsel. This study sought to provide this necessary empirical background against which to set subsequent inquiries concerning this process (i.e., are juveniles competent to waive rights in interrogation?).

Let us briefly outline the objectives of this study. First, one would wish to know how frequently juveniles are interrogated, and which juveniles are more or less likely to be interrogated when in the custody of police. Our preliminary observations indicated that interrogation in juvenile cases involving status offenses and misdemeanors was too infrequent to warrant detailed study. For this reason, the study examined interrogation only in reference to cases involving alleged felonies.[18]

Second, one would wish to know the frequency with which juveniles waive or assert their rights to silence and counsel, and whether that frequency suggests that juveniles are especially vulnerable to "inherent coercion" in police interrogations. Although one must assume variation across jurisdictions, the only study of adults' *Miranda* decisions in normal police cases found that 42.7% refused to waive the right to silence (Seeburger & Wettick, 1967). One would expect that juveniles' rate of refusal to talk would be less than that of adults. Driver (1968), for example, has summarized developmental, social status, and personality characteristics which were related to higher rates of compliance in social psychological studies employing laboratory situations. While many of

[17]The results of the study reported here have been published elsewhere (Grisso & Pomicter, 1977).

[18]A felony is defined here as any offense which would be so classified according to criteria applied in classifying offenses committed by adults. The term is considered in many jurisdictions to be a misnomer when applied to juvenile cases, since offenses referred to the juvenile court are not considered "criminal" under the Juvenile Code; but it is used here as a convenient label for a recognized category of offenses.

these characteristics—for example, low status vis-à-vis one's confronter, lack of external support, greater dependence—are found in varying degrees in adults, they may be especially characteristic of juveniles as a group when in the role of the interrogated. In addition, high rates of obedience and compliance, especially among adolescents of ages 11–14, have been documented in research by Costanza and Shaw (1966) and Patel and Gordon (1960).

Third, one would wish to know whether the aforementioned observations would vary in frequency under different conditions of procedural safeguards. We have noted earlier that over a period of three years, the juvenile court participating in the present study issued a series of changes in policies emphasizing greater safeguards of the rights of juveniles during interrogation. This provided the opportunities: (1) to examine changes in police applications of safeguards as specified by court policy changes; (2) to document any changes in rates of refusal to waive rights during less frequent versus more frequent application of procedural safeguards (for example, the presence of adult third parties); and (3) to determine whether the frequencies of interrogations, in general and for various types of juvenile cases, would be related to the degree of safeguards applied in interrogations.

Procedure

The data in this study were derived from a random sample of all felony referrals to the juvenile court in 1974, 1975, and 1976. The main sample years were 1974 and 1975; a smaller sample was drawn from 1976 to provide verification of trends obtained in comparisons of the two main sample years.

A computer printout was obtained which listed each felony referral made to the court during each of the three years, alphabetically arranged by name of the juvenile referred. From among the 2,573 and 2,909 listings made during 1974 and 1975, respectively, every tenth listing was selected for inclusion in the study. For the secondary sample in 1976, every twentieth listing was selected from among the 2,683 listings. When the juvenile selected had more than one felony referral for the year under study, data collected as described below were collected for each of the juvenile's felony referrals during that year.

The following data were obtained for each referral from the appropriate police report contained in the juvenile's social file: police departments making the referral; whether the report noted a reading of *Miranda* warnings; whether interrogation occurred (that is, questions were reported which were posed to the juvenile, or the report stated that questioning occurred); the place where interrogation occurred; whether the juvenile was reported to have waived rights (orally or by signature); whether the juvenile was reported to have refused to waive rights; whether the juvenile provided information to the police (that is, the report contained information other than personal identification, address, etc., reported to have been given by the juvenile); whether the report stated that the juvenile "refused to talk" (an alternative police notation implying refusal to waive right against self-incrimination); whether various adult third parties (including parents) were noted as present.[19]

For each juvenile, the following data were recorded: race, sex, address of parent, date(s) of referral(s), total number of felony referrals for the juvenile prior to the referral under investigation, and total number of referrals of any type prior to the referral under investigation. Age of the juvenile at the time at which the felony referral was made was calculated and recorded for each referral. Address of parent was used as an index of socioeconomic status. Prior to the study, county census tracts were rank-ordered on the basis of a composite index of median family income and median family education reported for each tract in the 1970 United States Census Bureau data. These rankings were used to divide the census tracts into four categories of socioeconomic status.[20]

When research forms for all cases were completed, all identifying information (e.g., name, address) was removed and all remaining information was prepared for computer analysis. The sample in the study was described in two ways: (1) the subject sample, defined as the juveniles involved in all felony cases in the study; and (2) the event sample, defined as the referral events in the study, and being greater in number than the subject sample due to multiple referrals for some juveniles in any given year.

Included in the main subject sample were 491 juveniles (237 in 1974 sample and 254 in the 1975 sample), including 450 males and 41 females, 380 whites and 111 blacks, and ages ranging from 6 to 17 years.

Since any subject in the sample could have been involved in more than one felony referral during a given sample year, the number of felony referrals (which we will call "events") in a sample year exceeds the number of subjects. For this reason, the sample description is presented in two ways in Appendix A: in Table A-1, a description of the

[19]It should be noted that the study was designed to examine whether juveniles "talked" to police or "refused to talk," but not to examine the rate of confessions (which is only one possible outcome of "talking") nor to determine the consequences of either rights waiver or confession. Examination of these important questions was beyond the capabilities of the methods employed in this study.

[20]For details of this system for defining the socioeconomic status of tracts and of juveniles' families, see Chap. 4, note 15.

subject sample; and in Table A-2, a description of the event sample. Chi-square tests revealed no significant differences between 1974 and 1975 (for both the subject description and event description) with regard to any of the demographic, referral history, or referral-type variables included in the tables.

An examination of Table A-2 in Appendix A will show that about a fourth of the referral events involved black juveniles. About 70% of the events involved juveniles aged 15–16. The low percentage of 17 year olds in the sample is due to a maximum jurisdictional age of 16 in Missouri. About half of the events involved juveniles who had no prior felony referrals, but the average number of prior felony referrals was 1.00 (1974) and 1.46 (1975), and the average number of total prior referrals of any kind was about 3.

Interrogation Variables

Our first objective was to examine variables representing operations controlled by the police or court personnel in the investigation of juvenile cases. During data analyses, we discovered systematic differences between 1974 and 1975 in terms of interrogation practices, and these will be noted as they arise during presentation of the analysis.

In the use of police records as a source of data, we encountered difficulties in defining "interrogation." Some records would state clearly that interrogation was attempted and/or carried out, while others would not. For example, reports often stated that a juvenile was apprehended, was read his rights, and "made the following statement." Although it may be inferred that questioning had occurred, there was no clear notation to that effect in such cases. Consequently, interrogation variables are described separately for "known" interrogations (Part I of Table 1) and for "inferred" interrogations (Part II of Table 1). Known interrogations are those in which police reports were sufficiently complete to have provided a notation that interrogation was attempted or carried out; that is, the police noted that they asked the juvenile to provide information or noted specific questions asked. Inferred interrogations are those in which no such notations occurred in police reports, but in which interrogation (or attempts to interrogate) could be inferred because the report included information subsequently provided to police by the juvenile, or stated that the juvenile would not talk.[21]

[21]Whether or not the information provided by the juvenile was a full confession or was incriminating was not relevant. For example, some cases included alibis and denials provided by the juvenile, and some included admissions of secondary or lesser involvement in offenses which the juvenile claimed were committed by other juveniles.

TABLE 1. INTERROGATION VARIABLES DURING THREE SAMPLE YEARS

Variable	1974	1975	1976	χ^2 (1974–1975)
N, total felony referrals	330	377	(116)	
% with known or inferred interrogations	74.5	64.2	(61.2)	
I. Known interrogations				
N	131	129	(39)	
% of total felony referrals	39.7	34.2	(33.6)	
% read rights	77.9	82.9	(89.7)	
Who present (% interrogation cases)				
Attorney	0.8	0.8	(0.0)	
Court representative	11.5	56.6	(71.8)	<0.001
Parent	50.4	69.8	(82.1)	<0.01
Adult friend and or relative	1.5	5.4	(0.0)	
Parent noted to be absent	11.5	5.4	(0.0)	
Unknown	35.9	18.6	(17.9)	<0.01
Where interrogated (% of interrogation cases)				
Court center	9.9	38.0	(48.7)	<0.001
Police station	38.2	28.7	(38.5)	
Home	21.4	8.5	(0.0)	<0.05
School	4.6	0.8	(0.0)	
At scene	14.5	10.3	(5.1)	
Unknown	11.4	12.4	(7.6)	
% with report that oral or signed waiver obtained	31.2	51.2	(61.5)	<0.01
II. Inferred interrogations				
N	115	113	(32)	
% of total felony referrals	34.8	30.0	(27.5)	
% read rights	89.6	83.4	(82.3)	
Who present (percent of inferred interrogation cases)				
Attorney	1.1	2.6	(3.0)	
Court representative	2.6	26.5	(43.7)	<0.001
Parent	40.0	43.4	(62.5)	
Adult friend and or relative	0.0	0.0	(0.0)	
Parent noted to be absent	13.0	7.0	(9.0)	
Unknown	45.2	46.0	(25.0)	

The results can be described as follows:

1. *Between 64% and 75% of the total felony referrals in a given year appeared to involve custodial interrogation by police.* Table 1 shows that known interrogations occurred in about a third of the total felony referrals, and inferred interrogations (see Part II of Table 1) accounted for an additional third. There was no significant difference between the two years in the frequency of either type of interrogation. *Miranda* rights warnings were reported to have been read in about 80% or more of the cases in all years for both known and inferred interrogations.

2. *The presence of court representatives (probation officer) and of parents at interrogations were more frequent during years when policy required a greater degree of procedural safeguards (1975 and 1976).* Table 1 shows that court representatives were present at significantly more known and inferred interrogations in 1975 than in 1974. There was also a significant increase in the presence of parents from 1974 to 1975 for known interrogations (though not for inferred interrogations). These trends clearly continued in 1976, the year when the requirements concerning the presence of parent and court officer were made explicit by statute. It would appear, then, that court directives and statutory changes had a predictable effect on police interrogation procedures with juveniles.

The marked absence of attorneys in known interrogations probably is an artifact of the procedures which were to be followed prior to interrogation attempts in this system. Especially in 1975 and 1976, police procedure called for notification of parents immediately after taking the juvenile into custody and prior to interrogation. It is likely that if parents indicated a desire for the involvement of an attorney, or if a public defender were on hand to advise the juvenile (as sometimes occurred even without a request for counsel by the juvenile), police would anticipate counsel's advice to the juvenile to remain silent. In such cases, the police would probably not bother to note in their report any intentions they might have had regarding interrogation, and the case would not qualify as a known interrogation attempt. Unfortunately, then, these data do not indicate either the frequency of the presence of attorneys or, of course, differences between sample years in regard to such frequencies.

3. *In 1974, when procedural safeguards were least emphasized, the majority of known interrogations occurred at police stations (38.2%) and in juveniles' homes (21.4%).*[22] These sites are the most convenient for the police and

[22]Data regarding site of interrogation for inferred interrogations are not available, due to an oversight in the data collection process. It was not possible to return to court files at a later date to correct the oversight, because by then many files would have been removed

probably served important tactical functions. The atmosphere of a police station can be conducive to cooperation by juveniles because of the authority symbolized by the setting. A juvenile's home can also be conducive to cooperation because its informality might allow a juvenile to let down defenses. These considerations, as well as matters of convenience, might account for the relative infrequency of interrogations at the court (detention) center (see Table 1).

4. *Interrogation at the court (detention) center significantly increased, and at juveniles' homes significantly decreased, in the years involving more explicit policy regarding procedural safeguards.* This was undoubtedly due to the requirement in 1975 and 1976 that juveniles be brought to a court officer (probation officer) before interrogation. Table 1 also shows that interrogations at police stations decreased from 1974 to 1975, and then increased again in 1976; this is probably because, in 1976, the court placed probation officers in police stations which had a record of more frequent interrogations, in order to make statutory compliance easier for these police departments.

Summary. Custodial interrogation by police in juvenile felony cases was common practice in this jurisdiction. Prior to explicit court policy and statutory requirements which increased procedural protections (that is, in 1974), parents were present at juveniles' interrogations in only about half of the cases; probably the greater number of the remaining cases involved no "friendly" third-party assistance for juveniles. It is clear that changes in juvenile court rules in 1975 produced a different set of interrogation behavior by police, involving greater procedural protection in the form of third-party monitors and more formal and controlled interrogation sites. The trend toward greater safeguards was even further augmented in 1976, commensurate with new statutory rules for interrogation procedures.

Interrogations for Different Referral Types

Table 2 shows the frequency of interrogations for various types of juvenile cases, defined by demographic characteristics of the juveniles and by classes of alleged offenses under investigation. We will focus primarily on the data from 1974 and 1975, since the small sample in 1976 (71 interrogations) produces unstable data when divided among several demographic classes.

---

by the court in the course of general court operations. But a later partial sampling of inferred interrogation cases did reveal trends similar to those shown for known interrogations.

TABLE 2. PERCENT OF FELONY REFERRALS WITHIN DEMOGRAPHIC GROUPS INVOLVING KNOWN AND INFERRED (*K* AND *I*) INTERROGATIONS COMBINED, AND KNOWN (*K*) INTERROGATIONS ALONE

	K and *I* combined			*K* only		
Variable	1974	1975	(1976)	1974	1975	(1976)
Age						
12 or younger	88.0	72.4	(46.1)	52.0	51.7	(51.3)
13	80.2	77.8	(61.5)	48.4	38.9	(30.8)
14	74.5	70.5	(54.5)	42.6	45.5	(36.4)
15	77.5	60.7	(62.7)	37.1	33.3	(33.3)
16	72.5	66.2	(62.8)	35.1	30.1	(35.3)
Number of prior felony referrals						
0	75.5	71.0	(59.7)	37.8	33.9	(31.3)
1	72.0	68.4	(56.3)	41.2	41.8	(37.5)
2	78.9	70.5	(60.0)	42.1	35.0	(40.0)
3	73.7	45.5	(75.0)	36.8	36.4	(25.0)
4 or more	80.0	52.8	(66.0)	48.0	22.6	(40.0)
Felony investigated						
Against person	78.7	41.7[a]	(62.5)	31.9	17.1	(37.5)
Against property	80.7	69.9	(64.8)	43.4	38.8	(33.0)
Possession	54.5	62.0	(33.3)	30.9	24.1	(33.3)
Race						
White	79.3	74.4	(68.3)	43.9	40.6	(38.0)
Black	65.3	41.4[b]	(45.9)	25.3	18.9	(24.3)
For known interrogation cases, proportion interrogated at various sites, by race						
White						
Court center				9.6	38.8[a]	(58.6)
Police station				36.4	28.7	(31.0)
Home				23.5	9.2	
School				5.2	0.9	
At scene				15.8	9.2	
Unknown				12.2	13.0	
Black						
Court center				10.5	34.2	(22.2)
Police station				57.8	28.7	(66.6)
Home				15.7	4.7	
School				0.0	0.0	
At scene				10.5	19.0	
Unknown				5.3	13.3	

[a] χ^2 indicated significant difference ($p<0.001$) between 1974 and 1975.
[b] χ^2 indicated significant difference ($p<0.01$ between 1974 and 1975). Also, in 1975, black versus white proportions interrogated were significantly different ($p<0.001$).

5. *Younger juveniles were somewhat more likely to be interrogated than were older juveniles.* Although the percentages were not significantly different statistically, interrogation rates were consistently higher for juveniles of ages 13 or 12-and-younger than for older juveniles, in both of the two main years and when calculated for known interrogations or for known plus inferred interrogations.

6. *Number of prior felony referrals and type of alleged felony were not consistently related to likelihood of interrogation.*

7. *Juveniles with a relatively greater number of prior felony referrals tended to be interrogated with less frequency in 1975 than in 1974, as were juveniles in cases involving alleged felonies against persons.*

It will be recalled that in 1975 the juvenile court began requiring that police officers bring juvenile suspects to the court (detention) center before interrogation (to allow a court officer to monitor the interrogation proceedings). This made interrogation much more difficult than was the case in 1974, due to the need to transport juveniles to the court center and to delay interrogation until the arrival of parents. It is possible, therefore, that police responded to such added complexities by decreasing the rate of interrogations in cases where confessions would be of secondary importance as evidence. Thus, a juvenile with multiple past felonies may have been viewed as sufficiently suspect, because of his past history, to warrant detainment without evidence which might be gained by a time-consuming interrogation. Regarding offenses against persons, direct evidence from testimony and identification provided by the victim is more often available in such cases than in cases involving offenses against property. Again, given the increased complexity of interrogation procedures in 1975, the police might have reduced their rate of interrogation in such cases, given the availability of evidence other than confessions.

This explanation gains support from data in Table 2 which indicates that in 1976 the rate of interrogation in such cases returned to the higher 1974 rate. Early in 1976, the juvenile court decided to make court officers available for monitoring interrogations in police stations. This served to reduce the effort required by the police in satisfying procedural requirements and can account for the increase in interrogation in the cases in question in 1976.

9. *In all years, the probability of interrogation for black juveniles was less than for white juveniles.* The difference was statistically significant in 1975.

10. *The rate of interrogation of black suspects decreased significantly from 1974 to 1975, while it did not for whites.*

Workers in the present court system suggested to us that interrogation of black juveniles is generally perceived by the police to be less fruitful than interrogation of white juveniles. Past studies of black self-identity (Kardiner & Ovesey, 1962) and interpersonal dynamics between black juveniles and authority figures both white (Katz, 1973) and black (Grambs, 1964) suggest that black juveniles could be expected to react to police in an inhibited and distrustful manner, perhaps more so than whites (Palermo, 1959). Police might expect more denial of guilt or resistance, and therefore less "reinforcement" for energy expended in the interrogation of black juveniles. Thus, both of the statistical observations might be reflections of the same general consequence noted earlier: that the anticipated effort required for interrogation (and the anticipated lack of valuable outcome) decreased the likelihood of interrogation.

In addition, the requirements regarding the presence of court representatives and parents at interrogations in 1975 may have had an especially greater impact in cases involving blacks. Court workers observed that it was more difficult in many instances to notify black parents that their immediate presence was needed. The majority of such parents were less advantaged financially than were white parents, and therefore would be more likely to lack phones, to have problems in transportation to a court center, or to have types of occupations which put the parent out of contact during the working day. It is noteworthy that in 1976, when court representatives were made available at police stations, interrogation of blacks began to return to the 1974 level. Being located in neighborhoods, such sites were more accessible to black parents and would have offered fewer transportation and communication problems for police and families than in 1975, when travel to the court center was required. The final entry in Table 2 is consistent with this explanation. The necessity of a court representative's presence in 1975 coincided with a decrease in the use of police stations for known interrogations for cases of both whites and blacks, but the decrease was much more dramatic for blacks. The use of police stations for interrogation of blacks markedly increased again in 1976, when court representatives were made available at police stations.

Juvenile Suspects' Responses

We will now examine the frequency with which juveniles waived their rights to silence. One will recall that court policy demanded greater procedural safeguards in interrogations in 1975 than in 1974. In fact, procedural safeguards were significantly more in evidence in 1975, according to our earlier data on the presence of court officers and parents and the sites of interrogations. Thus, we are in a position to examine whether the frequency of rights waiver was related to the degree of procedural safeguards provided to juveniles.

TABLE 3. JUVENILE SUSPECTS' RESPONSES

Variable	1974-1975	1974	1975	(1976)
Total felony referrals (*N*)	707	330	377	(116)
Known/inferred interrogations (*N*)	488	246	242	(71)
Number of interrogations including:				
Talking	442	222	220	(67)
Refusal to waive or to talk	46	24	22	(4)
Percent of refusal for:				
Total felony referrals	6.5	7.9	5.8	(3.4)
Known/inferred interrogations	9.4	9.7	9.1	(5.6)
Known/inferred interrogations when rights known to have been read	11.3	11.7	10.9	(6.3)
Known interrogations	2.3	3.0	1.5	(2.5)
Inferred interrogations	17.5	17.4	17.7	(9.3)

A juvenile was considered to have "talked"—waived the right against self-incrimination—when a police report contained information provided by the juvenile other than mere identifying information. Since the primary purpose of this portion of the study was to examine the decision regarding waiver of the right to remain silent, no distinction was made concerning whether talking involved confession or denial so long as the juvenile's statement addressed itself to the alleged offense which was under custodial investigation by the police.[23] "Refusal," or laying claim to the right against self-incrimination, was defined as a notation in police reports that the juvenile had refused (orally or in writing) to waive rights, or merely that the juvenile had refused to talk after being taken into custody. These juveniles were considered to have made the decision to remain silent.

The following observations are derived from data in Tables 3 and 4

[23]For a random selected portion of the cases in which juveniles "talked," an attempt was made to categorize their statements as confessions, partial confessions, denials, etc. Approximately 85–90% of the cases appeared to contain some level of admission to the alleged offense, and 10% were denials of any involvement. However, we arrived at no criterion for "admission" which would allow us to report with any confidence on the rate of confession in these cases. Thus, for purposes of the present study, juveniles were viewed as having placed themselves in a potentially incriminating position by having "talked" (that is, waived rights and made some statement), whether or not they confessed.

Table 4. Rate of Refusal to Talk within Demographic Classes, Expressed as Percentage of Known and Inferred Interrogations Combined

Variable	1974	1975	(1976)
Age			
12 or younger	0.0	0.0	(0.0)
13	5.5	0.0	(0.0)
14	0.0	3.2	(0.0)
15	13.0	10.4	(12.5)
16	13.7	12.9	(6.1)
Number of prior felony referrals			
0	9.5	6.9	(4.8)
1	8.0	9.1	(0.0)
2	12.9	14.3	(0.0)
3	0.0	20.1	(16.6)
4 or more	14.3	11.5	(10.0)
Current referral			
Against person	15.8	16.6	(10.0)
Against property	7.6	8.4	(5.2)
Possession	13.3	8.6	(0.0)
Race			
White	7.9	9.6	(3.6)
Black	15.7	6.4	(11.7)

showing juveniles' responses to the waiver decision for 1974 and 1975 (combined and separately) and for the smaller 1976 sample.

11. *For known and inferred interrogations combined* (Table 3), *the rate of refusal to talk in 1974–1975 was 9.4%.* Juveniles chose to talk, and thus potentially to incriminate themselves by confession or denial, in the remaining 90.6% of the cases. The obtained refusal rate for juveniles is considerably smaller than that for adults (42%) reported by Seeburger and Wettick (1967).

Occasionally juveniles are known to provide information to police prior to being informed of their rights by a reading of *Miranda* warnings. These cases might constitute "spontaneous confessions" before police have the opportunity to present the warnings, or might result from police negligence. Whatever the reason, one would wish to know the rate of refusal to talk specifically in those cases where juveniles were known to be informed of their right to remain silent. Of the 405 cases meeting this criterion (see Table 3), refusal to talk occurred in 11.3% of the cases, a rate which is only slightly different from the more general refusal rate noted above.

12. *The rate of refusal to talk was not related to the degree of procedural safeguards.* That is, there was no difference in the refusal rates between 1974 and 1975, in spite of the greater prevalence of procedural safeguards in the latter year. This result is confirmed by the refusal rate in the smaller sample of cases in 1976.

13. *Refusal to talk was virtually nonexistant below age 15, and occurred in about 12–14% of interrogations involving 15- and 16-year olds* (see Table 4).

14. *The rate of refusal to talk tended to increase with the number of prior felony referrals at the time of interrogation, and tended to be greater in cases involving offenses against persons (assault, armed robbery) than in property or possession cases.* These results are consistent with the generally held assumption that more sophisticated juveniles (older, or having more prior contact with police and court procedures) are somewhat more ready to assert rights in the context of police investigations, due either to greater familiarity with the meaning of the rights or to lesser intimidation by police authority. Additionally, one might speculate that assertion of rights will be more likely in juvenile cases when circumstances (e.g., being accused of a serious assaultive offense) suggest to the juvenile the expectancy that "conviction" is likely to lead to more serious consequences.

15. *Data in Table 4 suggest a higher rate of refusal to talk for black juveniles than for white juveniles.* The exception to this trend was in 1975, when police apparently became more selective in the interrogation of black juveniles (see Result 10 above) because of new procedures and system circumstances which made interrogation generally more difficult. Police might have decided to expend the added effort for interrogation of blacks only when they sensed some chance of less resistance on the part of a black suspect, thus producing the statistical reduction in the refusal rate during 1975.

Implications

The overall rates of interrogation and refusal to talk described here can be generalized to other jurisdictions only with great caution. Some other jurisdictions will contain populations of juvenile felony referrals which are proportionately different from the present samples in one or more of the demographic variables. It must be assumed, too, that police investigative procedures may differ from one metropolitan area or state to another. Yet, a careful consideration of the juvenile sample and the interrogation policies described earlier in this report should provide some estimate of the degree to which the present statistical results can be generalized to other specific jurisdictions.

In spite of these limitations, this investigation does provide empirical documentation which gives meaning and importance to the study of juveniles' rights in interrogation.[24] In the present jurisdiction—and we assume in many others as well—the interrogation of juveniles occurs in about three-quarters of cases involving alleged offenses which are serious enough (that is, felonious) to present the possibility of delinquency adjudication (and therefore placement in a juvenile correctional institution). In addition, interrogation is as likely to be employed with younger and less experienced juveniles as with older ones, although for younger juveniles the consequences of a confession might involve pressure to accept diversion treatment rather than full adjudication and correctional placement. In fact, interrogation was shown to be normative, rather than exceptional, for all classes of juveniles in the study, even in those classes which had lower rates of interrogation compared to other classes. In studying juvenile interrogation, then, we are not responding to the law's concerns about a rare event, but about a practice the consequences of which influence hundreds of juveniles in the present jurisdiction each year and many thousands of juveniles nationally.

The results of the study echo a question which has been raised by scores of courts and legal commentators, and which was the impetus for the investigations described later: Are juveniles capable of providing a meaningful waiver of their rights to avoid self-incrimination and to obtain legal counsel? Only about 10% of the juveniles in the present study asserted their right to silence, compared to 42% of adults in earlier research (Seeburger & Wettick, 1967). Is the "average" juvenile as capable as the "average" adult suspect of understanding the *Miranda* warnings or their implications? Or is the lower rate of assertion of rights by juveniles possibly a consequence of poorer understanding? Alternatively, might the higher rate of rights waiver by juveniles be due to increased intimidation as a consequence of developmental or social vulnerability vis-à-vis police authority? The data, then, provide an empirical justification for questioning the competence of juveniles to make a meaningful decision—voluntary and with reasonable understanding—about the waiver or assertion of rights in interrogation.

If it is found that a substantial proportion of juveniles indeed do lack the necessary competence to make these decisions, as some courts have

[24]In this section we review only those implications which provide a general background for the subsequent studies in our project. A more detailed examination of the implications of the study were provided in an earlier publication by Grisso and Pomicter (1977), and the interested reader is referred there for a more comprehensive review.

argued, then the question of special legal safeguards of juveniles' rights in interrogation becomes imperative. The present data concerning rates of rights assertion under conditions of more or fewer legal safeguards raises doubts about whether present trends in legal remedies—monitoring by court officers, presence of parents, greater formality and control in the site and manner of interrogation—provide the protection which some courts have intended. Even with these safeguards, the rate of rights assertion by juveniles was not comparable to that found for adult suspects, and indeed was no different than the rates for juveniles who had not been provided special due process. These results alone need not be interpreted as evidence of inadequate protection; there are other plausible explanations which we will examine later. But together with the concern of some courts regarding the role of parents in juvenile interrogations, the results call for an examination of parents' capacities to promote the welfare of their children in the context of police and court investigations.

At the broadest level, these were the questions which we addressed in the studies to be reported in the subsequent chapters of this book. But before the studies themselves could be designed, it was necessary to engage in a process which identified and translated the legal standards and concepts into researchable psychological measures and methods. We turn now to a description of that process.

3

From Legal Standard to Psychological Measurement

The purpose of this chapter is to describe our translation of the legal standards and concepts for competence to waive rights into methods for assessing that competence. It was our goal to develop measures which would be conceptually related as closely as possible to the requirements and concerns of the law when a court weighs the validity of suspects' waiver of *Miranda* rights. The experimental measures which we planned to develop were intended to provide the necessary tools for obtaining empirical information about which types of juveniles were more or less competent to waive their rights to silence and counsel. This information could then be used by legislators in forming law controlling the procedures of police and juvenile courts when dealing with interrogation issues. In addition, the results would provide attorneys and judges with an empirical basis with which to weigh the difficult question of the validity of waiver in individual juvenile cases. It was not our intention to develop tools or results which would replace judicial discretion in such matters. As we will explain later in this chapter, the question of the validity of a juvenile's waiver requires a consideration of more factors than the competence of the juvenile alone. In addition, experimental research can rarely take into account all of the individual characteristics of juveniles which might be relevant in certain cases. The measures, then, were designed to provide results which could stand as guidelines for judicial decisions, thereby improving the consistency and rationality of decision making.

Moving from the legal standards for waiver competence to criterion measures of competence required a thorough review of the relevant statute and case law, as well as intimate familiarity with legal process and the juvenile justice system. This background had to be integrated with a knowledge of psychological constructs, the development of psychological measures, and research design. The task clearly called for the joint efforts of psychologists and experts in juvenile law.

The conceptualization which follows, then, was the product of formal collaboration between lawyers and psychologists which extended over a period of several months. Among the legal professionals participating at various stages were judges, attorneys in private practice with juvenile cases, juvenile court attorneys, public defenders in juvenile courts, attorneys in a juvenile litigation center and in legal aid offices in various geographic areas of the country, and law professors. Participating psychologists included some who were faculty and student researchers, as well as psychologists employed by juvenile courts. Their areas of expertise represented clinical, developmental, and social psychology, as well as personality measurement and evaluation research methodology. The many perspectives represented by these individuals created difficult communication challenges. The result, however, was a set of research tools which could produce reliable, empirical information of a type that would be relevant and applicable to the law, legal process, and the legal system.

In what follows, we will begin with a conceptualization of the legal meaning of competence to waive rights. In this conceptualization, we will find that the law has considered competence to include several major types of understanding on the part of suspects—what we will call *components* of competence to waive rights. Then, for each component, we will propose *indicants* of the type of understanding with which the component is concerned— that is, observable behaviors which would allow one to infer that a suspect's understanding in the component area satisfies legal requirements. Finally, in each of the component areas, the project's development of experimental *measures* of the indicants will be described. These measures, then, served as the assessment tools in the studies of juveniles' competence to waive rights which are reported in subsequent chapters.

INTERPRETING THE LEGAL STANDARDS: COMPETENCE AND ITS COMPONENTS

THE LEGAL CONCEPT OF COMPETENCE

In *Miranda* v. *Arizona*, 384 U.S. 436 (1966), the Supreme Court required that a confession would be admissable in court only if the suspect had provided a valid waiver of the rights to silence and legal counsel.

The standard for a waiver's validity was whether the waiver was the product of a knowing, intelligent, and voluntary decision by the suspect. The Court in *Miranda* then focused primarily on the procedural requirements which had to be met in obtaining a waiver—that is, informing the suspect of the rights to silence and legal counsel and avoiding any semblance of threat or coercion in obtaining the waiver. These, then, were the circumstances to be weighed in determining the validity of rights waiver. Subsequent courts and legislation established other procedural requirements and circumstances to be met in the interrogation of juveniles; these were noted in Chapter 2 and will be further reviewed in subsequent chapters.

In re Gault, 387 U.S. 1 (1967) and *People* v. *Lara*, 432 P.2d 202 (1967) established an additional, *nonprocedural* circumstance to be weighed in determining the validity of juveniles' waiver of rights. That is, the greater vulnerability of some juveniles required that judges consider whether or not a juvenile in question had the *ability* to make a knowing, intelligent and voluntary waiver of rights. In essence, consideration was to be given not only to the procedural events and other circumstances surrounding the interrogation, but also to the cognitive and emotional characteristics of the juvenile which might suggest diminished ability to meaningfully decide to waive rights.

In the present project, we identified the latter circumstance—juveniles' capacities or abilities to waive rights knowingly, intelligently, and voluntarily—as the primary focus for our studies. This legal concept was labeled "competence to waive rights," a term which has appeared in many rulings involving juvenile suspects.

It is important to keep in mind the distinction between the validity of waiver and competence to waive rights. Competence is but one of several types of circumstances which courts must weigh in determining the validity of a juvenile's waiver. It can be argued that a juvenile who is not competent is quite unlikely to have produced a valid waiver (unless, perhaps, he or she received an advocate's assistance). In contrast, a juvenile who is competent to waive rights might also be found to have provided an invalid waiver, based on a consideration of other circumstances of the interrogation. Thus, competence will play an important role, but not always a determining role, in decisions about the validity of juveniles' waivers.

The Components

A scrutiny of relevant legal cases, beginning with *Haley* v. *Ohio*, 332 U.S. 596 (1948), was the first step in defining the concept of competence to waive rights. The analysis and interpretation of these cases to arrive at an adequate definition made heavy use of legal consultants to the project. It was determined that the definition would require consideration of more than one type of understanding and abilities. We refer to these as the components of the concept.

The first component was labeled *comprehension of rights.* This component involves the suspect's ability to understand what rights are available. In Chapter 4, which will describe our assessment for this component, a large number of court cases are reviewed in which reference was made to juveniles' abilities or inabilities to "understand," "comprehend," or "be cognizant of" the rights of which they were informed. Thus, courts have not equated the mere fact of having been told one's rights (a procedural matter) with knowing one's rights. For example, one court [*United States ex rel. Simon* v. *Maroney,* 228 F.Supp. 800 (1964)] remarked that the fact that *Miranda* warnings were properly given to a retarded, 18-year old suspect was "irrelevant" in light of the suspect's incapacities, which argued against his ability to understand what he was told.

The second component was labeled *beliefs about legal context.* Reviews of legal cases in Chapters 6 and 7 will document that many courts have been concerned about more than juveniles' understanding of what their rights are. They have also questioned how juveniles believe the rights function in the context of the legal process, and what they believe might be the consequences of rights waiver or assertion. A meaningful waiver, many courts have reasoned, requires both knowing one's rights and appreciating the significance of the rights or understanding how the rights work. It is one thing, for example, to know that one has a right to consult a lawyer, and perhaps quite another thing to know what a lawyer does or what the potential consequences of calling for a lawyer might be.

To the extent that some juveniles might bring to the interrogation certain uninformed, misperceived, or distorted beliefs about interrogation and how their rights function, they may be unprepared to make an informed and voluntary decision about those rights. Thus, the Court in *Gault* urged that "the greatest care must be taken to assure that [the confession] was voluntary, in the sense *not only* that it was not coerced or suggested, but also *that it was not the product . . . of adolescent fantasy, fright or despair*" (387 U.S. at 55; italics added).

Therefore, juveniles' knowledge of their rights and also their beliefs about the roles which those rights play in the context of the legal process were the two major components of the concept of competence to waive rights.

Two other potential components were considered. A brief description will show why we adopted one of them for exploration rather than more controlled study, and why the other was excluded.

A few courts, referring to juveniles' abilities to "weigh" the information they have or to "consider" certain consequences, seem to have been concerned with the cognitive capacities of juveniles to deal with complex choices and decisions. Similarly, psychologists have found differences between children of various ages in the number of possible options they are capable of considering at a given time, the range of consequences of any option which they are capable of weighing, and their ability to consider both short-range and long-range consequences when making decisions (Spivack, Platt, & Shure, 1976).

Therefore, a third component entitled *problem-solving capacity* would be a possible addition to the two existing components of competence to waive rights. In contrast to the two major components, however, the issue of problem-solving capacity has not played a leading role in legal cases or legal standards regarding juveniles' competence. For this reason, the problem-solving component was included as a secondary or exploratory component which we will meet again only briefly in Chapter 7.

Finally, some courts have employed terms such as "dependency," "immaturity," "compliance," "deference," and "degree of sophistication" when discussing juveniles' competence. We considered whether a component entitled "personality factors" should be included, but the consensus of opinion of the project's consultants was to avoid such a component. A scrutiny of the ways in which such terms were used by judges indicated that they either served as summary words to describe factors which were already included in the two primary components or were employed in judges' attempts to explain the reasons for juveniles' deficiencies in the realms of the two primary components. Thus, it was decided that to the extent that they could be validly measured, such personality dimensions could at some later time be evaluated concerning their relationships to the phenomena subsumed under the two major components, but that no separate component regarding personality variables should be constructed.

The next three sections of this chapter describe the development of behavioral *indicants* and experimental psychological *measures* for the concept of competence to waive rights. Each of these sections corresponds to one of the aforementioned components.

COMPONENT I: COMPREHENSION OF RIGHTS

The Supreme Court in *Miranda* specified the rights and entitlements about which suspects must be warned. The first Component of these rights requires that a suspect understand the warnings which the court ordered to be presented to suspects.

Chief Justice Warren described these warnings in two places in the Court's opinion. The first listing (*Miranda* v. *Arizona,* 384 U.S. at 444–445 (1966) contains four distinct warning elements, while the second listing (at 478–479) can be interpreted to contain five warnings. The four which appear in both places are worded somewhat differently in the two versions, but refer to warnings that the suspect has the right to remain silent, that statements made can be used as evidence against the suspect, that the suspect can have an attorney present, and that an attorney can be appointed if the suspect cannot afford one.

In the first version, this listing is followed by a statement of the standard for effective waiver of the rights (voluntary, knowing, and intelligent), and then by the pronouncement that the rights to silence and legal counsel can be invoked at any stage of the process, even after the suspect has answered some questions or volunteered some statements. The position of this pronouncement in the sequence of the opinion does not suggest that it was intended as one of the warnings to suspects.

In the second version, however, the listing of the four warnings is followed immediately by: "Opportunity to exercise these rights must be afforded to him throughout the interrogation. After such warnings have been given . . . the individual may knowingly and intelligently waive these rights" [384 U.S. 478–479 (1966)]. This suggests that the Court intended this fifth element to be included in the warnings, not merely to be a part of postwaiver protections as suggested by the first version.

This ambiguity concerning the fifth element caused us to define comprehension as an understanding of the rights and realities in the four basic warnings alone. Only these were clearly defined by the Court as being essential, and the fifth element was not usually referred to by courts in the cases of juvenile waiver which we will review in subsequent chapters. In retrospect, we consider our decision to have been less than ideal, in that it renders subsequent project results less complete in this regard. But we believe that in the last analysis the omission will be found not to have rendered the results of the project any less useful. At most it suggests that our estimates of the types and frequencies of juveniles who do not meet the standard of competence would err on the conservative side, a situation which in our opinion is preferable to overestimation. These points will be addressed further, however, in the interpretation of results.

Indicants

The next step in the conceptual process was to identify behavior (observable phenomena) which could be used to infer the presence of a person's understanding or misunderstanding of the four *Miranda* warnings. Discovering the appropriate indicants for understanding of a set of verbal messages is not an easy task, because comprehension itself is not a unitary function. For example, Miller (1965) notes that the meaning of a verbal message is not simply the sum of the meanings of each word in the message, and that single-word understanding is not necessarily a sign of adequate understanding of semantic content.

A second problem in identifying appropriate indicants concerns the mode of response to be required. Stated simply, if one asks juveniles (or others) to tell what they know about a piece of verbal material, some may not be able to express what they know. The verbal expressive difficulties of many delinquent juveniles have been well-documented (e.g., Corotto, 1961; Weins, Matarazzo, & Gaver, 1959), so that the problem was especially salient given the population with which our project was concerned.

Therefore, the project employed several indicants of comprehension of the warnings. Ebel (1972) and Gronlund (1968) have described two types of indicants of comprehension. The first is to have persons supply their own expression of their understanding of a content area in question. The project decided on two indicants using this mode of expression: (1) accurately paraphrasing each of the *Miranda* warnings; and (2) accurately defining critical words appearing in the *Miranda* warnings. The second type of indicant recommended by both Ebel and Gronlund is to have persons select an answer from a variety of alternative answers which have been preconstructed, as in multiple-choice or true-or-false items. Thus, the third indicant of *Miranda* comprehension was: (3) an identification of preconstructed sentences with meanings similar to the *Miranda* warnings.[1]

All three of these indicants have inherent strengths and weaknesses for assessing understanding. The two indicants requiring verbal expression are subject to juveniles' verbal expressive difficulties, which might interfere with the assessment of comprehension. The third indicant

[1]Interestingly, all three of these indicants have been employed on occasion in various legal cases involving questions of juveniles' understanding of *Miranda* warnings. For example, in *In re Holifield,* 319 S.2d 772, 473 (1975), a juvenile was asked to define the word "rights," which he did inadequately. He was then provided with an incorrect definition, which he identified as being correct. Finally, he was read the warning pertaining to the right to consult with an attorney before and during questioning, and was asked to paraphrase its meaning. He responded, "If you want the lawyer to defend you, you got to tell him what it's about." Recognizing that the juvenile's testimony might be self-serving, the court nevertheless felt that substantial questions were raised concerning his competence to waive rights. Similar attempts at assessment in the courtroom can be found in *Coyote* v. *United States,* 380 F.2d 305, 308 (1967), *People* v. *Baker,* 292 N.E.2d 760, 763 (1973), and *In re Morgan,* 341 N.E.2d 19 (1975).

(identifying correct responses) has the advantage of requiring no verbal expression, but does not guarantee that the "chosen" answer has been fully understood. It is because of such problems that the use of multiple indicants for a single construct has been strongly recommended by methodologists in the social and behavioral sciences (Kerlinger, 1973). Perhaps no indicant of any psychological phenomenon is immune from observational error produced by certain properties of the method of measurement. Using several indicants (and thus several measures) of understanding allows one to verify one's results across measures, thereby lending confidence that the research conclusions are not merely artifacts of any one method of measurement.

Measurement

Three measures of *Miranda* comprehension were developed, corresponding to the three indicants of the comprehension component. In this section, we will describe the process by which each measure was developed, and we will provide the information about administration and scoring of measures which is necessary for understanding the reports of research results in Chapters 4 and 5. More detailed information will be found in Appendicies B, D, and E.

Comprehension of Miranda Rights (CMR)

The development of this measure began with a specification of several objectives: (1) to examine understanding of the four primary *Miranda* warnings by way of the paraphrase indicant; (2) to develop a standard and reliable method for administering the procedure and obtaining responses; (3) to provide participant juveniles with every possible opportunity to reveal what they understood the warnings to mean, within the constraints of standardized administration; (4) to develop an objective scoring system, providing adequate reliability, and offering a minimum of chance that participant juveniles would be penalized for lack of verbal expressive sophistication; and (5) to develop criterion definitions for scoring of responses which would represent the consensus of opinion of a panel of attorneys and psychologists concerning the essential meaning of each of the *Miranda* warnings.

Administration of the CMR, described in detail in Appendix B, employs a reading of the four *Miranda* warnings, which are also displayed on printed cards, and after each, requires the juvenile to say "in your own words" what it is that the warning says. During the development and refinement of the instrument, specific rules were developed for the examiners in asking juveniles to clarify or elaborate on their initial responses when those responses were of questionable adequacy. The rules also allow for standardized inquiry regarding phrases which the juvenile employs "verbatim" from the *Miranda* warnings and regarding slang or colloquial terms and confusing sentence constructions which might inadvertently reduce scoring credit. The intention in this procedure was to provide juveniles with every opportunity to express what they knew, but to provide for a sufficiently standardized way of inquiring so that juvenile participants would not be provided with suggestions of the correct answers. Thus, if a juvenile's response to such inquiry results in an adequate response, the juvenile receives full credit even though his or her initial response was less than adequate.

The wording of the *Miranda* warnings presented to juveniles in this administration (see Appendix B) was selected in deference to the forms employed in the St. Louis metropolitan area at the time of the study. It will be recalled that in *Miranda* the Court offered two slightly different wordings, and there does not seem to be a single, standard form for *Miranda* warnings across U.S. jurisdiction. To the best of our knowledge, the wordings which we used are employed identically or with slight variations in most other jurisdictions.

Separate scoring criteria (i.e., definitions of adequate and inadequate responses) were developed for each of the four *Miranda* warnings. To develop these criteria a large number of sample responses collected from juveniles were reviewed by our consultants. Over several sessions, they engaged in a process of arriving at consensus both regarding logical categorization of responses and criterion statements and regarding the degrees of accuracy of understanding which in their opinion were represented by each category. It became apparent during this process that not all responses could be clearly classifiable as adequate or inadequate, and that an intermediate, "questionable" level of response adequacy would be needed in order to classify some responses.

There were four steps in the process of refining these initial criterion statements and adequacy classifications. First, a new sample of responses was obtained from juveniles, and considerable changes were made in the scoring criteria resulting from attempts to employ the initial system in scoring these new responses. Second, this modified scoring system was reviewed independently by lawyers in private and court practices in the St. Louis area, and their recommendations produced further modifications in the criterion statements. Third, the scoring system with all prior modifications was submitted for independent review to five attorneys in academic settings and juvenile legal service agencies in four other geographic areas of the country. This step was the final one aimed at producing criteria for adequate and inadequate understanding, which represented the consensus of a range of experts familiar with juvenile law and with juveniles in contract with the justice system. Fourth, the scoring system (with revisions incorporated from the comments of the national panel) was used by research assistants, heretofore unfamiliar with the system but newly trained in its use, to score a new set of sample responses. Scoring reliability figures were calculated to determine the degree of agreement between all pairs of scorers, and subsequent discussions of scorer disagreements led to final clarifications in the description of scoring criteria.

The final scoring system is presented in Appendix B. Each *Miranda* item is evaluated according to different specific scoring standards, but in each case responses are given 2 points (adequate understanding), 1 point (questionable or partial understanding), or 0 points of credit (inadequate understanding). Thus, total CMR scores may range from 0 to 8. Scoring is aided not only by descriptive statements regarding what is included within each response class, but also by a listing of many abbreviated examples of responses which meet the described requirements.

Subsequent to the aforementioned investigation of scorer reliability, four separate tests of independent scoring reliability were performed in the course of the project. Three of these involved several pairs of trained scorers immediately prior to, and at early and late phases of data collection for the study employing the CMR. The fourth involved a new set of scorers compared to one of the more experienced scorers. Generally, Pearson r coefficients between scorers were .80–.97 for various CMR items (i.e., *Miranda* warnings), and .92–.96 for CMR total scores, indicating a very high degree of independent interscorer agreement. (Specific coefficients are presented in Appendix B.)

Understanding of *Miranda* warnings should not change markedly over the span of a few days or weeks under normal conditions. One would hope that the CMR would be sufficiently uninfluenced by situational changes and therefore would produce correspondingly consistent scores for a juvenile. Thus, test–retest reliability was examined by administering the CMR to 24 juveniles during their first day in detention custody and again during their third day. The sample represented a broad range of IQ scores (69–117, mean = 97.2) and CMR scores ranged from 0 to 8 on both administrations. Twelve juveniles obtained the same scores on the original test and the retest, nine obtained scores one or two points higher on the retest, and the remaining three obtained scores one point lower on the retest. These results indicate that the test–retest procedure produced a "practice effect" which made scores on retest somewhat higher. However, the difference between the mean scores of the group for the two administrations was not statistically significant. Further, juveniles tended to maintain their scoring position relative to each other, as shown by the Pearson *r* coefficient of .84 indicating considerable stability of scores produced by the CMR.

Comprehension of Miranda Rights, True or False (CMR-TF)

The CMR-TF was developed to assess comprehension of Miranda warnings in a way that would require virtually no construction of verbal responses on the part of participating juveniles. The project staff generated a pool of accurate and inaccurate rewordings of each of the four *Miranda* warnings. From this item pool, items were selected for each of the *Miranda* warnings. Preference was given to items that were worded very simply and, in the case of "false" items, to those that represented errors in interpretation which had been in evidence in juveniles' responses to pilot administrations of the CMR paraphrase instrument.

The resulting items, presented in Appendix B, include three for each of the four *Miranda* warnings; thus, there is a total of twelve items, half of which are false and half true. A juvenile is presented with a card on which the standard *Miranda* warning is printed and it is read aloud by the examiner. Then the juvenile is told that the examiner will say some other sentences which use different words and that some of the sentences will "mean the same thing" as the printed sentence while others will not. The juvenile is to say "true" or "same" when the meanings are similar, and "false" or "not the same" when they are dissimilar to the standard *Miranda* warning in question. Total scores can range from 0 to 12. Comparison of scores between the CMR and CMR-TF will be provided in a subsequent discussion of research results with these measures in Chapter 4.

Comprehension of Miranda Vocabulary (CMV)

The purpose of the CMV was to assess respondents' abilities to accurately define the critical words in the *Miranda* warnings. While accurate definition would not allow one to infer that a person could comprehend the warnings themselves, deficiencies in word comprehension would strongly suggest deficiencies in understanding the *Miranda* warnings containing these words.

Within the standard *Miranda* warning statements employed in constructing the CMR, nine words were subjectively seen as offering potential difficulty for juveniles: consult, attorney, interrogation, appoint, entitled, right, statement, silent, and court. In pilot work in which juveniles were asked to define these words, it was our subjective evaluation that there were invariably adequate responses to the last three words (statement, silent, court). Therefore, these three words were discarded, and work was begun to develop a system for administration and evaluative scoring of a test of the understanding of the remaining six words. The process for developing the instrument is described in Appendix B, as are the details of administration and scoring. Generally, we followed a process similar to that described earlier for development of the CMR.

Administration of the CMV involves presenting a word audibly and printed on a card, presenting the juvenile with a sentence in which the word is used, and asking the juvenile to "tell me in your own words what the word means." As in the CMR, there are specific rules for inquiring about or requesting clarification of word definitions from the juvenile when the initial response is vague or when it would be scored as "questionable or partial" understanding if uncorrected by further elaboration. If the juvenile's response to inquiry corrects the vagueness or partial deficiencies in the initial response, full credit for the word definition is received.

The scoring criteria which met the consensus of opinion of our consultants regarding adequacy and inadequacy in understanding used a 2-point, 1-point, and 0-point format similar to that described earlier for the CMR, allowing total CMV scores to range from 0 to 12 points. The scoring system provides general criterion statements for each scoring possibility for a word, and offers many examples of actual responses conforming to the scoring criteria. Appendix B will show that sophisticated wording in juveniles' definition responses is not needed to achieve maximum credit, as long as the essential meanings are conveyed.

A series of tests of the reliability (degree of agreement) in scores between pairs of independent, trained scorers produced Pearson *r* coefficients of .89–.98 for the various individual *Miranda* words, and coefficients of .97–.98 for total CMV scores. Thus, trained scorers are capable of using the scoring criteria to produce highly reliable, consistent scores.

The three measures which we have described—CMR, CMR-TF, and CMV—were used in our project to assess comprehension of *Miranda* warnings and to determine the relationships between *Miranda* comprehension and various characteristics of juveniles such as age, race, and intelligence. This use of the measures is reported in Chapters 4 and 5. Before leaving these measures, we should note that it was not intended that some mathematical combination of scores on the three measures would be used in evaluating juveniles' comprehension of *Miranda* rights. Rather it was assumed that the three measures, being relatively independent assessments of a common content area, would allow us to avoid drawing conclusions about juveniles' capacities on the basis of any one index which employed a single mode of response.

COMPONENT II: BELIEFS ABOUT LEGAL CONTEXT

In the course of conceptualizing the content of the beliefs component, it became apparent that two subcomponents needed to be formed. First, it was decided by the panel of lawyers and psychologists that an intelligent, knowing, and voluntary waiver would depend in part on juveniles' *perceptions of the intended functions of the Miranda rights.* Second, juveniles' *perceptions of the probable consequences of decisions* to waive or to assert rights might in some cases be of a nature which would not meet the legal standards for competence. In the following sections, we will define these subcomponents and examine the indicants and measures developed in relation to them.

Perceptions of Function of *Miranda* Rights

The first subcomponent of the beliefs component concerns juveniles' perceptions of the function and significance of the rights specified in the *Miranda* warnings. It was reasoned that although a juvenile might possess an adequate understanding of the information expressed in the *Miranda* warnings, his or her ability to consider these rights intelligently might nevertheless be impaired by vague or faulty perceptions of the way such rights function in the context of interrogation and the significance they have in his or her potential interactions with legal personnel.

For example, some juveniles might clearly understand their right to consult an attorney; but their ability to make a reasoned decision about the right would be diminished if they possessed vague or faulty perceptions of the attorney–client relationship. Likewise, a juvenile might understand the right to silence in interrogation and that anything said might be used against him or her in court; but if the juvenile believes that judges are empowered to require juvenile defendants to answer questions in court, the significance of the *Miranda* warnings may be considerably reduced. This subcomponent, then, deals with contextual matters which are not explained in the *Miranda* warnings, but which are critical for grasping the significance of the warnings themselves.

Although courts have frequently expressed general concerns about juveniles' perceptions of the interrogation situation, very few courts have discussed their specific concerns regarding the critical perceptions which might be related to competence to waive rights. Thus, the project consultants logically arrived at three perceptions which were felt to be critical aspects of the subcomponent in question.

First, the significance of all of the *Miranda* warnings can be appreciated only if one correctly perceives the nature of interrogation and related legal processes. The accusatory quality of such processes is implied in the *Miranda* warning informing the suspect that statements may be "used against you," but it is not self-evident that all suspects (especially juveniles) perceive police as being in an adversary role in relation to themselves. Second, the right to legal counsel can be appreciated only if one correctly perceives the nature of attorney–client relationships and the general functions of a defense attorney. Third, the right to remain silent should be perceived as an irrevocable protection from self-incrimination. That is, one should realize that the powers of police, judges, or other authorities do not include the power to lawfully waive or revoke that right, to apply coercive pressure on the juvenile to do so, or to demand a response to questioning after a suspect has laid claim to that right.

Thus the "perceptions of function" subcomponent includes three content areas: (1) accurate perception of the nature of interrogation; (2) accurate perception of the attorney–client relationship; and (3) accurate perception of the irrevocable protection from self-incrimination.

Indicants

For a variety of reasons (e.g., the participating court's concern about interference with legal processes), it was not feasible for us to observe juveniles' behavior in actual interrogations or in contacts with defense attorneys. An alternative would have been to systematically observe juveniles' behavior and responses in "staged" interrogations or attorney–client situations; we believed, however, that this procedure might be too stressful for some juveniles.

It was finally decided to ask juveniles to express their beliefs and perceptions about the three content areas in an experimental procedure, offering them hypothetical situations and requiring them to respond in the third person to the situations. The accuracy of their perceptions of the function of rights in the three content areas could be inferred by asking them to define the roles of the participants (for example, police, lawyer, judge), to define the formal purposes of the legal processes involved, and to define what they believed was or was not legally allowable with regard to the behavior of the participants.

Measurement

An instrument entitled *Function of Rights in Interrogation* (FRI) was developed to assess the perceptions of juveniles concerning the functions and significance of *Miranda* rights. The instrument was designed to fulfill two requirements for assessing this subcomponent: (1) assessment stimuli were needed which would present the context in which *Miranda* rights have a function; and (2) a response format was needed in which juveniles' responses could be evaluated regarding the presence or absence of the critical indicants.

It was decided to present the important contexts (interrogation, attorney–client consultation, court hearing) in the form of verbal descriptions of hypothetical situations and also pictographically, so as to enhance the contextual set and to maximize subjects' attention to the contexts. Thus the FRI stimuli consist of four drawings, each of which is accompanied by a brief story which is verbally presented by the examiner. Two of the drawings depict interrogation scenes, a third depicts a youth and an attorney in consultation, and the fourth displays a courtroom scene. The content of the 15 FRI items (five for each of the three content areas), as well as their administration, are described in Appendix D and in Chapter 6, so they will not be detailed here.

The content of the questions and the criteria for scoring evolved through a process of collecting sample responses to be evaluated by the project's consulting lawyers and psychologists, much as has been described earlier for other measures. Each question has scoring criteria (see Appendix D) which allow for credit assignments of 2, 1, or 0 points. Three subscores are produced, corresponding to the three content areas of the instrument (nature of interrogation, attorney–client relationship, right to silence sanctions); thus, subscores can range from 0 to 10 and total FRI scores from 0 to 30. In a series of tests of the interscorer reliability with the FRI scoring system, pairs of trained scorers obtained Pearson r coefficients of agreement of .71–1.00 for various items, .80–.94 for various subscales, and .94–.96 for total FRI scores.

Expectancies about Decision Consequences

The second subcomponent of the beliefs component was juveniles' expectancies about the consequences of decisions to waive or assert their rights to silence and counsel. In discussing the beliefs component earlier, we noted the concern of courts regarding the effects of "adolescent fantasy, fright, or despair" on a juvenile's decision regarding *Miranda* rights. Other courts have registered concern specifically about the consequences which juveniles imagine might follow as a result of the decision to waive or assert their rights, and how this might influence their decisions [e.g., *Gallegos* v. *Colorado,* 370 U.S. 54 (1962); *Cooper* v. *Griffin,* 445 F2d 1142 (1972)]. Rotter's (1954) social learning theory holds that one's behavior is in large part a function of one's expectancies regarding the likelihood of positively or negatively valued consequences of the alternative behaviors available. In the present context, juveniles' "fantasies" about the consequences of rights waiver or assertion—that is, their expectancies about outcomes—might have a strong bearing on their decisions and could potentially cloud their ability to make a rational choice.

In defining the critical content of the expectancy subcomponent, the question before us was this: what expectancies about the consequences of the rights waiver decision are critical for inferring the ability or inability to make a knowing, intelligent, and voluntary decision?

The right to silence was intended to allow one to avoid the consequence of self-incrimination. But there are potentially many consequences of the decision to waive or assert that right which go far beyond the issue of self-incrimination. For example, many attorneys told us that in their opinion, most juveniles with whom they had worked were concerned primarily with whether they would spend the night following their arrest in a detention facility or at home, and that their expectancy regarding the effects which "silence" or "confession" might have on this discretionary matter played a large part in their decisions. Such expectancy issues were said to occur generally without any mention by police of physical detainment or the threat of detainment.

Can this expectancy be said to signify greater or lesser competence of the juvenile to decide whether or not to invoke rights? Some attorneys said yes. That is, they felt that juveniles who focused on a consequence such as detainment versus returning home were not considering the most important consequence of rights waiver—that is, self-incrimination—and therefore were not engaged in a rational decision-making process. Other attorneys were not so sure. They reasoned that there may be circumstances—for example, the combination of an especially insignificant alleged offense, a first-time offender, and a particularly offensive detention facility with the possibility of psychological damage to the juvenile if held overnight—in which it might be quite appropriate for a juvenile to consider what effect the decision about rights waiver or assertion might have on detention.

In short, we were not able to systematically arrive at a consensus regarding the set of expectancies which would contribute to or detract from one's competence to waive rights. The problem was compounded by the lack of guidance from the legal case comments of past courts.

Further, we were ignorant regarding even the basic *types* of expectancies which juveniles might have.

Therefore, it was decided to develop a method to systematically explore the range and types of juveniles' expectancies concerning outcomes of the rights decision and the reasoning they employed in arriving at that decision. The measures discussed earlier were designed to be evaluative, in the sense that they might define qualities of adequacy and inadequacy. In contrast, it was decided that the method associated with the expectancy subcomponent would be exploratory and descriptive, leaving questions of adequacy or appropriateness to persons who might later use the results derived from this descriptive method.

The instrument which we developed to explore juveniles' expectancy and reasoning concerning the waiver decision was called the *Waiver Expectancy Interview* (WEI). A semistructured interview was chosen for this exploratory task, partly because this format had proved to be useful in studies of juveniles' reasoning in other areas (Kohlberg, 1963; Tapp and Levine, 1974). The interview schedule is presented in Appendix E and will be described in more detail in Chapter 7.

PROBLEM-SOLVING STYLE (SECONDARY COMPONENT)

It will be remembered that the problem-solving component was viewed as secondary and exploratory in nature, since there was not sufficient evidence in court decisions to support its inclusion as a formal component of the competence standard.

Spivack, Platt, and Shure (1976) have offered a model for examining the effectiveness of problem-solving in adapting to interpersonal problem situations. The model focuses on five cognitive operations: (1) awareness of the existence of a problem; (2) generating alternative responses to the problem; (3) articulating the means for carrying out various types of alternative responses; (4) considering the consequences of various optional responses or solutions; and (5) appreciating the influence of one's responses on others' feelings and actions.

We decided to focus primarily on two of these skill areas: generating alternative responses or solutions to problems and considering the consequences of various optional solutions. The primary reason for this selection was that the Waiver Expectancy Interview would provide information relevant to both of these skill areas. The WEI asks juveniles to report all possible responses to the *Miranda* warnings and police requests for information and also asks them to reflect on the probable consequences of each alternative. The number of optional responses juveniles were capable of considering could suggest whether this aspect of their problem-solving skills reflected the necessary flexibility and productivity to consider responses other than mere compliance (waiver of rights). Similarly, the range of different types of consequences which they considered might reflect their degree of rigidity or flexibility when thinking about various decisions, the latter quality theoretically being the more effective in solving problems.

In Chapter 7, where we report the study employing the WEI, we will describe in detail the way in which interview responses were coded to meet these objectives.

PREPARATION FOR THE STUDIES OF COMPETENCE

The various instruments which we have described were used to evaluate juveniles' abilities in relation to the legal standards for competence to waive rights. Chapters 4 through 7 describe four separate studies in which the measures were used. (Chapters 8 and 9 address questions of adequate protection for juveniles in interrogation.) Each chapter begins with a review of relevant case law, revealing judicial assumptions (or assumptions evident in state statutes) about juveniles' capacities in relation to the legal standards. This is followed by a review of relevant social science research findings. Then we describe the use of our measures to empirically examine the performance of juveniles with various demographic characteristics and backgrounds. Those results are used to test the validity of the aforementioned judicial and statutory assumptions about juveniles' capacities. Finally, the results are interpreted so as to be of assistance in future legal decision making regarding the waiver of rights by juveniles.

4

Juveniles' Comprehension of *Miranda* Warnings

Many courts have addressed the question of juveniles' abilities to understand the *Miranda* warnings which preceded their waiver of rights and confession. As we noted in foregoing discussions, almost all courts faced with such matters have held steadfastly to the test which requires examination of the "totality of circumstances" in each case, following *Gallegos* v. *Colorado*, 370 U.S. 49 (1962) and *People* v. *Lara*, 432 P.2d 202 (1967). Even when a court has based a decision on a juvenile's specific age, IQ score, or other information, it will usually have been careful to cite reliance on the totality test and to admonish that the specific age or IQ in the instant case should not be applied alone as a test in future cases.

How, then, do judges and attorneys arrive at their conclusions concerning a juvenile's ability to understand *Miranda* warnings? Our case-by-case review of courts' decisions in this regard revealed two types of guidelines which appear to structure judicial decision making.

First, such cases have repeatedly set forth certain classes of circumstances which the courts believe were important concerning the question of juveniles' abilities to understand *Miranda* warnings. To use the terminology introduced in Chapter 3, these can be referred to as *legal indicants*—that is, classes of observable or easily verifiable phenomena (e.g., age, measured intelligence) which are assumed to relate logically to superordinate psychological attributes such as "understanding" or "awareness."

Second, across the history of such cases, judicial determinations of "lack of comprehension" can be identified with certain specific values of these classes, which we may call *indicant values*. That is, the cases involve critical circumstances such as specific ages or a particular IQ score which, when cases are viewed collectively, seem to represent critical dividing points for decisions of capacity or incapacity to understand *Miranda* warnings. Court reports themselves rarely acknowledge such critical dividing lines per se with regard to any indicant, so one cannot tell whether such collective "norms" enter into judicial decision-making, or if so, whether they enter by judges' unintentional or conscious yielding to consensus. These norms, then, represent "hypothetical assumptions" in law, in that they can be discerned through careful analysis of many cases but are not explicitly acknowledged.

In this chapter, we will review the relevant legal cases to identify judicial assumptions concerning relationships between the attribute in question (understanding of *Miranda* warnings) and both types of guides for judicial decisions (legal indicants and indicant values). Then we will describe a study which employed several measures of *Miranda* comprehension to test these judicial assumptions and to provide empirical guidelines for legal decisions about juveniles' capacities to understand *Miranda* warnings.

LEGAL ASSUMPTIONS

Legal Indicants

A few cases widely cited in later court decisions have provided lists of circumstances to be weighed in rights waiver cases. Often the circumstances in these lists have included not only the characteristics of the defendants, but also procedural circumstances—for example, whether the defendant was held incommunicado or the method and length of interrogation [see for example *West* v. *United States,* 399 F.2d 467 (1968)]. This is because procedural circumstances are important for weighing the broad question of the validity of a defendant's waiver. As described in Chapter 3, the competence of the defendant is but one of several matters which bear on the validity of waiver. Here we will focus only on circumstances which courts have suggested for weighing the defendant's competence to waive rights: that is, the defendant's capacity to waive *Miranda* rights knowingly, intelligently, and voluntarily. Let us first examine a few of the most widely cited lists of circumstances required or recommended by courts in some leading cases.

Courts which have dealt with juvenile waiver cases sometimes have cited lists of circumstances which were provided in two adult cases. The earliest, *Johnson* v. *Zerbst*, 304 U.S. 458 (1938), recommended that a defendant's "background, experience, and conduct" were circumstances to weigh in judging the defendant's capacity to provide a knowing, intelligent, and voluntary waiver. In *Coyote* v. *United States*, 380 F.2d 305 (1967), the court proposed a test including consideration of the age, intelligence, and "background" of the defendant.

By far the most frequently cited list in juvenile cases is from *West* v. *United States*, 399 F.2d 467 (1968). Of the nine circumstances referred to in *West*, seven were procedural and therefore not directly relevant for weighing juveniles' competence *per se*. The two circumstances referring to characteristics of juveniles themselves were age and education. Finally, in a list developed by the court in *State* v. *White*, 494 S.W.2d 687 (1973), three more characteristics of juveniles were added: physical condition, mental age or intelligence, and previous experience with the police or the justice system.

A composite set of characteristics from these four lists, then, would include: (1) age, (2) intelligence, (3) education, (4) prior experience with police, (5) physical condition, (6) "background," and (7) "conduct." Again, these characteristics were provided in lists of circumstances recommended by the four courts for addressing the general question of any defendant's competence to waive *Miranda* rights.

We turn now to an examination of the use of these circumstances in cases involving the more specific question of juveniles' abilities to understand the *Miranda* warnings. Forty cases in which this specific question was addressed were discovered in a review of appellate cases from 1948 to 1978. Confessions were ruled invalid due to lack of understanding of the warnings in about half of these cases and were ruled valid due to a finding of adequate understanding in a third of them. In the few remaining cases, judges offered strong opinions regarding juveniles' lack of understanding, but the cases were decided on other issues (primarily procedural ones).

The most common juvenile characteristic noted as a circumstance in the cases was age, followed closely by level of general intelligence. IQ scores, mental ages, or intelligence labels (e.g., "mentally retarded") were referred to in over half of the cases. In about one-third of the cases, the courts cited juveniles' levels of education as a circumstance which was weighed, while degree of prior experience with the justice system was also noted in about one-third of the cases.

Three of the characteristics noted earlier in frequently cited lists of circumstances were mentioned in only a negligible number of cases concerned with juveniles' understanding of *Miranda* warnings. These were the physical condition, "conduct," and "background" variables.

These three variables will not be dealt with in subsequent discussions, nor were they investigated in the research to be described. This was because of the infrequency with which they were referred to in the relevant cases, and because there was no rational way to define the variables, since the courts did not discuss what they meant when they used them.

The review of cases concerning juveniles' understanding of *Miranda* warnings produced two variables, however, which were not in the list of seven recommended circumstances. One of these, language ability or "literacy," was referred to in nearly a quarter of the cases. The other, mentioned in only a few cases (and therefore not to be dealt with further by us), was psychiatric condition (for example, "sanity," "absence of psychosis").

Indicant Values

Now let us examine specifically how each of the major characteristics (age, intelligence, experience, education, and literacy) have been employed by courts to decide on a juvenile's understanding of *Miranda* warnings. Before doing this, it is important to point out some general conclusions from this review.

First, nearly all courts addressing the issue of juveniles' understanding have affirmed the position, stated by the court in *West* v. *United States*, 399 F.2d 467 (1968), that no single variable, circumstance, or characteristic of a juvenile is ever an absolute sign of the juvenile's competence or incompetence.[1] The matter is to be decided on a case by case basis considering the totality of circumstances. They affirm that no specific age, IQ score, or any other sign is to be viewed as automatically excluding a confession by reason of inadequate understanding of the *Miranda* warnings. Second, nearly all courts addressing this issue have in fact cited more than one variable or characteristic as having influenced their decisions about juveniles' understanding. Therefore, in reading any given case, it is not possible to weigh any one variable as having had more or less influence on the decision than any other variable.

One must therefore read the following reviews with caution. For

[1]A few jurisdictions, though, have taken the rigid position that no juvenile confession is valid unless a parent, attorney, or guardian was present to help them decide concerning rights waiver. At the same time, they have refused to rule that juveniles themselves never waive rights knowingly and intelligently. This has prompted one judge [*Commonwealth* v. *Webster*, 353 A.2d 372 (1976)] to note that the situation "confounds all logic," since the former ruling implies that juveniles as a class cannot effectively waive rights without assistance, a point which courts nevertheless will not concede.

example, we will note that judges tended to decide that juveniles' understanding was adequate in cases involving juveniles above a certain age. We do not mean, however, that age was the controlling factor in these cases. Age will have been only one of several factors noted by the judges. A mere relationship between age (or any other variable) and a particular judicial decision does not imply that the variable in question was the deciding factor. The following is an examination of those relationships.

Age

Relevant cases have involved juveniles from ages 9 to 19. Understanding of *Miranda* warnings was considered to be lacking in almost all of the cases which involved juveniles of 12 years of age or younger.[2] In contrast, understanding was found to be sufficient in about three-quarters of the cases of juveniles 16 to 19 years of age.[3] Cases involving the intermediate ages of 13, 14, and 15 were more variable in outcome than were the other two age groups, and produced more dissenting opinions by judges.[4]

Intelligence or Mental Age

As in the case of age, judges have emphasized that no particular IQ score—not even mental retardation—is alone indicative of inadequate understanding of *Miranda* warnings [see *People* v. *Lara,* 432 P.2d 202 (1967)]. Thus, in one case, a suspect with an IQ score of 55 was consid-

[2]See *In re R.,* 345 N.Y.S.2d 11 (1973); *In re S.H.,* 293 A.2d 181 (1973); *People* v. *Baker,* 292 N.E.2d 760 (1973); *In re C.W., Jr.,* 508 S.W.2d 520 (1973).

[3]See *United States ex rel. Lynch* v. *Fay,* 184 F.Supp. 277 (1960); *United States ex rel. Simon* v. *Maroney,* 228 F.Supp. 800 (1964); *People* v. *Lara,* 432 P.2d 202 (1967); *State* v. *Prater,* 463 P.2d 640 (1970); *People* v. *Stanis,* 200 N.W.2d 473 (1973); *State* v. *Thompson,* 214 S.E.2d 742 (1975); *State* v. *McConnell,* 529 S.W.2d 185 (1975); *State* v. *Young,* 552 P.2d 905 (1976); *Doerr* v. *State,* 348 So.2d 938 (1977).

[4]See *Gallegos* v. *Colorado,* 370 U.S. 49 (1962); *In re Estrada,* 403 P.2d 1 (1965); *Lopez* v. *United States,* 399 F.2d 865 (1968); *In re L.,* 287 N.Y.S.2d 218 (1968); *Commonwealth* v. *Darden,* 271 A.2d 257 (1970); *People* v. *King,* 183 N.W.2d 843 (1970); *Thomas* v. *State,* 447 F.2d 1320 (1971); *Commonwealth* v. *Cain,* 279 N.E.2d 706 (1972); *United States* v. *Miller,* 453 F.2d 634 (1972); *Cooper* v. *Griffin,* 455 F.2d 1142 (1972); *In re Roderick P.,* 500 P.2d 1 (1972); *State* v. *White,* 494 S.W.2d 687 (1973); *Coney* v. *State,* 491 S.W.2d 501 (1973); *Commonwealth* v. *Youngblood,* 307 A.2d 922 (1973); *In re Stiff,* 336 N.E.2d 619 (1975); *M.K.H.* v. *State,* 218 S.E.2d 284 (1975); *State ex rel. Holifield,* 319 So.2d 471 (1975); *In re Morgan,* 341 N.E.2d 19 (1975); *Riley* v. *State,* 226 S.E.2d 922 (1976); *People* v. *Carpenter,* 347 N.E.2d 781 (1976); *State* v. *Toney,* 555 P.2d 650 (1976); *Williams* v. *State,* 232 S.E.2d 535 (1977); *Parker* v. *State,* 351 So.2d 927 (1977); *Tennell* v. *State,* 348 So.2d 937 (1977).

ered to have sufficient understanding of his rights when he was found to be able to read at a fifth grade level [*State* v. *Thompson*, 214 S.E.742 (1975)].

Despite this philosophy of the courts, a review of the relevant cases in which IQ scores were in evidence (about half of all the relevant cases) demonstrated a relationship between judges' decisions and IQ scores of the juveniles involved. That is, almost all of the cases in which requisite understanding of warnings was considered to be lacking involved juveniles with IQ scores below 75.[5]

Prior Experience with the Justice System

Generally, courts have considered a juvenile's lack of prior contacts with police and the courts as weighing against sufficient understanding of *Miranda* warnings, especially when viewed in combination with other variables supporting such a conclusion.[6] Similarly, extensive prior experience has sometimes been cited by judges as suggesting greater understanding of *Miranda* warnings due to more frequent exposure to them and familiarity with court processes [*In re Morgan*, 341 N.E.2d 19 (1975)]. In *State* v. *Prater*, 463 P.2d 640 (1970), the fact that the juvenile had 15 prior arrests was seen by the court even to reduce the importance of the police officer's hasty and incomplete reading of the *Miranda* warnings; the court concluded that "a warning as to his rights was needless" (at 641).[7]

Education and Literacy

Cases in which school grade level or reading ability were mentioned used this information in either of two ways. First, enrollment in a classroom for retarded students was sighted in a few cases in which juveniles' understanding was viewed as inadequate. The classroom placement, then, was used as evidence suggesting very low intelligence.

[5]IQ below 75, see *United States ex rel. Lynch* v. *Fay*, 184 F.Supp. 277 (1960); *United States ex rel. Simon* v. *Maroney*, 228 F.Supp. 800 (1964); *Thomas* v. *State*, 447 F.2d 1320 (1971); *In re P.*, 500 P.2d 1 (1972); *Cooper* v. *Griffin*, 455 F.2d 1142 (1972); *People* v. *Stanis*, 200 N.W.2d 473 (1973); *People* v. *Baker*, 292 N.E.2d 760 (1973); *Commonwealth* v. *Youngblood*, 307 A.2d 922 (1973); *State ex rel. Holifield*, 319 So.2d 471 (1975). IQ above 75, see *Commonwealth* v. *Darden*, 271 A.2d 257 (1970); *Coney* v. *State*, 491 S.W.2d 501 (1973); *In re Stiff*, 336 N.E.2d 619 (1975); *People* v. *Carpenter*, 347 N.E.2d 781 (1976); *State* v. *Toney*, 555 P.2d 650 (1976); *Parker* v. *State*, 351 So. 2d 927 (1977).

[6]*United States ex rel. Simon* v. *Maroney*, 228 F.Supp. 800 (1964); *In re P.*, 500 P.2d 1 (1972); *Cooper* v. *Griffin*, 455 F.2d 1142 (1972); *Commonwealth* v. *Cain*, 279 N.E.2d 706 (1972).

[7]See also *State* v. *Toney*, 555 P.2d 650 (1976).

Second, reading comprehension scores at a fifth grade or higher level were cited in a few cases, resulting in judgments of adequate understanding. Here again, grade levels were used as an index of general intellectual capacity.[8]

Summary and Hypotheses

The review indicated that courts generally refuse to acknowledge that any single indicant, or any particular indicant value, is always a sign of adequate or inadequate understanding of *Miranda* warnings. In addition, courts usually do not specify the relative importance of each of several indicants cited by them in any given case. Nevertheless, a composite of the relevant cases suggests certain relationships between each of the indicants and case outcomes. As explained early in this chapter, these relationships can be viewed as "hypothetical assumptions" which are not formally recognized in law: that is, as assumptions which might underlie judicial decision making when weighing whether certain juveniles understand *Miranda* warnings. These assumptions can be translated into hypotheses to be tested in our experimental investigation of juveniles' understanding of *Miranda* warnings.

Specifically, there was a tendency for judges to conclude a lack of understanding in cases involving juveniles of ages 12 and below, adequate understanding in cases of juveniles of ages 16 and above, and mixed decisions in the middle adolescent ages. If the judicial assumptions which we infer to underlie these tendencies are valid, we would expect to find a positive relationship between juveniles' ages and scores on our experimental measures of *Miranda* comprehension.[9] By the same process of reasoning, we would expect to find a positive relationship between IQ scores and *Miranda* comprehension scores, with an espe-

[8]*Commonwealth* v. *Youngblood*, 307 A.2d 922 (1973); *United States ex rel. Simon* v. *Maroney*, 228 F.Supp. 800 (1964).

[9]One empirical study (Ferguson & Douglas, 1970) investigated the abilities of 46 juveniles (in public schools and training schools) to describe "what you understand your rights to be," after each juvenile was taken individually and without explanation to a room where the experimenters formally read the *Miranda* warnings. Juveniles aged primarily 14–16 were represented in the study. Scores were assigned to responses, but there were no objective criteria for deciding on scores. The study employed no tests of statistical significance of differences in scores between ages. A clear view of juveniles' abilities to understand the various warnings cannot be obtained from the results, since the juveniles were required not only to understand the warnings but also to remember all of the warnings after having heard them read once in succession. Thus, although the study did find markedly low scores in many cases and found better scores at age 16 than age 14, the results have little meaning and questionable validity.

cially marked lack of comprehension to be associated with IQ scores below 75. In addition, if there is validity in the apparent judicial assumption of adequate understanding in almost all juveniles of ages 16 and above, then IQ scores at this age should be less predictive of experimental *Miranda* comprehension scores than at ages 15 and below.

Finally, judges' views of the effects of experience which a juvenile has had with the justice system would suggest that (other things being equal) juveniles with more police or court contact should demonstrate better understanding of *Miranda* warnings than should less experienced juveniles.

We did not feel justified in forming hypotheses about education and literacy, since no clear pattern of use of these variables emerged in the legal review. In the study to be reported below, we also did not examine the relationships of these variables to experimental measures of *Miranda* comprehension. This was because of methodological and procedural complications. Specifically, we encountered ambiguity in determining juveniles' present grade levels in many cases. In addition, the inclusion of a reading comprehension test would have unduly lengthened the experimental sessions with juveniles. We did, however, subject the four standard *Miranda* warnings to a readability formula developed by Fry (as described by Grunder, 1978, and involving a formula using sentence lengths and syllables per 100 words). The wording of the *Miranda* warnings was identified as being at the eighth grade level of reading difficulty, corresponding to the reading ability of the average 14-year-old.

THE RESEARCH METHOD

Given these hypotheses, we decided to administer the three measures of understanding of *Miranda* warnings (see Chap. 3) to a large number of juveniles, aged 10 to 16, and to examine relationships between scores on these measures and several demographic and social history variables. Our decision to perform the study with juveniles who had recently been taken into custody by police was based on several factors. First, it was only by testing juveniles within the juvenile justice system that we could be assured the availability of accurate information on such variables as number of prior referrals ("arrests") through access to court records. Second, by testing juveniles in the court's detention center soon after they had been taken into custody (rather than, for example, a random sample of a public school population), our sample could be more representative of the population with which courts have been concerned when addressing the issue of juveniles' waiver of *Miranda* rights.

This decision raised many complex practical, ethical, and legal problems, however, the resolutions of which required prolonged discussion and negotiation involving project personnel, various representatives of the court where the study was performed, and many third parties whose opinions were sought because of their interest in the welfare of juveniles in custody.

Among the practical problems was the fact that three-quarters of the juveniles detained in this court system remained in detention no more than three days, with the average stay being nearer to two days. Thus, testing had to be accomplished soon after a juvenile's admission to detention if we were to obtain a representative sample of juveniles. On the other hand, consideration for the emotional welfare of juveniles dictated against testing during the first 24 hours of detention, even though this would cause us to "lose" potential participants who were in detention less than a day. Such practical problems of scheduling, as well as the need to have effective relationships with the court and a high level of accountability for our activities, required that we place a full-time research associate at the court and detention site for the two years during which this and subsequent studies were being performed.

Among the many research ethics issues that we dealt with were the development of procedures to ensure that juveniles' participation would be voluntary, establishment of the autonomy of our research functions while working within the court system, maintenance of confidentiality in terms of both protecting juveniles' identities outside the court system and avoiding knowledge by the court of juveniles' responses and test scores, screening of potential participants for emotional suitability to participate, and establishment of public accountability and monitoring of the research process. The ways in which we dealt with these and other issues are detailed in Appendix G. It is unlikely that even our stringent resolutions of these issues would have sufficed to warrant research testing of juveniles in detention had it not been demonstrated that the research procedure itself presented an extremely low risk of harm to subjects and offered very great potential for producing results which might be of benefit to these juveniles and others like them in the future.[10]

[10]Throughout the two years of our data collection in the detention setting, there was no incident of undesirable emotional reaction to participation by any juvenile, nor were there complications or complaints from attorneys regarding legal issues in relation to our testing. This was especially gratifying since more than 700 juveniles participated in the several studies. During the two years, about 1 in 12 juveniles who were "eligible" to be research subjects did not participate, either because of their own refusal or as a result of the project's procedure for screening out juveniles who were at the time too emotionally unstable to participate.

A pressing legal concern was that the research project should not interfere with the ongoing legal process in relation to the juveniles who were research participants. For example, neither we nor the court wanted our research procedure to occur within the context of the actual preinterrogation process for juveniles. In addition, the court required that we not test juveniles who were presently being detained in relation to a felony charge. Among these juveniles would be some who might later be certified to stand trial as adults, and the necessity for more stringent control of the legal process in such cases resulted in the court's decision to restrict us from testing this group.[11]

As a consequence of these various considerations, the 359 juveniles tested in the court detention center for this study were almost all of the juveniles during an 11-month period who met the following requirements: (1) remained in detention for at least 24 hours; (2) were not presently being held on a felony charge; (3) were not screened out by reason of present emotional state; and (4) volunteered to participate. All were tested prior to 72 hours in detention. Nearly all had been read *Miranda* warnings when they were taken into custody, but only a minority had actually been interrogated (or were ever to be interrogated by police) concerning their present alleged offense prior to research testing. Another 72 juveniles were tested in a boys town and a boys school facility, bringing the total sample to 431 juveniles. The latter juveniles were included in order to increase the sample size of certain age and race groups. In addition, we wished to compare their performance to that of juveniles tested in detention, to assess for possible nonspecific effects of the "detention experience" on test performance.

Each juvenile was seen individually by trained research assistants under conditions clearly described to the juveniles as research, and as having no bearing on their future in detention or with the court or other agency having custody. We recognized, of course, that these conditions were quite different from those in which juveniles normally would be asked to consider their rights as expressed in *Miranda* warnings. Thus, it was anticipated that we would interpret the results as reflecting understanding under relatively optimal conditions rather than under the more stressful conditions of actual interrogation procedures.

Tests administered to all subjects were Comprehension of Miranda Rights (CMR), Comprehension of Miranda Vocabulary (CMV), and Similarities, Vocabulary, and Block Design subtests of the Wechsler Intelligence Scale for Children-Revised (WISC-R), from which an IQ

[11]This restriction did not prohibit us from testing juveniles whose prior referrals to the court had included felonies, so long as their present charge was not a felony. Thus, the restriction did not jeopardize the possibility of obtaining a representative sample of the juvenile detention population, as will be seen in our later description of the sample.

score was prorated.[12] The last 105 juveniles tested during data collection were administered the Comprehension of Miranda Rights, True or False (CMR-TF) measure in addition to the aforementioned measures.[13] Finally, the court's computer storage of juveniles' files allowed us to obtain the following information for each juvenile subject: (1) age, (2) sex, (3) race,[14] (4) local address, which was used to classify the subject in a socioeconomic group,[15] (5) number of prior felony referrals (arrests); (6) number of prior misdemeanor referrals; (7) number of prior referrals for

[12]These three WISC-R subtests were chosen because they had been consistently found to produce the highest correlations with Full Scale IQ of any subtests (Wechsler, 1974), and there is evidence that an IQ prorated on the basis of these three subtests correlates with Full Scale IQ in the .90s (Wechsler, 1955). In addition, we had the opportunity to compare the prorated IQ scores of 33 boys town juveniles to their Full Scale IQ scores obtained from administration of the full WISC-R by various social service agencies prior to these juveniles having been sent to the boys town. Our prorated IQ scores correlated .86 with the Full Scale IQ scores. This compares favorably with correlations between full administrations of Wechsler tests at widely discrepant time intervals.

[13]Only this later portion of the total sample received this measure because an earlier version of the CMR-TF, administered to the first 150 juveniles and including a smaller number of items than the final TF measure, proved to be nondiscriminating because of the extreme homogeneity of scores. Thus, redevelopment and piloting of the measure delayed its use in data collection.

[14]Courts have never listed race of defendant as a variable to be weighed in cases where a juvenile's understanding of *Miranda* warnings was in question. Yet, it is assumed that the "totality of circumstances" test would allow race, as well as socioeconomic class, to be included if they were seen to be relevant. We were especially interested in examining relationships between race and various *Miranda* comprehension scores, since psychological studies have suggested that when many black children are given information input in standard English, they must perform a transformation of the information which is not necessary for most white children (Williams & Rivers, 1976). Thus one might expect black juveniles on the average to have greater difficulty in understanding the wording of the *Miranda* warnings than would white juveniles as a group, even when the effects of differences in IQ scores are statistically controlled.

[15]Census information (1970) on median income and education in the 291 census tracts in St. Louis and St. Louis County was used to rank order the tracts, with separate rankings for income and for education. The mean of these two rankings constituted the SES rank for a tract. The tracts were then divided into four groups on the basis of SES ranks, with each of the two middle groups containing approximately one-third of the total tracts and the two extreme groups containing the highest one-sixth and the lowest one-sixth of the total tracts. SES labels were assigned to each of these groups in accordance with the probable socioeconomic status which would have been associated with the groups' mean incomes and educational levels in 1970. But assumptions about the relationship between these labels and the labels assigned on the basis of other systems for describing socioeconomic status must be approached with caution. The following data define the SES labels used herein by mean income and mean education in 1970: upper-middle—$17,406, 14.50 years; middle—$11,863, 12.21 years; lower-middle—$9,285, 10.28 years; lower—$6,307, 8.82 years. A subject's SES classification was determined by using his or her street address to find the tract of residence, and then to assign the tract's SES label as the SES classification for the subject.

TABLE 5. SAMPLE DESCRIPTION: NUMBER OF SUBJECTS, AND PERCENT OF SAMPLE (IN PARENTHESES), IN CATEGORIES FOR DEMOGRAPHIC VARIABLES

Variable	Category translation	Category 0	Category 1	Category 2	Category 3	Category 4	Category 5	Mean (standard deviation)
Age	0=10 and 11; 1=12; 2=13; 3=14; 4=15; 5=16	8 (1.8)	18 (4.2)	56 (13.0)	111 (25.8)	122 (28.3)	116 (26.9)	14.55 (1.24)
Sex	0=male; 1=female	256 (59.4)	175 (40.6)					
Race	0=white; 1=black	316 (73.3)	115 (26.7)					
Socioeconomic status	0=upper middle; 1=middle; 2=lower middle; 3=low; 4=not classified	68 (15.8)	141 (32.7)	99 (23.0)	31 (7.2)	92 (21.3)		
IQ	0=70 or less; 1=71–80; 2=81–90; 3=91–100; 4=101+	47 (10.9)	92 (21.3)	105 (24.4)	92 (21.4)	95 (22.0)		88.39 (16.12)

Total prior referrals	0=0 1=1-2 2=3-4 3=5-7 4=8+		80 (18.6)	139 (32.2)	106 (24.6)	54 (12.6)	52 (12.0)	3.38 (3.47)
Total prior felonies	0=0 1=1	2=2 3=3+	290 (67.3)	71 (16.5)	38 (8.8)	32 (7.4)		0.65 (1.26)
Total prior misdemeanors	0=0 1=1 2=2 3=3+		266 (61.7)	84 (19.5)	45 (10.4)	36 (8.4)		0.79 (1.47)
Total prior status offenses	0=0 1=1 2=2 3=3+		133 (30.9)	100 (23.2)	66 (15.3)	132 (30.5)		1.92 (2.13)
Total prior detentions	0=0 1=1 2=2 3=3+		246 (57.1)	69 (16.0)	53 (12.3)	63 (14.4)		1.05 (1.72)

		Percent in IQ classifications					
		0–70	71–80	81–90	91–100	101+	Mean IQ
Race	white	4.7%	17.4	24.1	25.3	28.3	92.75 (14.56)
	black	27.8%	32.2	25.2	10.4	4.3	76.40 (14.02)

"status offenses"; (8) total number of prior court referrals; and (9) number of prior detentions. Each of the five offense history variables was used independently as an index of amount of prior experience with police and the juvenile justice system.

An examination of Table 5 will provide an overview of the characteristics of the 431 juveniles in the study. The sample included a wide range of IQ scores and degrees of prior involvement with the justice system, with prior felony charges in about one-third of the sample. There were no significant differences between age groups in the proportions of blacks and whites, males and females, or of subjects in the various IQ classifications. Males and females contained similar percentages of blacks and whites and nearly identical percentages of subjects in each IQ classification. Blacks and whites differed only in IQ; as shown in the last entry in Table 5, whites were overrepresented in the higher IQ classifications and blacks were overrepresented in the lower IQ classifications, in proportion to their numbers in the total sample.

It will be recalled that our research procedures did not allow us to test juveniles who remained in the court detention center less than 24 hours, nor to test juveniles who were in residence there due to present felony charges. Thus, it was necessary to examine whether the sample of tested juveniles, which accounted for less than a third of all juveniles admitted to the detention center during the data collection period, might be different in composition from the total detention population. We did this by collecting demographic information on *all* juveniles entering the detention center during the first three months of the 11-month data collection period, and comparing these data to the demographic composition of the tested sample.

Table C-1 in Appendix C shows, for the three-month period, the demographic compositions of tested juveniles, of juveniles not tested because of current felony charges, and of juveniles not tested because their detention stay was too brief. Table C-1 also shows the demographic composition of the total three-month detention population (that is, the former three groups combined), and allows for comparison of that detention population to the 431 juveniles (which includes the smaller boys school and boys town subsamples) tested during the 11-month data collection process. There were clearly some differences in offense history variables between the group tested during the three months and the group not tested because of current felony charges or brief stay. However, when the composition of the total three-month detention population was compared to the composition of the final sample of tested subjects, there were no significant differences between the two groups on any demographic or offense history variable. We can conclude that the tested sample probably was representative of this jurisdiction's detention population from which the majority of the sample was drawn.

Now let us review juveniles' performance on the three *Miranda* comprehension measures, first without reference to types of juveniles, then in relation to their characteristics.

PERFORMANCE ON THE THREE *MIRANDA* MEASURES

Comprehension of *Miranda* Rights (CMR)

Table 6 shows three ways to conceptualize juveniles' performance on the CMR. First, about 20% of the juveniles obtained perfect total scores on the CMR; that is, they demonstrated adequate (two-point) understanding of all four *Miranda* warnings. Another 20% received less than half the obtainable credit on the CMR (total scores between 0 and 4). Second, zero-point credit (demonstration of inadequate understanding) was obtained on one or more of the *Miranda* warnings by about 55% of the juveniles. Therefore, depending on which definition of comprehension one employs, either four-fifths of the sample (with less than perfect scores) or slightly more than one-half of the sample (with one or more zero credits) can be seen as having been deficient in critical understanding of the *Miranda* warnings.[16]

Third, we may look at the percentage of subjects demonstrating adequate and inadequate understanding of each specific *Miranda* warning statement (see Table 6). Warnings I (right to silence) and IV (right to appointed attorney) were paraphrased adequately by the greatest number of juveniles (89% and 85%, respectively) and were inadequately paraphrased by only about 9% and 5%, respectively. When Warning I was inadequately understood, it was usually completely misconstrued (e.g., "You have to remain silent").

Greater difficulty in understanding occurred on Warnings II (statement will be used in court) and III (right to attorney before and during interrogation). Adequate understanding of Warning II was demonstrated by nearly two-thirds of the juveniles, but nearly a fourth of them provided clearly inadequate definitions. When definitions were inadequate, it was usually because juveniles interpreted the phrase, "anything you say," to refer to "swearing" or "lying," and interpreted "will be used against you in court" to mean that such disrespect or

[16]The issue of selecting an appropriate psychometric definition ("cut-off score") of adequate understanding for various practical purposes is discussed later.

TABLE 6. CMR: TOTAL SAMPLE

Category	Number	Percent of sample
Total scores		
8	90	20.9
7	82	19.0
6	123	28.5
5	46	10.7
4	46	10.7
3	12	2.8
2	20	4.6
1	4	0.9
0	8	1.9
Obtained zero-point credit		
On one item	156	36.2
On two items	55	12.8
On three items	19	4.4
On all four items	8	1.9
On one or more items	238	55.3
Adequate (2-point) responses on items		
I	385	89.3
II	272	63.1
III	129	29.9
IV	369	85.6
Inadequate (0-point) responses on items		
I	38	8.8
II	103	23.9
III	193	44.8
IV	21	4.9

Note. Range = 0–8; Mean = 5.86; *S.D.* = 1.85.

disobedience would result in negative consequences. While this belief may not be unrealistic, as an interpretation of Warning II it ignores the critical meaning regarding self-incrimination in the giving of information about an alleged offense.

Warning III was clearly the least understood of the warnings, with only about 30% of the juveniles demonstrating adequate understanding and 44% providing clearly inadequate (zero credit) responses. When understanding was inadequate, it was usually due to errors and confusion concerning time and place an attorney can be obtained. Interrogation was often misconstrued as the court hearing at which adjudication or other judicial decisions are made,[17] and occasionally the issue of

[17]When courts have examined misunderstanding of specific *Miranda* warnings, the most common error noted in such cases has been suspects' mistaken interpretations that they were being told they could have an attorney at their court hearing, and their apparent

availability of counsel "before and during" questioning was inadequately understood or simply unspecified, even after inquiry by the examiner.

Correlations between the responses on the four CMR items (see Appendix C, Table C-2) were relatively low, with five of the six coefficients being in the .20s and low .30s. This suggests that a juvenile's understanding of any one warning would not be especially predictive of the level of understanding of any other warning. The relatively more substantial correlations between individual CMR items and total CMR scores (.55–.73) do suggest some commonality between items, but the nature of this common factor cannot be discerned from the correlations themselves.

Comprehension of *Miranda* Vocabulary (CMV)

On the CMV (see Table 7), only a very small percentage of juveniles obtained a perfect score of 12 points, which required a fully adequate, two-point response for each of the six *Miranda* vocabulary words. Scores generally formed a more normal distribution than on the CMR, with very few juveniles at either extreme and a clustering of juveniles in the middle range.

A better sense of the juveniles' performance on the CMV is obtained by examining the percentages of subjects who obtained zero point credit on various numbers of CMV words (Table 7). Nearly two-thirds of the juveniles demonstrated inadequate understanding of one or more vocabulary items. Comparing these figures to their counterparts on the CMR (Table 6), it appears that vocabulary definition was somewhat more difficult than was defining the warnings themselves.

Examination of the percentages of two-point and zero-point responses on each of the vocabulary items (Table 7) reveals three patterns of scores. First, on the words attorney (II), entitled (III), and appoint (IV), there were relatively high percentages of juveniles providing adequate definitions and relatively low percentages demonstrating clearly inadequate understanding of the words. Second, the word interrogation (V) provided the opposite situation, with 37% offering adequate definitions and about 60% showing lack of understanding. Most errors in the definition of interrogation were of two types: defining it as a court hearing or being unable to provide any definition. Third, the

---

failure to understand that the warning referred to counsel in relation to the immediately impending process of police interrogation [see *Coyote* v. *United States,* 380 F.2d 305 (1967); *In re Morgan,* 341 N.E.2d 19 (1975); *People* v. *Baker,* 292 N.E.2d 760 (1973)].

TABLE 7. CMV: TOTAL SAMPLE

Category	Number	Percent of sample
Scores		
12	25	5.8
11	41	9.5
10	77	17.9
9	57	13.2
8	60	13.9
7	58	13.5
6	37	8.6
5	30	7.0
4	20	4.6
3	7	1.6
2	8	1.9
1	9	2.1
0	2	0.5
Obtained zero-point credits		
On one item	129	29.9
On two items	83	19.3
On three items	33	7.7
On four items	13	3.0
On five items	13	3.0
On six items	2	0.5
On one or more items	273	63.3
Adequate (2-point) responses on items		
I Consult	122	28.3
II Attorney	279	64.7
III Entitled	332	77.0
IV Appoint	346	80.3
V Interrogation	161	37.4
VI Right	115	26.7
Inadequate (0-point) responses on items		
I Consult	121	28.1
II Attorney	29	6.7
III Entitled	40	9.3
IV Appoint	36	8.4
V Interrogation	258	59.9
VI Right	39	9.9

Note. Range = 0–12; Mean = 7.93; *S.D.* = 2.62.

words consult (I) and right (VI) were clearly understood and clearly misunderstood by relative minorities of juveniles. That is, "questionable" or "partial" understanding (one-point credit) was demonstrated by a large percentage of juveniles on these words (consult, 43.6%; right, 62.9%). When juveniles demonstrated only partial understanding of the word consult, it was usually because they understood that it meant "to talk to" someone, but failed to sense the advisory, assisting, or decision-making purpose which distinguishes "consult" from words such as "converse" or "communicate." The word right was most often defined by some variation of the following phrases: "You can do it," "It's up to you, if you want to do it you can do it," "You can do anything if it's your right." Even with inquiry questions used by examiners to elicit further elaboration of meaning, most of the juveniles did not include the idea that a right is protected (for example, "You can do it *no matter what*" or "Nobody can't tell you that you can't do it, if it's your right"); they spoke of rights merely as allowances or choices.[18]

As in the CMR, correlations between CMV items (see Appendix C, Table C-2) were relatively low and correlations between individual items and total CMV scores were more substantial (from .51–.72). Two of the words that were understood by the fewest juveniles (consult and interrogation) produced the highest correlations with CMV total scores, suggesting that CMV performance may be related to general fund of word knowledge.

Comprehension of *Miranda* Rights, True or False (CMR-TF)

It will be recalled that this measure consists of three true or false items for each of the four *Miranda* warnings. Table 8 shows the CMR-TF results. As in the CMR, Warning III appeared to be the most difficult for juveniles to understand. But whereas Warning IV was dealt with relatively adequately by most juveniles in the CMR measure, responses to IV in the CMR-TF were only slightly better across juveniles than in Warning III. An examination of typical errors on Warning IV in the CMR-TF revealed that many juveniles that otherwise did well on the measure had endorsed the CMR-TF item, "If you don't have the money for a lawyer, the court will appoint a *social worker* to help you," as synonymous with the *Miranda* warning, "If you cannot afford an *attorney*, one will be appointed for you."

Before examining comprehension scores in relation to various demographic variables, the relationships between the three comprehen-

[18]Melton (1979) studied children's definitions of a right, using objective criteria based on Tapp and Levine's (1974) study of the development of legal concepts in children's thinking. Melton found that, even in children in the fifth and seventh grades, a frequent response was to confuse a right with an allowance provided by authority, rather than as a privilege which is legally protected against the whims of authority.

TABLE 8. CMR-TF SCORES: STUDY I SUBSAMPLE (N=105)

Category	Number	Percent of sample
Total scores		
12	12	11.4
11	17	16.2
10	29	27.6
9	16	15.2
8	11	10.5
7	14	13.3
6	4	3.8
5	2	1.9
Subscores		
Miranda I (mean=2.48)		
3	63	60.0
2	31	29.5
1	10	9.5
0	1	1.0
Miranda II (mean=2.48)		
3	58	55.2
2	40	38.1
1	7	6.7
0	0	0.0
Miranda III (mean=2.08)		
3	33	31.4
2	51	48.6
1	18	17.1
0	3	2.9
Miranda IV (mean=2.32)		
3	42	40.0
2	55	52.4
1	8	7.6
0	0	0.0

Note. Range = 5–12; Mean = 9.38; *S.D.* = 1.76.

sion measures should be noted. CMR total scores correlated substantially with CMV scores (r = .67), more so than either did with IQ (IQ and CMR, r = .47; IQ and CMV, r = .59). Similarly, CMR scores correlated more substantially with CMR-TF scores (r = .55) than either did with IQ (IQ and CMR, r = .47; IQ and CMR-TF, r = .43). Thus, similar abilities or knowledge may have contributed to performance on all three measures, and it would appear that some aspects of the common content of the measures rendered performances which were not solely a consequence of general intellectual ability.

COMPREHENSION IN RELATION TO JUVENILES' CHARACTERISTICS

Now let us examine the *Miranda* comprehension scores in relation to the various demographic and offense history characteristics. The first part of the discussion will focus primarily on results with the CMR and CMV.

Age and Intelligence

The two variables which we found to be most closely related to CMR and CMV scores were age and intelligence (IQ score). The increases in mean CMR and CMV scores as one proceeds upward in age and in IQ are clearly seen in Table 9, and both types of relationships are statistically significant on both measures. In the subsample of 105

Table 9. CMR, CMV, and CMR-TF Mean Scores by Age and IQ

Variable	CMR[a]		CMV[a]		CMR-TF[b]	
Age						
10 and 11	3.75[c]	(1.48)	4.50	(1.69)	8.25	(1.70)
12	4.66	(2.52)	5.83	(2.77)	9.11	(2.20)
13	5.64	(1.79)	7.00	(2.55)	9.23	(1.75)
14	5.84	(1.85)	7.45	(2.75)	8.96	(1.75)
15	6.04	(1.84)	8.55	(2.29)	10.00	(1.76)
16	6.11	(1.65)	8.73	(2.30)	9.78	(1.43)
F and (p)	4.57	(<.001)	12.10	(<.001)	1.57	(N.S.)
r	.19		.34		.21	
Partial r[d]	.22		.44		.27	
Intelligence score						
70 or less	3.70	(2.37)	4.61	(2.71)	7.25	(1.83)
71-80	5.29	(1.83)	6.82	(2.29)	8.81	(1.76)
81-90	5.97	(1.50)	7.67	(2.06)	9.03	(1.62)
91-100	6.34	(1.30)	8.98	(2.03)	10.23	(1.18)
101 or more	6.88	(1.27)	9.89	(1.51)	10.17	(1.55)
F and (p)	35.66	(<.001)	63.41	(<.001)	8.06	(<.001)
r	.47		.59		.45	
Partial r[d]	.39		.57		.41	

[a] $N = 431$.
[b] $N = 105$.
[c] Mean, with *S.D.* in parentheses.
[d] Partial correlations controlled for combinations of age, race, and IQ.

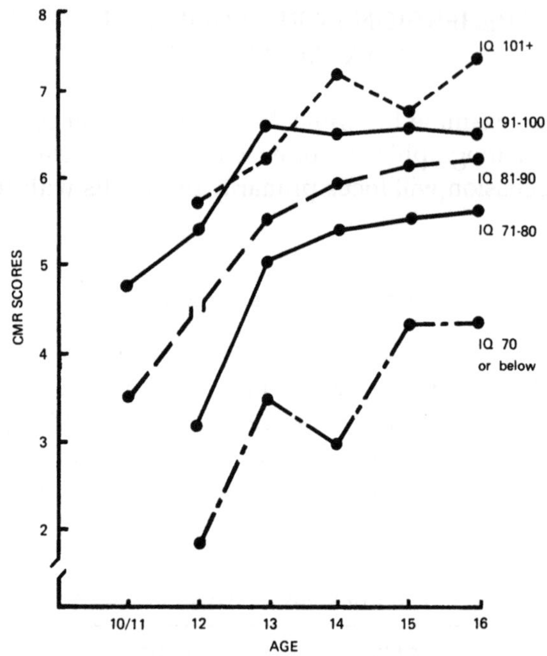

Fig. 1. CMR means by age and IQ classification.

juveniles, the differences between IQ classifications in CMR-TF scores were significantly different, but age did not show a significant effect.

The actual correlations between these measures and age are only low to modest (CMR, $r = .19$; CMV, $r = .34$; CMR-TF, $r = .21$), while they are more substantially related to IQ score (CMR, $r = .47$; CMV, $r = .59$; CMR-TF, $r = .45$). Together these results would suggest that IQ score accounts for more of the individual differences between juveniles in CMR and CMV performance than does age and therefore might be a better indicator of understanding of *Miranda* warnings.[19]

One of the reasons that age was not more closely related to CMR scores is graphically demonstrated in Figure 1, where mean CMR scores for each IQ classification are plotted by age. Within each of the IQ classifications above IQ of 71, CMR means scores were very similar from one age to the next after about age 14, while CMR means scores increased more dramatically from ages 10 and 11 through 13. In other

[19]Results of the multiple regression analysis separately for both *Miranda* measures appear in Appendix C, Tables C-3 and C-4. For the CMR, IQ accounted for about 25% of the variance in scores, while age accounted for only about 4%. For the CMV, IQ accounted for 37% of the variance, and age 13%.

words, a plateau in CMR performance was reached by about age 14, so that age is related to CMR performance only for ages 13 and below. The plateau seems to develop somewhat later in the lowest IQ classification.[20]

Returning to Table 9, note that the partial correlations (partial r) between the *Miranda* measures and both age and IQ are relatively similar to (and in one case, stronger than) the simple correlations (r).[21] This suggests that both age and IQ might have independent "power" to contribute to any attempts at producing more refined indicators than either would provide alone.[22] In fact, in a multiple regression analysis,[23] the combination of age and IQ correlated .54 (multiple r) with CMR scores, which is a somewhat better relationship than was found for IQ alone. Similarly, age and IQ correlated .71 (multiple r) with CMV scores, substantially better than age or IQ alone. Overall, the results suggest that better predictions about *Miranda* comprehension could be made by considering both variables simultaneously than by using either variable independently.

Tables 10 (CMR) and 11 (CMV) show the progression of *Miranda* mean scores with increasing age and IQ combined. Table 10 also shows

[20]An alternative explanation for the plateaus could be the argument that as more juveniles at higher age levels obtain perfect (8-point) scores, this might create a ceiling for age-group CMR means. But the plateau is apparent even in the lowest IQ classifications (71–80, 70 and below), where only about 20–30% of juveniles of ages 14–16 obtained perfect CMR scores.

[21]For the nonscientist, we would explain partial r as a statistical technique which is used when variable X is known to be related to variable Y, but when this relationship might be due primarily to their relationship in common with one or more other variables. The partial r technique allows one to statistically "hold constant" the third (or more) variable, to examine whether the relationship of variables X and Y remains high or is diminished to secondary or incidental status. In the present instance, the relationship between age and *Miranda* scores was examined with IQ and race held constant, since other procedures had suggested some interrelationships between these variables in our sample. In testing the relationship between IQ and *Miranda* measures, partial r was calculated with age and race held constant.

[22]Age and IQ were also suggested as independent sources of variance in two-way analyses of variance for CMR scores (age: $F = 6.98$, 5/403, $p<.001$; IQ: $F = 39.65$, 4/403, $p<.001$; interaction: $F = 1.44$, $p<.10$) and for CMV scores (age: $F = 22.40$, 5/403, $p<.001$; IQ: $F = 80.30$, 4/403, $p<.001$; interaction, $F = 0.70$, *N.S.*).

[23]In the multiple regression analyses (Appendix C, Tables C-3 and C-4), the amount of variance in CMR scores accounted for by age and IQ was 29%, and in CMV scores, 51%. The only other variables accounting for any notable amount of variance was race (about 1.8% for CMR scores and 1.3% for CMV scores). Since the combination of all demographic and offense history variables in this study accounted for just 33% of CMR variance and 53% of CMV variance, it is clear that IQ and age were the most critical variables in this study in terms of their relationships to *Miranda* scores.

TABLE 10. CMR MEANS FOR AGE BY IQ CLASSIFICATIONS, AND PERCENTAGE WITH NO ZEROS ON ANY CMR ITEMS (IN PARENTHESES)

	IQ classification					
Age	70 or less	71-80	81-90	91-100	101+	Total
10 and 11	—[a]	—[a]	3.50 (00)	4.66 (33)	—[a]	3.75 (12)
12	1.50 (00)	2.80 (20)	—[a]	5.33 (00)	5.75 (30)	4.66 (27)
13	3.40 (00)	5.00 (25)	5.58 (41)	6.57 (50)	6.15 (38)	5.64 (35)
14	2.92 (14)	5.39 (34)	6.00 (40)	6.41 (58)	7.10 (70)	5.84 (46)
15	4.38 (23)	5.56 (39)	6.10 (41)	6.51 (58)	6.69 (69)	6.04 (49)
16	4.30 (30)	5.67 (28)	6.17 (51)	6.29 (54)	7.45 (81)	6.11 (47)
Total	3.70 (19)	5.29 (31)	5.97 (42)	6.34 (53)	6.88 (65)	5.86 (45)
						S.D. =1.85

[a] Insufficient number of subjects.

the percentage in each age–IQ group who received no zero credits on any of the four *Miranda* warnings. These tables offer several interesting observations. First, the figures suggest that the performance of the average 10–12-year-old was markedly deficient compared to the average for the overall sample of juveniles. Second, the performance of 15- and 16-year-olds in the lowest IQ classification (70 or less) was no better than that of 12-year-olds overall. Third, referring to the percentage of juveniles with CMR records containing no zeros, only slightly more than one-third of juveniles in the 71–80 IQ class or the 81–90 IQ class with ages 15 or below, produced records with no zero-credit responses. At ages 14–16, these percentages increased to about 50% in IQ class 91–100,

TABLE 11. CMV MEANS FOR AGE BY IQ CLASSIFICATIONS

	IQ classification					
Age	70 or below	71-80	81-90	91-100	101+	Total
10 and 11	—[a]	—[a]	4.50	5.66	—[a]	4.50
12	2.00	4.00	—[a]	7.33	8.75	5.83
13	4.00	5.16	6.50	8.21	9.00	7.00
14	3.42	6.43	7.44	8.58	9.50	7.45
15	5.46	7.34	8.34	9.64	10.11	8.55
16	5.69	8.14	8.37	9.50	10.90	8.73
Total	5.69	6.82	7.67	8.98	9.89	7.93
						S.D. =2.62

[a] Insufficient number of subjects.

and reached a substantial majority (70–80%) in the upper ages at the highest IQ level. Generally, the figures confirm the value of employing both age and IQ in examining juveniles' performance on these measures. Later we will examine the implications of these results for legal issues raised earlier.

Prior Experience with Justice System

To examine the relationships between *Miranda* scores and amount of prior contact with the justice system, we used several indexes independently: number of prior referrals (arrests), number of prior felony referrals, number of prior misdemeanor referrals, number of prior "status offenses," and number of times previously held at the detention center. We found no significant differences in CMR or CMV mean scores (analyses of variance) between more and less experienced juveniles as defined by any of these indexes. Juveniles with many referrals were no more likely to demonstrate better understanding of the warnings than were inexperienced juveniles, even though juveniles presumably had been read the *Miranda* warnings nearly every time they came in contact with police or detention personnel.

We examined possible relationships between prior experience and CMR performance in combination with a number of other demographic variables as well. These analyses produced one interesting finding. Among whites, mean CMR scores increased as the number of prior felony referrals increased, especially when the referral record included three or more felony events. But among black juveniles, mean CMR scores *decreased* as the number of prior felony referrals increased, so that black juveniles with three or more felony referrals had a lower CMR mean score than did black juveniles with 0, 1, or 2 prior felony referrals. This differential relationship between prior felony referrals and the two race groups was statistically significant.[24] A detailed examination of mean CMR scores indicated that the aforementioned results applied to each of the different levels of IQ. No similar results were found for CMV

[24]Mean CMR scores for number of prior felonies for whites were 0 = 6.12, 1 = 6.47, 2 = 6.55, 3 or more = 7.22; and for blacks, 0 = 4.75, 1 = 5.47, 2 = 5.05, 3 or more = 4.00. A three-way analysis of variance (race by number prior felonies by IQ) for CMR scores revealed a statistically significant race effect and a significant IQ effect (as detailed elsewhere in the results), and a nonsignificant felony effect ($F = 2.59$, $p<.06$). But a statistically significant race by prior felony interaction effect was found ($F = 3.17$, $p<.02$), with IQ by felony and race by IQ interactions being nonsignificant statistically. In the multiple regression analyses of CMR and CMV scores, no experience variable accounted for other than negligible amounts of variance in scores.

scores. The interpretation of these results is problematic and will be taken up in our discussion of the results.

Race and Socioeconomic Status

We noted earlier the much lower mean IQ scores of black juveniles as compared to white juveniles in our sample. Therefore, given the substantial relationship between IQ and *Miranda* scores, it was not surprising to find that blacks as a group performed significantly poorer than did whites on all three *Miranda* measures (Table 12). The importance of the IQ effect can be seen in the partial correlations (partial *r*) between race and *Miranda* scores; when controlled for IQ and age, the race/CMR and race/CMV partial correlations were much lower than the simple correlations. In our opinion, however, the partial *r* coefficients still revealed a weak but potentially important relationship between *Miranda* scores and race, even apart from the mean difference between blacks and whites in IQ. Confirmation of that possibility is offered in the remainder of Table 12. Within nearly every IQ classification, the mean CMR and CMV scores of blacks were below those of whites. These differences, however, were pronounced only in the IQ classes below 90.[25] In other words, at lower IQ classifications, blacks tended to perform more poorly than whites on these measures of *Miranda* comprehension even when their IQ scores were similar.

Before exploring the reasons for the race differences in *Miranda* performance, we examined the relationships between *Miranda* scores and socioeconomic status (SES), since this variable also was modestly related to race in our sample.[26] Correlational analyses indicated some relationship between SES and both CMR ($r = .27$) and CMV ($r = .27$) scores. However, this was apparently due to relationships between SES and both race and IQ, because when correlations were examined with race and IQ controlled, there was no relationship between SES and either CMR (partial $r = .04$) or CMV (partial $r = .00$). In contrast, with IQ and SES controlled, some relationship still existed between race and

[25]Race and IQ both appeared as significant sources of variance in two-way analyses of variance for CMR scores (race: $F = 15.83$, 1/421, $p<.001$; IQ: $F = 21.64$, 4/421, $p<.001$; interaction: $F = 1.56$, $p<.18$) and for CMV scores (race: $F = 17.63$, 1/421, $p<.001$; IQ: $F = 41.02$, 4/421, $p<.001$; interaction: $F = 0.64$, *N.S.*). The reader is again referred to Appendix C, Tables C.3 and C.4, to examine the proportion of variance accounted for by race in multiple regression analyses.

[26]All analyses involving socioeconomic status were performed with a sample size of 333 juveniles, since juveniles with unknown socioeconomic status were deleted from these analyses. When SES was not known, it was because the juvenile was from outside the metropolitan St. Louis area which had been SES-classified prior to the study.

TABLE 12. CMR AND CMV MEANS FOR RACE BY IQ CLASSIFICATION, AND PERCENTAGE WITH NO ZEROS ON ANY CMR ITEMS (IN PARENTHESES)

	CMR		CMV		CMR-TF[a]	
IQ	White	Black	White	Black	White	Black
70 or below	4.86 (26)	3.15 (15)	5.46	4.21		
71-80	5.65 (40)	4.75 (18)	7.27	6.16		
81-90	6.10 (43)	5.62 (38)	8.02	6.75		
91-100	6.36 (53)	6.25 (50)	9.10	8.25		
101+	6.92 (65)	6.20 (60)	9.87	10.20		
Total	6.26 (51)	4.74 (28)	8.57	6.16	9.61	8.40
F and (p)	64.84 (<.001)		84.84 (<.001)		8.13 (<.001)	
r	.36		.44		.27	
partial r	.18		.19		.13	

[a] The CMR-TF was employed only with a subsample of 105 juveniles. Thus the number of juveniles was not large enough to describe mean scores by two independent variables.

Miranda performance (race and CMR, partial $r = .19$; race and CMV, partial $r = .21$).

The inclusion of SES with IQ and race in an inspection of CMR means did provide a clue to the nature of the relationship between race and CMR. Unfortunately, statistical tests of significance between the groups formed by these variables were not possible due to small cell sizes. It will be remembered (see Table 12) that lower CMR mean scores for blacks than for whites occurred primarily in IQ levels below 90. We found, however, that among upper-middle and middle class juveniles in that IQ range, the difference between the CMR mean scores of blacks (mean = 5.48) and whites (mean = 6.27) was less dramatic than was the difference between CMR means of blacks (mean = 4.22) and whites (mean = 5.91) in the lower-middle and lower classes and with IQ scores below 90. For juveniles with IQ scores above 90, CMR mean scores were nearly identical for both races at both SES levels (CMR means ranged from 6.14 to 6.83). The race difference in performance, then, seemed to be confined primarily to juveniles with a combination of subaverage intelligence and lower or lower-middle class background.

In reviewing these results, we recalled that many studies (e.g., Entwhisle, 1968; Labov, 1970) have pointed to linguistic differences between black and white children, especially in lower socioeconomic classes, and to the effects of such differences on performance in verbal tasks (Williams & Rivers, 1976). Is it possible that black juveniles in this group tended to obtain lower CMR scores not because of poorer understanding, but because of the verbal expressive demands of the CMR task, which requires paraphrasing the meaning of the warnings? An inspection of the CMR and CMR-TF results for the subsample of 105 juveniles who received both measures suggested that if there were race differences in verbal expressive ability, they probably were not responsible for the CMR differences between blacks and whites. The CMR-TF requires no verbal expression. Therefore, if blacks' lower CMR mean scores were due to verbal expressive difficulties, one would expect a much lower correlation between race and CMR-TF scores than between race and CMR scores. But the race/CMR-TF correlation ($r = .27$) was nearly as great as the race/CMR correlation ($r = .34$). When controlled for IQ, the corresponding partial correlations (.14 and .19) were still nearly equal.[27]

An alternative explanation would suggest that the relatively formal words or phrasing of the *Miranda* warnings are less clearly understood by lower socioeconomic blacks than by other blacks or by lower socioeconomic whites, because of possible differences in cultural and linguistic backgrounds. We have no data to confirm this interpretation, but the aforementioned results are more consistent with this interpretation than with the one focusing on verbal expressive differences.[28]

Sex

We found no significant difference between males and females in CMR mean scores. Females did perform significantly better on the CMV than did males. The low correlation ($r = .10$) between CMV scores and sex of juvenile, however, was reduced to nearly zero in partial correlation analysis in which the effect of age was controlled, since females in our sample had a slightly higher mean age than did males.

[27]The demographic balance of this subsample of 105 was very similar to that of the total sample of 431 juveniles. Correlations between CMR and IQ ($r = .50$) and CMR and race ($r = .34$) in this subsample were nearly identical to those in the total sample ($r = .47$ and .36, respectively). Thus, we assume that results from analyses with this subsample would generalize to the total sample.

[28] We considered a third explanation. Lower SES blacks may have been less motivated to perform for white examiners in comparison to whites or middle-class blacks, as suggested by Kennedy and Vega (1965). Since any such motivational factors would be expected to influence performance on the intelligence test as well as the CMR, the CMR/race relationship should be nullified when controlled for IQ if this explanation is valid. It was noted earlier, however, that a small but significant CMR/race correlation remained when partial r technique was used to control for IQ. Thus the motivational explanation is found lacking.

Administration Setting

One would wonder whether the setting or context within which the *Miranda* measures were administered might have had some general effect on the scores obtained. For example, we were curious whether emotional factors associated with recent arrest and detainment might have impaired the performance of juveniles tested in the detention setting, since they were seen by examiners usually within 24–48 hours after their arrest.

It will be recalled that 72 juveniles were tested not in detention, but in a boys town and a boys school where they had been placed due to earlier court referrals for delinquent behaviors. Both of these settings offered greater freedom of movement for juveniles than did the detention setting, and most juveniles in these nondetention settings probably had made initial adjustments to them, having been in residence there for at least a few months prior to our contact with them. We decided to compare the performance of these nondetention juveniles to the detention juveniles in order to examine possible effects of circumstances associated with the detention setting.

For each nondetention juvenile, we selected from our detention sample a juvenile who was of the same sex, race, and age, whose IQ score was within five points of the nondetention juvenile's IQ score, and who had the same (plus or minus one) number of prior court referrals.[29] We found no significant differences between the boys school sample and its matched detention sample in CMR or CMV mean scores. The boys town sample, however, did significantly poorer than did its matched detention sample on the CMR, but the two samples were not different on the CMV.[30] The results suggested that administration setting, and the fact of being tested soon after admission to detention, did not produce lower *Miranda* comprehension scores than if juveniles were tested in other controlled but less restrictive settings.

[29]A series of t-tests comparing both of the nondetention samples to their matched detention samples on all demographic and offense history variables not used in the matching revealed no significant differences except: (1) a significantly greater mean number of prior felony referrals for the boys school sample (mean = 1.26) than for its matched detention sample (mean = 0.52) ($t = 3.04$, $p < .003$); and (2) a significantly greater mean number of total referrals for the detention sample (mean = 3.20) than for the matched boys town sample (mean = 1.64) ($t = 2.89$, $p < .005$).

[30]For boys school ($N = 39$) versus matched detention sample ($N = 39$): CMR, boys school mean = 4.73, detention mean = 5.23, $t = 0.98$, p = *N.S.*; CMV, boys school mean = 6.00, detention mean = 7.05, $t = 1.84$, $p < .07$. For boys town ($N = 33$) versus matched detention sample ($N = 33$): CMR, boys town mean = 5.11, detention mean = 6.17, $t = 2.38$, $p < .02$; CMV, boys town mean = 7.00, detention mean = 7.52, $t = 0.88$, p = *N.S.*

COMPARISON TO LEGAL ASSUMPTIONS

Before we examine the implications of these results for legal assumptions, it must be acknowledged that our data offer at least two ways to make evaluative statements about juveniles' abilities to understand *Miranda* warnings. First, one may evaluate the abilities of a particular class of juveniles (e.g., age 12) in relation to any other class of juveniles in the study (e.g., age 16), or in relation to the performance of the total sample of juveniles. For example, one can evaluate the performance of particular types of juveniles as deficient because their performance scores were markedly below the overall average of the sample. The difficulty with this approach, of course, is that it implies that the average performance of the total sample is adequate, an assumption which cannot be made without comparing the average performance to some more absolute standard.

Second, it will be remembered that in the development of the various *Miranda* measures, the criteria for scoring responses as indicating adequate or inadequate understanding were based on the opinions of a wide range of lawyers and experts in juvenile law. Thus, when a juvenile receives zero credit on one of the test items, the juvenile has not met the standard represented by the judgments of the expert panel concerning "sufficient" understanding. The scoring system itself, then, can be used as a standard for making evaluative statements about adequacy of understanding. For example, assuming that the court in *Miranda* intended that all four of the *Miranda* warnings must be understood, zero credit on any one of the *Miranda* warnings in the CMR can be interpreted as signifying a juvenile's lack of preparedness to make an informed decision about rights waiver.[31]

Using these standards, then, let us return to the legal issues which this study was designed to address, to examine whether the results support the prevailing legal assumptions about juveniles' abilities to understand *Miranda* warnings.

The results generally support the prevailing legal assumption that the mere fact of being a juvenile does not signify an inability to under-

[31]Although we will define adequate comprehension of *Miranda* warnings as "no zero credits on any CMR item," others might prefer to require "two-point credit on every CMR item" as the standard for adequate comprehension. But to employ "perfect score" as the standard assumes that one-point responses signify inadequate understanding, while in fact such scores were assigned when juveniles' responses were not clearly wrong but were insufficient to conclude that full understanding existed. The "no zeros" standard, then, reduces the likelihood of erroneously "penalizing" juveniles by concluding they do not understand when in fact it is not clear whether or not they do.

stand the *Miranda* warnings. Two of the warnings were understood over 80% of the time, the most difficult warning was understood by about 30% of the juveniles, and about 45% of the juveniles obtained no zero credits on any *Miranda* warnings.

The finding that no single demographic or offense history variable alone accounted for the full range of individual differences in CMR or CMV performance supports the general notion, implicit in the "totality of circumstances" approach, that judicial decisions concerning juveniles' rights waivers should be based on several factors or circumstances. Although IQ score was strongly related to understanding on the *Miranda* measures, other variables were found to qualify the conclusions which might be drawn on the basis of IQ alone.

Our review of cases revealed three legal indicants—age, intelligence, and prior justice system experience—which have been used with great frequency when weighing issues of juveniles' understanding of *Miranda* warnings. The substantial relationships between *Miranda* performance and both age and IQ score in our study validate legal assumptions about the relevance of these two indicants. The results also suggest that there may be some value to consideration of prior justice system experience of juveniles, but only in very limited and qualified ways which we will discuss below. Finally, certain findings concerning relationships between Miranda performance and both race and socioeconomic status raise the possibility that these variables should be weighed in some cases, although they have never been cited as relevant circumstances in past legal cases.

The most important application of the present results is as an empirical standard with which to evaluate the courts' uses of indicant values—that is, for evaluating implicit assumptions apparent in past court cases concerning critical ages or levels of IQ. Let us first compare the empirical results to judicial assumptions concerning age and *Miranda* understanding, adding other variables as we proceed.

We noted that courts have been reluctant to view understanding of *Miranda* warnings as being adequate among juveniles of ages 12 or below. Our results indicate that understanding is indeed deficient in this age range compared to the overall juvenile sample, with inadequate understanding present in about three of four cases in this age range (compared to about one of two for the total sample). The courts' record of more variable decisions in the 13–15 age range is consistent with our finding that approximately half of the juveniles of this age provided responses with no zero credits. But our results differ from the courts' general decision record regarding 16-year-olds. Although cases involving juveniles of this age have usually resulted in findings of adequate understanding of the *Miranda* warnings, we found that at least half of the 16-year-olds in our sample were deficient in this regard.

The most critical implication of these results, then, is that age itself is quite limited in its effectiveness as a guide for weighing decisions about juveniles' understanding. This was especially true at ages 14 through 16, where a plateau in performance was reached on the CMR measure, such that age itself ceased to account for individual differences in understanding. In addition, within any given age in this range, juveniles demonstrated a wide range of individual differences in both intellectual functioning and CMR performance.[32] Thus, while the study supports the combined use of age and intelligence as legal indicants, it strongly suggests that decisions should be weighed more heavily by considerations of intelligence within the 14–16 age range.

The results provide some dramatic consequences of this situation. For example, there is evidence that 15- and 16-year-olds with very low intelligence generally should be viewed as having no greater understanding of *Miranda* warnings than the average 10–12-year-old. In contrast, 15- and 16-year-olds of average intelligence (IQ above 100) are very likely to have adequate comprehension, with seven or eight of ten expected to produce "no zero" records.

Judging from our results, courts would appear in many cases to have underestimated the intellectual ability required to adequately understand the *Miranda* warnings. Court decisions have consistently viewed understanding to be adequate in cases where IQ scores above 75 were entered as evidence. But an examination of Table 10 reveals that among 14–16-year-olds in our sample, the probability of adequate understanding with IQ levels between 80 and 100 is no better than 50% and as low as 40% in some ages.

The courts' assumptions that juveniles with more prior experience with the justice system have a better understanding of *Miranda* warnings appear to be simplistic. Our results found no simple relationship between any of the indexes of amount of prior experience and any of the *Miranda* measures. The assumption is apparently based on the notion that increased exposure to a set of information leads to learning. But one can argue that the emotionally arousing conditions under which juveniles are exposed to the warnings during arrest might inhibit or

[32]These results are consistent with past developmental research (Kohlberg, 1969; Loevinger, 1976; Tapp & Levine, 1974), which has documented the considerable variance in cognitive and other developmental characteristics of children once they have achieved the age which is generally associated with the development of Piaget's "formal operations" stage.

impair incidental learning of the warnings.[33] Further, while repetition may lead to familiarity, it is not self-evident that it leads to understanding. In this light, it is not surprising that we found no direct relationship between amount of prior experience and *Miranda* comprehension, even with the use of many indexes of prior experience.

The one significant relationship which was found in this area suggested that more prior felony referrals were associated with better *Miranda* comprehension when the juvenile was white and poorer comprehension when the juvenile was black. This finding is intriguing but very difficult to interpret. The fact that these effects were apparent at every IQ level for whites and blacks suggests that the results are not due to differences in intellectual ability *per se* between groups of white and black high-felony juveniles. We can speculate that in the total population of black juveniles who engage in illegal behaviors, number of prior felonies may indeed be associated with increased *Miranda* comprehension just as it was for white juveniles, but that a particular type of black, high-felony juvenile was not represented in our sample. For example, suppose that some subset of high-felony juveniles "learn" from their experience and become legally sophisticated, while another type of high-felony juvenile does not. Any local police or court procedures which deal differently with black juveniles and white juveniles in this sophisticated subset of the high-felony group might produce differences in the composition of the black and white high-felony groups in our sample. Such a situation could occur if legally sophisticated ("street-wise") high-felony blacks are more likely to be certified to stand trial as adults than are similarly sophisticated high-felony whites. We have neither evidence nor any particular reason to believe that this is the case; but such jurisdictional circumstances could produce the results we obtained, since the black, sophisticated subset would have been outside the juvenile jurisdiction when data was collected and hence would not have been adequately represented in our sample. At any rate, the differential results for blacks and whites concerning the relationship between CMR scores and number of prior felony referrals must stand as an interesting finding which, however, cannot be seen as sufficiently conclusive to warrant recommendations for court policy or decisions.

No courts were found to apply race or subcultural background as a variable to be weighed in decisions about juveniles' comprehension of *Miranda* warnings. Clear warnings have been issued by social scientists

[33]The negative effects of anxiety on learning of verbal material have been researched and documented extensively (Sarason, 1960; Spence & Spence, 1966).

(Williams & Rivers, 1976) that when many black children are provided information input in standard English, they are being asked to perform a transformation of the information which is not necessary for most white children. That is, these black children may have learned and retained various information in the context of their own linguistic background (other than standard English), so that standard English cues do not facilitate the retrieval or recall of the information sought. Such a view is consistent with our findings regarding comparatively poorer CMR performance for lower socioeconomic blacks than for lower socioeconomic whites even within the same IQ range.[34] The results, then, suggest that race should be weighed as an indicant of poorer comprehension when IQ scores are below approximately 80–90 and when lower socioeconomic status applies.

In the next chapter of this book, we will address further the implications of the results of this study for rules and procedures in the juvenile justice system. At that time, we will address a question raised by the present data. That is, is the level of *Miranda* comprehension of the most proficient subjects in our sample—the older and intellectually adequate juveniles—sufficient to support the general assumption, apparent in courts' decisions, that older juveniles generally can understand the *Miranda* warnings?

The results we have just discussed offer two ways to address the question. Examining the information in Table 10, some would respond that even among 14–16-year-olds with IQ scores from 81 to 101 +, the probability for adequate understanding of *Miranda* warnings is little better than 50%, even under our "ideal" experimental conditions. They might conclude, then, that the courts' presumption of adequate understanding seems unwarranted.

But the data offer the possibility for a quite different argument. Figure 1 shows that the CMR performance of these same juveniles has reached a plateau around age 14. One might wonder whether this plateau signifies the achievement of the maximum probability for *Miranda* comprehension for these juveniles individually and as a group, so that the plateau would actually extend beyond age 16. If so, then these 14–16-year-olds might be demonstrating understanding which is not inferior to that of adults with similar intellectual capacities. Since courts generally have presumed that adults have the capacity to under-

[34]But it does not necessarily follow that a simplified or "black dialect" form of the *Miranda* warnings would improve *Miranda* comprehension scores for lower SES black juveniles. Several studies (Copple & Succi, 1974; Quay, 1971, 1974) have found little difference in black, lower SES children's understanding of standard English, and black nonstandard English forms of verbal material.

stand the warnings, the foregoing argument would suggest the validity of that presumption for 14–16-year-olds as well. The fact that some adults themselves might not achieve a level of comprehension deemed adequate by absolute standards (e.g., no zeros on CMR) need not deter such an argument. The law has often applied standards which are relative rather than absolute, as when judgment expected of "a reasonable man" is considered sufficient for fulfilling one's legal obligations.

This argument rests on the assumption that the plateaus in comprehension found for average 14–16-year-olds would extend into adult years and therefore represent an adult level of *Miranda* comprehension. The testing of this assumption was the objective of our next study.

5

Adults' *Miranda* Comprehension

A STANDARD FOR JUVENILES' COMPETENCE

The results of the study in the foregoing chapter indicated that juveniles at any given age varied considerably in the extent of their understanding of *Miranda* warnings, commensurate with a wide range of intellectual abilities at any specific age. In general, however, mean comprehension scores increased at each successive age level from 10 and 11 to about 14, beyond which a plateau in mean comprehension scores extended through age 16. These results indicated the need for a similar study of adults' comprehension of *Miranda* warnings in order to determine whether this plateau signified the attainment of a level of comprehension generally associated with an adult level of understanding.

The appropriate procedure for measuring adult comprehension appeared to be a straight forward replication of procedures employed in the study with juveniles. The CMR, CMV, and CMR-TF items, procedures, and scoring criteria had been designed in relation to legal concepts which apply to criminal law as well as juvenile law. Pilot administration of the three measures to a sample of college students and adults in halfway houses for offenders indicated no difficulties in the use of scoring criteria or response examples in the manual, even though the development of the manual had been based on responses obtained from juveniles. Interrater reliability in the scoring of adults' protocols proved to be very similar to the reliability coefficients obtained in scoring juveniles' protocols (as described in Chap. 3).

We had decided in the earlier research to study court-referred juveniles instead of a random sample of juveniles from the community, because court-referred juveniles represented that portion of the juvenile population for whom the issue of *Miranda* comprehension was most important. Similarly, in selecting an adult sample, we reasoned that the juveniles ought to be compared to adults for whom *Miranda* comprehension was most relevant—that is, adults who had been arrested. While it would have been desirable to test adult volunteers soon after they had been arrested, as we had done with juveniles, several circumstances did not allow us this opportunity. Therefore, we decided on a sample of adult offenders residing in halfway houses where they had been placed either while on probation or when returning to the community after prison or jail terms.[1]

These adults, of course, would be expected to have much more experience with police, courts, and the *Miranda* warnings than would most of the juveniles. Therefore, if they were found to be superior to juveniles in *Miranda* comprehension, their greater understanding might be due either to their greater experience as adult offenders or to intellectual abilities related to their status as adults *per se.* Anticipating this difficulty in interpretation of the juvenile–adult comparison, we decided to obtain a nonoffender adult sample as well, one which would be relatively similar to the adult offenders in age and intelligence. Although this sample was obtained, it proved to be a difficult task, which resulted in a relatively small sample size.[2] Nevertheless, it was consid-

[1]In exploring the possibility of testing adults soon after their arrests, some of the difficulties we encountered were related to resistance by some officials to research activities in general in the settings we approached. In addition, the principal investigator was concerned for the security and safety of research assistants after examining the potential sites for data collection. In deciding not to test adults soon after their arrests, we also weighed the fact (demonstrated in Chap. 4) that juveniles who were tested soon after being taken into custody performed at about the same level on the *Miranda* measures as did boys residing in juvenile rehabilitation centers. This provided some indirect evidence that the procedure of testing juveniles soon after arrest and adults during their rehabilitation would not in itself contribute to juvenile–adult differences in performance on the *Miranda* measures.

[2]Part of the difficulty in obtaining an adequate sample of nonoffenders was the necessity to match the age and intellectual heterogeneity of the offender sample. There proved to be no single occupational or organizational group available in the community which might match this heterogeneity. Our first attempt was to obtain subjects from a technical school for young adults. While this satisfied the necessary racial and SES requirements, we found that these subjects tended to be more intellectually capable than was the offender sample as a group. Consequently, the nonoffender group was finally composed of citizens from various walks of life who were obtained as research volunteers in a range of different occupational settings. The relatively small size was a result of difficulties in obtaining cooperation of work supervisors. Workers themselves seemed quite willing to volunteer once we were given the opportunity to approach them with our request.

ered sufficient to serve the purpose of addressing the aforementioned problem in interpreting any differences between juveniles and adults in *Miranda* comprehension.

THE ADULT SAMPLES

The offender sample consisted of 203 male and female volunteers residing in four halfway houses managed by the Magdala Foundation of St. Louis. This private organization accepts referrals from the local court and from state and federal correctional agencies. The residents were either on probation or on parole from jail or prison terms. The primary objective of the halfway houses is to provide a temporary residential and counseling base for offenders while they develop initial occupational, residential, and social stability in the community.

Halfway house residents were approached by research assistants generally within the first week of their residence. The information obtained from each volunteer included: age, race, sex, whether on probation or parole, and socioeconomic status (see footnote 15, Chap. 4, for a description of the method for determining socioeconomic classification). In addition, each of the subjects in the sample had consented to the researchers' examination of the subject's files to determine the number of prior felony arrests, the number of prior misdemeanor arrests, and the total number of prior arrests. These did not include arrests prior to the subject's seventeenth birthday, since juvenile arrests were not included in most files. Arrests rather than convictions were recorded, since these data were intended to be indexes of the amount of prior experience with the police and, therefore, with the *Miranda* warnings. Procedures for administering the *Miranda* comprehension measures and intelligence test were identical to those described for the juvenile study, except that the three intelligence test subtests (Vocabulary, Similarities, Block Design) were from the Wechsler Adult Intelligence Scale.

The nonoffenders were 57 male and female volunteers obtained in a variety of settings: custodial services, maintenance workers at a university and in a hospital (kitchen workers, laundry crews, grounds maintenance workers), and college freshmen with inner-city backgrounds. Information was obtained on age, race, sex, and socioeconomic status. There was no way to verify whether or not a subject in this sample had ever been arrested. But it is safe to assume that the great majority of the nonoffender subjects would not have had the amount of contact with police and courts typical of the offender sample. Procedures with the nonoffenders were identical to those used with the offenders. Testing occurred at the place of a subject's employment, or for students, at the university.

The demographic composition of both of the adult groups are shown in Tables A-3 and A-4 (Appendix A). In both samples, the mean ages were in the mid-twenties, with ages ranging from 17 to 50. In contrast to the juvenile sample, the majority of subjects in both of the adult samples were black, with the upper-middle and middle SES categories underrepresented. The mean IQ score of the adult offenders (89.35) was very similar to the mean IQ in the juvenile sample, but slightly (nonsignificantly) lower than the mean IQ for adult nonoffenders (91.74).

ADULTS' PERFORMANCE ON THE THREE *MIRANDA* MEASURES

Adults' performances on the CMR, CMV, and CMR-TF are shown in Tables 13, 14, and 15, respectively. The data for juveniles, which have

TABLE 13. CMR DATA FOR ADULT AND JUVENILE SAMPLES (ALL NUMBERS IN PERCENTAGES)

Category	Offender adults (*N*=203)	Nonoffender adults (*N*=57)	Total adult sample (*N*=260)	Juveniles (*N*=431)
Total scores				
8	42.4	42.1	42.3	20.9
7	26.1	29.8	26.9	19.0
6	12.3	7.0	11.5	28.5
5	10.3	17.5	11.9	10.7
4	4.4	1.8	3.8	10.7
3	1.0	0.0	0.8	2.8
2	2.0	0.0	1.5	4.6
1	0.5	1.8	0.8	0.9
0	1.0	0.0	0.4	1.9
Adequate (2-point) responses on items				
I	86.7	93.0	88.5	89.3
II	71.4	56.1	68.1	63.1
III	65.0	70.2	66.5	29.9
IV	83.3	91.2	85.4	85.6
Inadequate (0-point) responses on items				
I	5.4	5.3	5.0	8.8
II	8.9	7.0	8.5	23.9
III	15.3	14.0	14.6	44.8
IV	4.4	0.0	3.1	4.9
Obtained zero-point credit on one or more items	23.2	22.8	23.1	55.3

TABLE 14. CMV DATA FOR ADULT AND JUVENILE SAMPLES (ALL NUMBERS IN PERCENTAGES)

Category	Offender adults (N=203)	Nonoffender adults (N=57)	Total adult sample (N=260)	Juveniles (N=431)
Total scores				
12	12.8	15.8	13.5	5.8
11	24.6	29.8	25.8	9.5
10	21.2	19.3	20.8	17.9
9	13.8	17.5	14.6	13.2
8	11.8	3.5	10.0	13.9
7	7.9	10.5	8.5	13.5
6	1.5	3.5	1.9	8.6
5	1.0	0.0	1.2	7.0
4	1.0	0.0	0.8	4.6
3	1.5	0.0	1.2	1.6
2	1.5	0.0	1.2	1.9
1	0.0	0.0	0.0	2.1
0	1.5	0.0	0.8	0.5
Adequate (2-point) responses on items				
I Consult	43.8	42.1	43.5	28.3
II Attorney	78.8	78.9	78.8	64.7
III Entitled	88.7	94.7	90.4	77.0
IV Appoint	77.8	91.2	80.8	80.3
V Interrogation	71.9	75.4	72.7	37.4
VI Right	42.4	45.6	43.1	26.7
Inadequate (0-point) responses on items				
I Consult	8.4	1.8	6.9	28.1
II Attorney	1.5	1.8	1.5	6.7
III Entitled	5.9	5.3	5.7	9.3
IV Appoint	9.4	3.5	8.1	8.4
V Interrogation	22.7	21.1	22.3	59.9
VI Right	19.2	8.8	16.5	9.9
Obtained zero-point credit on one or more items	39.0	33.2	37.3	63.3

been included in these tables to facilitate comparison, were taken from the similar tables which appeared in Chapter 4.

On all three measures, a far greater percentage of adults attained the highest possible scores on the measures than did the juveniles. For example, CMR scores of 7 or 8 were made by 69.2% of the adults, compared to 39.9% of the juveniles. CMV scores of 10, 11, or 12 were made by 60.2% of the adults, compared to 33.2% of the juveniles. An examination of the percentage of subjects giving inadequate responses

TABLE 15. CMR-TF DATA FOR ADULT AND JUVENILE SAMPLES (ALL NUMBERS IN PERCENTAGES)

Total CMR-TF scores	Offender adults (*N*=203)	Nonoffender adults (*N*=57)	Total adult sample (*N*=260)	Juveniles (*N*=431)
12	38.9	24.6	35.8	11.4
11	25.6	31.6	26.9	16.2
10	12.3	17.5	13.8	27.6
9	7.4	12.3	8.5	15.2
8	6.9	8.8	7.3	10.5
7	3.0	3.5	3.1	13.3
6	3.9	0.0	3.1	3.8
5	2.0	1.8	1.5	1.9

to various CMR items shows that most of the differences between adults and juveniles occurred on Warnings II (use of incriminating information in court) and III (right to counsel before and during interrogation). Judging from the percentages for adequate and inadequate responses to various CMV items, adult–juvenile differences were manifested across vocabulary items in the CMV. Before examining the differences between adults and juveniles more closely, let us examine differences between the adult samples.

COMPARISONS OF ADULT OFFENDERS TO NONOFFENDERS

An examination of the percentages in Tables 13–15 suggests that there were few if any remarkable differences in performance between the adult offenders and nonoffenders. To examine this assumption, we performed a series of two-way analyses of variance; each analysis employed the two adult groups (offenders and nonoffenders) as one independent variable, the other variable being age classification, race, sex, SES, or IQ. These were performed separately for CMR scores, CMV scores, and CMR-TF scores.

Regarding CMR and CMR-TF scores, there were no significant differences between groups (that is, adult offenders and adult nonoffenders) in any of these analyses. One significant group difference in CMV scores was found, however, in one of the CMV analyses (group × age); that is, when differences in age composition between the two groups were statistically controlled, nonoffenders were found to perform significantly better on the CMV than did offenders.[3]

[3]In a two-way analysis of variance of CMV scores: offenders vs. nonoffenders, $F = 6.00$, $df = 1/250$, $p<.01$; age, $F = 5.91$, $df = 4/250$, $p<.0001$.

The results indicate that the offenders' greater degree of experience with police and courts did not appear to improve their comprehension of *Miranda* warnings beyond that which would be expected of other, less-experienced adults of similar age, IQ, socioeconomic status, and race. For this reason, we combined the offenders and nonoffenders into a single adult sample for most of the remaining analyses.

Comprehension in Relation to Adults' Characteristics

In one-way analyses, CMR scores were significantly related to race, IQ, and SES, but not to age or sex. In a three-way analysis involving race, IQ, and SES, however, only IQ maintained a significant relationship to CMR scores.[4] Therefore, while the mean CMR score was inferior for blacks compared to whites and inferior for lower SES than for higher SES groups, these results were related primarily to the lower mean IQ of blacks and lower SES subjects in the adult sample. Identical results were obtained in similar analyses of the CMR-TF scores of the adults. Thus, it can be concluded that differences among adults in understanding of the *Miranda* warnings are related primarily to differences among them in general intellectual ability.

Similar analyses of CMV scores revealed a different picture. In one-way analyses of variance, CMV scores were significantly related to age, race, and IQ, but not to SES or sex. In a three-way analysis of variance involving age, race, and IQ, both age and IQ maintained significant relationships to CMV scores, while race was not significantly related to CMV scores when age and IQ were controlled.[5] The ability to define *Miranda* words, then, varies not only in relation to general intellectual abilities of adults, but also in relation to age, with older adults on the average being able to better define the *Miranda* words than are younger adults.

The relationships between the amount of prior police and/or court experience and various *Miranda* measures was investigated using the data from the offender group alone. Within the adult offender group, number of prior felony arrests was significantly related to CMR scores (but not CMV or CMR-TF), when the effect of IQ was statistically con-

[4]For one-way analyses of variance of adults' CMR scores: race, $F = 10.53$, $df = 1/258$, $p<.001$; IQ, $F = 21.22$, $df = 4/255$, $p<.0001$; SES, $F = 3.80$, $df = 3/197$, $p<.01$. For three-way analysis of variance using the same data: race, $F = 0.26$, $df = 1/169$, *N.S.*; IQ, $F = 12.55$, $df. = 4/169$, $p<.0001$; SES, $F = 1.84$, $df = 3/169$, *N.S.*

[5]For one-way analyses of variance of adults' CMV scores: age, $F = 4.99$, $df = 4/255$, $p<.0007$; race, $F = 10.90$, $df = 1/258$, $p<.001$; IQ, $F = 37.44$, $df = 4/255$, $p<.0001$. For three-way analysis of variance using the same data: age, $F = 4.17$, $df = 4/216$, $p<.003$; IQ, $F = 33.08$, $df = 4/216$, $p<.0001$; race, $F = 0.37$, $df = 1/216$, *N.S.*

trolled.[6] Offenders with more prior felony arrests generally performed more adequately on the CMR than did offenders with fewer prior felony arrests. These results suggest that an earlier conclusion should be qualified. It will be recalled that offenders did not exceed nonoffenders on any of the *Miranda* measures. This suggested that greater experience acquired during arrests did not result in more adequate *Miranda* comprehension. Although this might be true for offenders as a group, it appears from this latter analysis that those offenders with a large number of felony arrests (a great deal of police or court experience) do acquire a greater understanding of *Miranda* warnings than do nonoffenders or less experienced offenders.

COMPARISON OF JUVENILES TO ADULTS

The final set of analyses addressed the central question for which data on adults had been obtained: How do subjects in the juvenile ages compare to subjects at various adult ages on the *Miranda* measures? The most appropriate method of comparison was considered to be two-way analyses of variance of the CMR and CMV scores of all subjects (N = 691, composed of 431 juveniles and 260 adults), employing eleven age groups (six juvenile and five adult age categories) and five IQ classifications. It was understood that blacks, males, and the lower SES categories comprised a somewhat greater proportion of the adult age groups than of the juvenile age groups. But these variables had rather consistently been found not to be related to CMR or CMV scores when controlled for IQ and age. This was the justification for using age and IQ alone in this final analysis.

Tables 16 and 17 show the CMR means and CMV means, respectively, for each juvenile and adult age-by-IQ group. (The data for juveniles are repeated from a similar table in Chap. 4.) Accompanying these tables are graphs which plot the means shown in the tables (for CMR, Figure 2, and for CMV, Figure 3).

CMR Comparison

The CMR means in Table 16 and Figure 2 demonstrate in general that CMR mean scores were higher in the adult ages than in the juvenile ages, at every IQ level. The age differences are not as great at the two

[6]For a three-way analysis of variance of adult offenders' CMR scores: number of prior felony arrests, $F = 2.48$, $df = 4/162$, $p<.04$; IQ, $F = 15.55$, $df = 4/162$, $p<.0001$; race, $F = 0.04$, $df = 1/162$, *N.S.*

TABLE 16. CMR MEANS FOR AGE BY IQ CLASSIFICATIONS, INCLUDING ALL ADULTS AND JUVENILES (N = 691)

Age	IQ classifications					Total age means
	70 or less	71-80	81-90	91-100	101+	
10 and 11	—[a]	—[a]	3.50	4.66	—[a]	3.75
12	1.50	2.80	—[a]	5.33	5.75	4.66
13	3.40	5.00	5.58	6.57	6.15	5.64
14	2.92	5.39	6.00	6.41	7.10	5.84
15	4.38	5.56	6.10	6.51	6.69	6.04
16	4.30	5.67	6.17	6.29	7.45	6.11
17-19	—[a]	5.22	6.83	7.52	7.50	6.64
20-22	5.00	5.80	7.00	7.15	7.75	6.65
23-26	4.16	7.00	7.13	7.23	7.54	6.91
27-31	—[a]	—[a]	6.64	7.00	7.63	6.86
32+	6.00	7.20	6.23	7.06	7.20	6.82

[a] Insufficient number of subjects.

highest IQ levels (91–100, 101+) as at the lower IQ levels. One will note that the CMR means for each age group (at the right side of Table 16) continue to rise beyond age 16, and to reach a plateau at the 23–26 age group. Juveniles of ages 15 and 16 with average IQ scores (91–100, 101+) performed about as well on the whole as did adults with IQ scores of 90 or below.

TABLE 17. CMV MEANS FOR AGE BY IQ CLASSIFICATIONS, INCLUDING ALL ADULTS AND JUVENILES (N = 691)

Age	IQ classifications					Total age means
	70 or less	71-80	81-90	91-100	101+	
10 and 11	—[a]	—[a]	4.50	5.66	—[a]	4.50
12	2.00	4.00	—[a]	7.33	8.75	5.83
13	4.00	5.16	6.50	8.21	9.00	7.00
14	3.42	6.43	7.44	8.58	9.50	7.45
15	5.46	7.34	8.34	9.64	10.11	8.55
16	5.69	8.14	8.37	9.50	10.90	8.73
17-19	—[a]	7.88	8.22	10.23	11.00	8.74
20-22	5.66	8.33	9.09	9.65	11.37	9.05
23-26	6.33	9.37	9.20	10.11	11.09	9.56
27-31	—[a]	—[a]	9.92	10.81	11.09	10.06
32+	9.00	9.40	10.15	10.75	10.70	10.34

[a] Insufficient number of subjects.

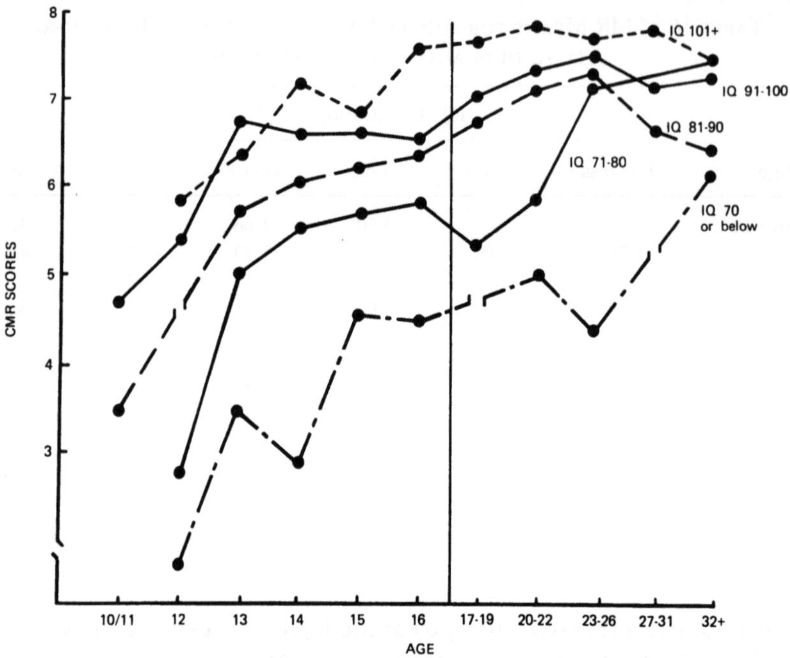

Fig. 2. CMR means by age and IQ classification for juveniles and adults.

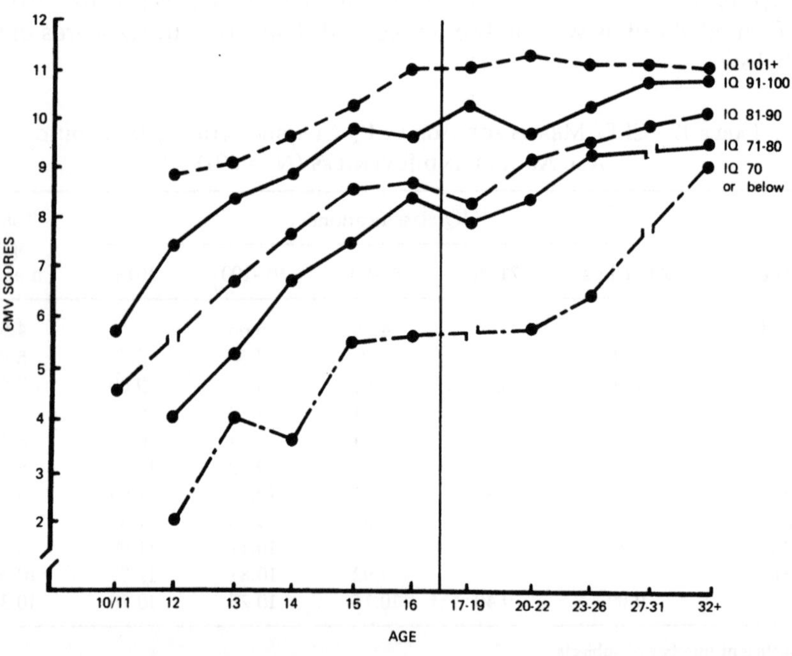

Fig. 3. CMV means by age and IQ classification for juveniles and adults.

A two-way analysis of variance (age × IQ) of CMR scores indicated that CMR performance was significantly related to both age and IQ.[7] (The same result was obtained in a similar analysis of CMR-TF scores.) Age and IQ together accounted for 33% of the variance of CMR scores. A multiple range test[8] revealed the following significant differences ($p<.05$) between age groups in CMR scores: (1) 10- or 11- and 12-year-olds' scores were significantly lower than scores at all other age groups; (2) 13-, 14-, and 15-year-olds' CMR scores were significantly lower than the scores of age groups of 17 and above; (3) the scores of 16-year olds were *not* significantly different from those of subjects 17–22 years of age, but were significantly different from those of subjects 23 years or older; and (4) there were no significant differences between any of the age groups of 17 and above.

CMV Comparison

Table 17 and Figure 3 demonstrate the higher CMV scores of adult age groups compared to juvenile age groups of similar IQ. As in the CMR, the differences between adult and juvenile age groups are not as great at higher IQ levels as they are at lower IQ levels. Unlike the CMR, CMV means for each age group (at the right side of Table 17) do not reach a plateau by the middle 20s; they continue to rise with each successive adult age group.

A two-way analysis of variance (age × IQ) of CMV scores indicated that CMV performance was significantly related to both age and IQ.[9] Age and IQ together accounted for 52% of the variance of CMV scores. A multiple range test revealed the following significant differences ($p<.05$) between age groups in CMV scores: (1) 10- or 11- and 12-year-olds' scores were significantly lower than scores in age groups of 14 and above; (2) 13- and 14-year-olds' CMV scores were significantly lower than the scores of age groups of 15 and above; (3) 15- and 16-year-olds'

[7]In a two-way analysis of variance (age × IQ) of CMR scores (N = 691): age, $F = 8.77$, df = 10/638, $p<.0001$; IQ, $F = 61.31$, df = 4/638, $p<.0001$. For CMR-TF scores: age, $F = 4.71$, df = 10/638, $p<.001$; IQ, $F = 41.02$, df = 4/638, $p<.0001$.

[8]This procedure would be meaningful only if there were no marked IQ differences between the eleven age groups themselves. A one-way analysis of variance of IQ scores across the eleven age classifications revealed that there were no significant differences between ages in IQ scores. The range of mean IQ scores was 87.3 (for age group 20–22) to 93.2 (ages 27–31), with juvenile age groups all having IQ means of 87–90. Standard deviations of IQ scores ranged from 12 to 16 in the various age groups. The similarity of IQ compositions within the various age groups justified the use of the multiple range test for examining CMR and CMV differences between age groups.

[9]In a two-way analysis of variance (age × IQ) of CMV scores (N = 691): age, $F = 22.83$, df = 10/638, $p<.0001$; IQ, $F = 118.18$, df = 4/638, $p<.0001$.

scores were not significantly different from those of subjects 17–22 years of age, but were significantly different from the scores of subjects 23 and older; and (4) the scores of 17–19- and 20–22-year-olds were significantly lower than those of subjects 23 years of age or older.

CONCLUSIONS

We mentioned in Chapter 4 that there were several standards with which to judge the adequacy of juveniles' abilities to understand *Miranda* warnings. When we judged juveniles' CMR and CMV performances against absolute standards—that is, no incorrect responses as defined by the scoring criteria for these measures—we concluded that the probability of adequate understanding of *Miranda* warnings is little better than 50%, even among 14–16-year-olds with IQ scores above 80.

The present, direct comparison of adults' and juveniles' performances was intended to provide data relevant to a different standard, one which employs an "adult level of understanding" as the criterion for judging adequacy of understanding of *Miranda* warnings. Two of our findings relate specifically to that standard. Sixteen-year-olds' comprehension of the *Miranda* warning statements, and 15- and 16-year-olds' comprehension of *Miranda* words, did not differ significantly from the level of comprehension manifested by 17–22-year-olds of similar intelligence. In contrast, juveniles in age groups below 15 obtained significantly lower mean scores on the *Miranda* measures than did subjects who were 17 years of age or older. Therefore, the "plateaus" in comprehension observed in the older juvenile ages in Chapter 4 were confirmed; that is, *Miranda* scores at juvenile ages increase through the 14-year-old group, beyond which mean scores do not increase appreciably with successive age groups into the adult years.

Using the "adult level of understanding" criterion in a strict sense, then, juveniles at ages below 15 would not be seen to meet this standard for understanding of the *Miranda* warnings. Applying this information to policy recommendations concerning the competence of juveniles to waive rights, the results indicate that as a group, juveniles below age 15 are not competent to waive their rights to silence and counsel. Understanding of the warnings, of course, is only one of the components of competence to waive rights, as we outlined in Chapter 3. But without this understanding, one need look no further in addressing the issue of competence.

Fifteen- and sixteen-year-olds, on the other hand, are seen to meet the "adult level of understanding" criterion. Yet it would be premature to conclude that they are competent to waive *Miranda* rights. As we discussed in Chapter 3, competence to waive rights requires more than understanding of the warnings alone; it must also include an understanding of the significance of the rights in the context of the legal process. In Chapter 6, we will examine this second type of understanding among 15- and 16-year-olds (as well as younger juveniles).

In addition, some persons would argue that the standard which should be applied in juvenile cases is the absolute standard, which we discussed in Chapter 4, rather than the adult standard. The juvenile justice system has been predicated on an assumption that juveniles should receive special consideration often not provided in adult cases, because of juveniles' general emotional immaturity. The use of the absolute standard—a higher standard than the "adult level of understanding" criterion—might be seen as compensation needed in juvenile cases. Using the absolute standard, our results questioned the adequacy of understanding among nearly half of the juveniles in the 15–16-year-old range. These matters of interpretation will be revisited in the final chapter, after other results bearing on the question have been presented.

Before leaving the present study, two observations concerning the performance of the adults deserve mention. First, we found no significant differences between any of the adult age groups in CMR scores, but younger adults (ages 17–19 and 20–22) performed significantly more poorly on the CMV measure than did older adults in the sample (ages 23 and older). These results are generally consistent with what is known about the development of general intellectual and verbal abilities. That is, general intellectual ability has been found to increase until about age 16, after which time there is little increase until late middle age when abilities decline on the average (Wechsler, 1955). The acquisition of verbal information and the development of verbal expressive abilities, however, continue to develop well into adulthood (Jones & Conrad, 1933; Wechsler, 1955). This well-known fact might account for the increase in the ability to define *Miranda* vocabulary words in successive adult age groups in our sample.

Second, Table 14 shows that less than one-half of the adult subjects provided an adequate definition of the word "right." While more adults than juveniles did provide adequate definitions, the majority described a right as something one is allowed to do, and failed to express a sense of the protectedness of a right (see definitions in the CMV manual, Appendix B). In the next chapter, we will have the opportunity to examine in more detail both adults' and juveniles' perceptions of the nature of a right.

6

Perceptions of the Function of Rights

An understanding of the *Miranda* warning statements *per se* is not enough to prepare a suspect to make a knowing, intelligent, and voluntary decision to waive or assert his or her rights. The *Miranda* warnings are merely notifications of those rights. They inform a suspect that certain optional choices are available, but they do not explain how the rights work in the context of police and court procedure. To know that one has choices is of limited value if one does not also have an understanding of the significance and function of those choices within the legal system.

The courts have been mindful of this distinction between a knowledge of rights and an understanding of their function, especially in light of the greater vulnerability of juvenile suspects. For example, in a recent California Supreme Court case [*In re Patrick W.*, 148 Cal. Rptr. 735 (1978)], the court found that although the 13-year-old murder suspect "showed understanding of the *Miranda* admonitions as explained by deputies," he was not likely "to fully 'comprehend the meaning and effect of his statement'" (at 738). (The "meaning and effect" phrase was quoted from *People* v. *Lara,* 432 P.2d 202, at 215 (1967), a leading case which dealt in part with a juvenile's ability to understand the full implications of the right to silence and a waiver of that right.)

The United States Supreme Court, in *In re Gault,* 387 U.S. 1 (1967), expressed similar concerns. The Court commented on the complexities of the legal proceedings which face many juveniles and the possible detrimental effects of adolescents' fantasies concerning the consequences of the choice before them. Thus it has not been uncommon for later courts to consider juveniles' understanding of the function and significance of their rights as an issue more or less distinct from their understanding of the *Miranda* warnings themselves.[1] Some courts have even questioned juveniles in the courtroom to determine whether they understood what manner of assistance they refused when they waived the right to legal counsel, or whether they even understood the concept of a right.[2]

These legal concerns led us to conceptualize a second major component of the legal standards for competent waiver, which we labeled beliefs about legal context. As described in Chapter 3, this component was further divided into two subcomponents. One of the subcomponents, to be discussed in Chapter 7, focused on juveniles' expectancies about the personal consequences of waiving or asserting *Miranda* rights. The other subcomponent involved juveniles' perceptions of the intended functions of the rights to silence and legal counsel. It is this subcomponent to which we now turn our attention.

POLICE, LAWYERS, AND THE POWER OF RIGHTS

Our review of case law provided almost no guidance in defining what knowledge is essential for a suspect to understand the function of the rights to silence and counsel. That is, judges have not been specific about their concerns for juveniles' comprehension of the "meaning and effect" of these rights. Our first task, then, was to determine what it is that a defendant ought to understand (apart from the *Miranda* warnings *per se*) in order to have a grasp of the intended significance and function of the rights. Consistent with the general approach throughout our studies, we went to legal and psychological consultants for the standards for defining the content of this subcomponent.

We asked juvenile law attorneys (project consultants) to arrive at a set of legal concepts, legal processes, and roles of participants in the legal process, the understanding of which would be essential for a knowing, intelligent, and voluntary waiver of rights. Consensus resolved to three content areas which were judged to be critical and which were not explained by the *Miranda* warnings themselves.

[1]For example: *In re L.*, 287 N.Y.S.2d 218 (1968); *Commonwealth* v. *Darden*, 271 A.2d 257 (1970); *Cooper* v. *Griffin*, 455 F.2d 1142 (1972); *In re Thompson*, 241 N.W.2d 1 (1976).

[2]For example: *Coyote* v. *U.S.*, 380 F.2d 305 (1967); *People* v. *Baker*, 292 N.E.2d 760 (1973); *In re C.W., Jr.*, 508 S.W.2d 520 (1973); *In re Morgan*, 341 N.E.2d 19 (1975); *In re Holifield*, 319 S.2d 471 (1975).

1. *The suspect should understand that the police, in their role as interrogators, are in an adversarial position and are attempting to discover the degree of the suspect's involvement in a law violation.* If one does not view the police as adversaries in their interrogation role, or does not understand the nature of the information they are seeking, one will not have a sense of potential jeopardy associated with the waiving of one's rights. The *Miranda* warning that "anything you say can and will be used against you" does of course refer to potential jeopardy. But the specific nature of that jeopardy and the information sought by police (that is, a confession which could be the primary or sole legal justification for severe penalties) must be inferred from the warning. While this inference might seem to be an easy one, it is not certain that it would be so for all juveniles.

2. *The suspect should perceive a defense attorney as an advocate, skilled in law, whose function is to provide legal advice and guidance in the interest and defense of the suspect.* Knowing that one can have an attorney has no relevance if one does not also understand generally what an attorney does and how a client may benefit from the attorney's skills. The *Miranda* warnings provide no direct information in this regard.

3. *The right to silence should be perceived as a privilege: that is, as an entitlement which should not and cannot legally be violated or revoked by authority.* The decision concerning whether or not to lay claim to one's right to remain silent is diminished in significance if one believes that the right generally can be revoked by the authorities at some future time, or that the authorities in some other way are allowed not to honor one's decision. The *Miranda* warnings do not inform a suspect of the nature of a right, especially its effect in binding the authorities to accept without question the decision of the person who validly lays claim to it.

In this chapter, we will describe what is known about juveniles' perceptions and understanding in these three areas. Then we will present our study designed to assess these perceptions in both juveniles and adults, and examine their implications for the legal question of juveniles' competence to waive rights.

Our general objective in this study was to examine whether juveniles are as prepared in the three aforementioned areas of belief as are adults for purposes of making decisions about waiving their rights. All of the results were derived from an assessment of 199 juveniles, 203 adult offenders, and 57 adult nonoffenders. The juveniles included 160 who were among the larger detention sample described in Chapter 4, as well as an additional 39 boys town and boys school juveniles who were not in the previous sample. The demographic composition of this sample was nearly identical to that of the sample described in Chapter 4. The adults in the present study were the same samples described in Chapter 5. The two adult samples were dealt with separately in the present analyses because, as we will show later, the two adult samples differed significantly in their level of understanding as measured in this study.

The measure which was used to assess subjects' perceptions of the function of *Miranda* rights was described in Chapter 3 and is called the Function of Rights in Interrogation (FRI).[3] It will be recalled that the FRI administration included the presentation of four brief hypothetical situations to the subject, with each situation accompanied by a picture stimulus depicting the situation described: two interrogation scenes, a lawyer–client consultation scene, and a courtroom scene. Characters in these scenes were depicted with a lack of facial or body cues which might signal any particular emotion or intent. Pictures shown to juveniles and adults were identical, except that the suspect in the picture was an adolescent in the juveniles' set of pictures and an adult in the pictures shown to adults. A series of questions was asked after each picture and situation was presented; only short answers were required. The fifteen questions pertained to three FRI subscales, one subscale for each of the three areas of understanding described earlier in this chapter; there were five questions for each subscale. Each response was scored 2 (adequate), 1 (questionable), or 0 (inadequate), according to objective criteria in the FRI manual. (See Appendix D for details of administration, wording of questions, and scoring criteria.) The FRI, then, yields three subscale scores, as well as a total FRI score which we will discuss at a later point in this chapter.

FRI SUBSCALE I: NATURE OF INTERROGATION

Rational for Subscale Content

This subscale of the FRI consists of two types of items: one's perceptions concerning the type of information police will seek in interrogation, and whether one perceives the policeman's role in interrogation as being benevolent or adversarial. Adequate responses, scoring criteria for which were defined by the project's legal and psychological consultants, include an awareness that an illegal act is being investigated by policemen who are in an adversarial role in relation to the suspect.

[3]The FRI was administered within a series of research procedures and was preceded by the CMR and CMV measures. Thus, all subjects had been exposed to the *Miranda* warnings within the experimental session prior to administration of the FRI.

Some critics might argue that a perception of the police as adversaries in juvenile cases is either inaccurate or inappropriate because the traditional philosophy of the juvenile justice system is to provide treatment, not punishment, in accordance with its concern for the best interests of the child. In *Kent* v. *U.S.*, 383 U.S. 541 (1966), however, Justice Fortas noted that "there is evidence, in fact, that there may be grounds for concern that in the juvenile justice system the child receives the worst of both worlds: that he receives neither the protection accorded to adults nor the solicitous care and regenerative treatment postulated to children" (at 556). The Supreme Court in *Gault*, 387 U.S. 1 (1967) spoke of the delinquency adjudication as having consequences which were "comparable in seriousness to a felony prosecution" (at 36), and remarked on juveniles' "loss of liberty for years" and their consequent need for "defense." The Court saw little to distinguish between the dispositional consequences of criminal court and juvenile court with regard to deprivation of liberty, and thus construed the juvenile court as manifesting in fact, if not in philosophy, an adversarial position in relation to alleged delinquent juveniles.

Police officers are often the ones to provide courts with the evidence to legally justify the deprivation of a juvenile's liberty. Thus, they share with the juvenile court the adversary-like position noted in *Gault*. There are undoubtedly many police officers who are genuinely concerned about juveniles' welfare, but this does not reduce the need for juvenile suspects to be aware of the formal adversarial nature of the police–suspect relationship in the context of the legal system as it has been described by the Supreme Court.

Empirical Background

There are no data directly addressing the question of juveniles' perceptions of the role and purpose of police in interrogation. Children's general attitudes toward the police have been studied by Torney (1977) in a large sample of 8–14-year-olds. Younger children had more positive attitudes toward police than did older children in the sample; they more often saw police officers as helpful and personally likeable. Rafkey and Sealey (1975) found that about half of nonarrested white juveniles endorsed positive questionnaire statements about police, as compared to only a quarter of black juveniles and of arrested white juveniles.

Barthel's (1977) journalistic account of the interrogation of Peter Reilly, a 17-year-old, demonstrates that juveniles can misperceive the role of interrogators. In this widely publicized case, the fatherless boy was accused of having murdered his mother, which evidence discovered much later indicated he had not done. Soon after Peter's arrest, interrogators offered themselves to him as confessors. They claimed that their primary interest was in helping him to "remember" the event, which they said he was repressing and which would cause him to "go crazy" under the burden of unconscious guilt. Believing their motives, Peter entered into a prolonged and guided search for his "repressed" memory, eventually "remembering" having murdered his mother. Peter experienced relief and gratitude toward the detectives. The total effect was probably enhanced by Peter's prior congenial acquaintance with the interrogators in this small, rural community.

Although this might be an unusual circumstance, friendly interrogation procedures designed to minimize the adversarial relationship between police officer and suspect are commonly described in police textbooks on interrogation (e.g., Inbau & Reid, 1967). Thus, it is of interest to know to what extent juveniles who have had police and court experiences perceive interrogators as benevolent or as adversarial in relation to a suspect.

Results

Mean Subscale I scores for juveniles, adult offenders, and adult nonoffenders are shown in Table 18. All three means were above 9; since

Table 18. Results on FRI Subscale I: Nature of Interrogation

Variable	Juveniles	Adult offenders	Adult nonoffenders
Mean score and *S.D.* (in parentheses), range 0–10	9.09 (1.19)	9.60 (1.04)	9.61 (0.81)
Percent of adequate (2-point) responses on items			
1. (Purpose of interrogation)	91.5	97.0	94.7
2. (Crime suspected)	94.5	99.0	98.2
3. (Information sought by police)	98.0	99.5	100.0
4. (Police affect)	68.8	88.7	87.7
5. (Suspect affect)	99.0	97.0	98.2
Percent of inadequate (0-point) responses on items			
1. (Purpose of interrogation)	7.5	1.0	1.8
2. (Crime suspected)	4.5	0.5	1.8
3. (Information sought by police)	1.0	0.5	0.0
4. (Police affect)	28.6	11.3	12.3
5. (Suspect affect)	1.0	3.0	1.8

the total maximum score was 10 points for the 5 questions combined, it is clear that even most of the juveniles demonstrated an adequate perception of the adversarial purposes of interrogation and the appropriate police–suspect role relationship. In none of the three groups were FRI Subscale I scores related significantly to age, IQ, race, or (in the juvenile and adult offender samples) number of prior felony referrals. When the juvenile and adult offender subjects were included in a two-way analysis of variance involving age and IQ score as independent variables, neither age nor IQ were significantly related to FRI Subscale I scores. Similar results were found for a similar analysis using juveniles and adult nonoffenders.

The percentage of adequate and inadequate responses to the five Subscale I items (see Table 18) were very similar for the three groups, except for a greater incidence (though not statistically significant) of juveniles attributing sadness or regret to the police officers (item 4).

In summary, the juveniles appeared to be as aware of the adversarial nature of interrogation as were the adults.

FRI SUBSCALE II: RIGHT TO COUNSEL

Rationale for Subscale Content

This FRI subscale contains two kinds of items. Some of the items examine one's understanding of the lawyer's role as a provider of legal assistance and as being different from the court's role in determining delinquency or guilt and the subsequent disposition of the case. Other items focus on one's understanding of the attorney–client relationship as involving helpfulness and as deserving of the client's trust. Generally, then, adequate responses were those which cast the attorney in the role of defender: providing friendly legal advice, offering confidentiality of communications, assuring that the state assumed the burden of proving allegations, and when necessary arguing for the least restrictive disposition or penalty. Subjects' responses did not have to be this specific to be scored as adequate (see Appendix D for scoring criteria), but the scoring criteria were developed with these definitions in mind.

There are those in juvenile courts who will disagree with our definition of the attorney's role in juvenile cases, for reasons which we will explain shortly. Nevertheless, a vigorous defense patterned after the role of the advocate attorney in criminal courts has been endorsed as appropriate in juvenile cases by the recent Juvenile Justice Standards Project (IJA-ABA, 1977). This position has been in large part a response to the Supreme Court's reasoning in *Gault* that the consequences of delinquency adjudication warrant a strong defense for juveniles in delinquency proceedings.

Empirical Background

The Juvenile Justice Standards Project (IJA-ABA, 1977) has asserted that "few juveniles have the experience and understanding to decide meaningfully that the assistance of counsel would not be helpful" (p. 92). An exploratory study by Catton and Erickson (1975), involving 22 juveniles who were represented by lawyers in delinquency hearings, demonstrated that many juveniles might not perceive advocacy as part of the attorney's role. When asked whether there had been anyone in the courtroom on their side, only 7 of them mentioned the defense lawyer, and only 4 identified the lawyer when asked who was the best person to tell "their side of the story" to the judge. Rafkey and Sealey (1975) found that half of their nondelinquent juvenile sample claimed to perceive lawyers as dishonest; that figure rose to 80% of black adolescents who had been arrested. In samples of juveniles who had been represented by attorneys in delinquency hearings, Connor (1972) found that two-thirds were disappointed in their lawyers' courtroom performance, and Walker (1971) reported that 30% admitted to researchers that they had not told their lawyers "the whole story" about their illegal activities. Stapleton and Teitelbaum (1972) discovered that delinquent juveniles perceived themselves as having more in common with their probation officers than with their defense attorneys.

The literature on the defense attorney in juvenile courts suggests three reasons why juveniles who have had experience with attorneys might not view them as helpful or as advocates.

First, while the years since *Gault* have seen a widespread introduction of defense lawyers into the juvenile courts, their role is a matter of much controversy. On the one hand are lawyers and judges who consider a strong legal defense for juveniles to be essential in assuring due process and fairness in the courts' handling of juvenile cases (IJA-ABA, 1977; McMillian & McMurtry, 1969–1970; Piersma *et al.*, 1977). On the other hand are those who view the attorney more or less as an officer of the court who shares the court's duty as *parens patriae.* Critical issues of defense and the safeguarding of due process are less important in this role than is the attorney's assistance to the court: helping to determine the facts of the case, determining the "treatment needs," and recommending a disposition. Thus, Ferster *et al.* (1970–1971) found that many defense attorneys claimed that they would report to the court any admission of guilt by their juvenile clients, even if the admission were in the context of a confidential communication.[4] That this view of the defense attorney's role has prevailed in many post-*Gault* juvenile courts is suggested by several other extensive studies (Kay & Segal, 1972–1973; Landsman & Minow, 1978; Stapleton & Teitelbaum, 1972). Juveniles who have had experience with this type of lawyer might be expected to develop a dim view of the advocacy potential in the attorney–client relationship.

A second problem which may lead to negative perceptions of attorneys by juveniles is that even the advocate lawyer is often faced with the necessity of adopting a position contrary to the expressed desires of the juvenile. This may occur as a result of the juvenile's immaturity and its effect on his or her rather short-sighted view of what is the most desirable outcome, or because of legal realities which are beyond the comprehension of the juvenile. Although a sensitive lawyer might be able to explain such matters to a juvenile, some juveniles may see the lawyer's well-meaning actions as a betrayal.

Third, commentators have questioned the abilities of most lawyers to develop good rapport with juveniles, to explain their own function and the relevant court processes in language understandable to juveniles, to perceive the situation through the juvenile's eyes, and to be sensitive to the juvenile's emotional needs (Genden, 1976; Landsman & Minow, 1978). Catton and Erickson (1975) reported that in only 2 out of the 22 observed sessions between public defenders and juvenile clients did the lawyers explain their function or purpose to the juveniles. In one case, the researcher observed a lengthy consultation between a public defender and a cooperative boy to whom the attorney had been assigned; at the end, the boy was heard to ask the public defender when his lawyer was going to arrive! Most attorneys are not prepared by law school training to establish working relationships with children, and

[4]Ferster *et al.* (1970–1971) documented the way in which some lawyers assume the function of finder of fact and determiner of disposition. They found that many attorneys made decisions regarding whether to "plead a juvenile guilty or not guilty" on the basis of their judgment of the juvenile as a "good kid" or a "bad kid" (defined primarily by the juvenile's attitude toward authority or the attorney) and on the juvenile's past record. They tended to "enter a plea of guilty" for bad kids in almost all circumstances in order to help the court process them toward reformatories and to "plead guilty" for good kids with no prior record on the assumption that they needed a scare to send them straight in the future. Good kids with prior records received the most adequate defense.

many children therefore can be expected to be at least ambivalent about the role of counsel or noncognizant of the type of advocacy which counsel could provide.

On the right to counsel subscale of the FRI, then, one might expect considerable variance among juveniles in their perceptions of the potential helpfulness of defense attorneys and of their function in relation to the juvenile and to the court.

Results

Table 19 shows that the mean Subscale II score for juveniles was lower than those for adult offenders and nonoffenders. To examine these differences, we included all of the juveniles and the adult offenders in a two-way analysis of variance (age × IQ) of Subscale II scores. The results indicated that the subscale scores were significantly related to age and to IQ.[5] A multiple range test showed that the Subscale II scores of 11-year-olds were significantly lower than those of 12–15-year-olds, which in turn were significantly lower than those of subjects 16 years of age or older. An age by IQ interaction effect indicated that differences in IQ scores were more strongly related to Subscale II scores at younger ages than in the adult age groups. That is, low IQ juveniles did more poorly than higher IQ juveniles on this subscale, while the differences between low IQ and higher IQ adults was less marked. A similar two-way analysis of variance including juveniles and adult nonoffenders produced similar results.[6]

The results indicated, then, that at each age below 16, subjects demonstrated significantly poorer understanding of the defense attorney's role and the attorney–client relationship than did subjects 16 years of age or older. An examination of the percent of adequate and inadequate responses (Table 19), however, shows that in an absolute sense the juveniles as a group demonstrated considerable understanding of certain aspects of the attorney's role. A sizable majority described the lawyer's potential to provide defense (items 6 and 10), were cognizant of the expectation that suspects were supposed to cooperate with their attorneys (item 7), and knew that the lawyer in turn is expected to

[5]In a two-way analysis of variance of FRI Subscale II scores of juveniles and adult offenders: age, $F = 9.03$, $df = 10/350$, $p<.0001$; IQ, $F = 9.19$, $df = 4/350$, $p<.001$; age × IQ, $F = 2.91$, $df = 51/350$, $p<.02$.

[6]In a two-way analysis of variance of FRI Subscale II scores for juveniles and adult nonoffenders: age, $F = 5.97$, $df = 10/210$, $p<.006$; IQ, $F = 6.67$, $df = 4/210$, $p<.025$; age × IQ, $F = 4.49$, $df = 31/210$, $p<.004$.

TABLE 19. RESULTS ON FRI SUBSCALE II: RIGHT TO COUNSEL

Variable	Juveniles	Adult offenders	Adult nonoffenders
Mean score and *S.D.* (in parentheses), range 0–10	8.54 (1.70)	9.25 (1.31)	9.07 (1.52)
Percent of adequate (2-point) responses on items			
6. (Lawyer's defense role)	80.4	89.2	86.0
7. (Client's role)	91.5	86.7	96.5
8. (Information sought by lawyer)	92.0	92.6	93.0
9. (Reason to seek truth)	67.3	88.7	80.7
10. (Lawyer's defense potential)	80.9	84.2	89.5
Percent of inadequate (0-point) responses on items			
6. (Lawyer's defense role)	10.1	0.5	3.5
7. (Client's role)	4.0	3.4	1.8
8. (Information sought by lawyer)	4.5	3.9	5.3
9. (Reason to seek truth)	28.1	6.4	10.5
10. (Lawyer's defense potential)	12.1	9.9	3.5

offer advice or will attempt to discover any relevant information about the alleged offense (item 8).

The one exception to this pattern was item 9, which asked subjects why the lawyer needed to know the truth from the suspect about the alleged offense. The idea that the lawyer needed this information in order to build a defense or otherwise help the suspect was offered by 67% of the juveniles, compared to 88% of the adult offenders. Inadequate responses were given by 28% of the juveniles compared to 6% of the adult offenders, a difference which did not quite reach statistical significance. Inadequate responses were significantly more frequent among juveniles with only one or no prior felony referrals (31%) than among those with two or more prior felony referrals (8%),[7] but were not related to any other subject variables.

Three types of inadequate responses accounted for most of the zero-credit cases on item 9. First, in about a fifth of these inadequate responses, juveniles said that the lawyer needed to know the truth from the suspect so that the lawyer could decide on guilt and punishment (for example, "So the lawyer will know whether to let him go or send him up"). Juveniles giving these responses apparently made no distinction

[7] $F = 2.75$, $df = 3/195$, $p < .05$.

between the role of the defense attorney and that of the court itself in decisions about adjudication and disposition. The second type of inadequate response, accounting for another fifth of the zero-credit responses, included the idea that the lawyer must know whether or not the juvenile committed the alleged violation because the lawyer would not advocate the interests of a juvenile who admitted to the violation. Finally, about three-fifths of the inadequate responses included the idea that the defense lawyer is required to report to the court any evidence of a juvenile client's responsibility for an alleged offense. The lawyer's obligation to do this was stated in either of two ways: (1) that the lawyer must enter a "guilty plea" if the juvenile admits responsibility for an offense to his or her attorney; or (2) that the lawyer must report any knowledge of a juvenile's wrongdoing to the judge (for example, "so the judge will know Tim really did it," "so he can say it in court, because it's his job to tell the court that Tim did it, if he did do the crime"). It will be noted that all three types of inadequate responses had a single message in common: that the defense lawyer's role is to advocate the interests of juveniles who claim to be innocent, but not of juveniles who admit to their attorneys that they were responsible for an offense.

Thus, for about one-third of the juveniles with little previous experience in felony-related court proceedings, the perception of the defense lawyer's role is that of a "fickle" advocate at best. While the potential for defense and helpful advocacy is generally understood, they see this as available primarily to the juvenile who is being wrongly "accused" by the court; if the juvenile is being rightly "accused," they believe that the lawyer's role is to assist the court in disposition of the case.

FRI SUBSCALE III: RIGHT TO SILENCE

Rationale for Subscale Content

The right to silence subscale of the FRI examines whether subjects understand that if a suspect asserts the right to silence, then the authorities (specifically the police and the juvenile court judge) are legally bound to accept that decision without penality or revocation and without applying persuasion to change the suspect's decision. That is, the right when claimed provides absolute protection. The items in this subscale focused on the permissible powers and impermissible reactions of police and judges to a suspect's claim to the right to silence. (For specific questions, see Appendix D.)

Objectively, of course, there is no such thing as an absolute right.

Friedman (1971) has defined a right subjectively (that is, in principle) as a claim against or through the authorities which must be granted to anyone who invokes the right. But realistically, Friedman pointed out, there is a limit to what any society or government can allow. The hypothetical assertion of any right by all persons to whom the right pertains would create chaos. Nevertheless, the position taken in the development of the FRI was that a person would be unprepared to make a knowing, intelligent, and voluntary waiver if he or she did not perceive the right to silence as functioning in an absolute sense. It was on this premise that the Supreme Court in *Miranda* and *Gault* provided the right to suspects in police and court proceedings.

Empirical Background

There are two areas of scientific inquiry which are relevant in evaluating juveniles' perceptions of the right to silence: their conceptions of a right and their views of the child in relation to legal authority.

Tapp and Levine (1977) have remarked on the near absence of empirical information about children's conceptions of a right. Tapp (1977) has proposed that ideas about rights follow a developmental sequence through childhood which parallels the stages of moral development conceptualized by Kohlberg (1964) and employed by Tapp and Levine (1974) in their studies of legal socialization. Generally, a right may be viewed early on in development (the preconventional stage) as something which one is allowed to do, but which is bestowed by persons in authority and is as easily taken away by the authorities. Development may proceed to a conventional view of rights as protections which are part of the legal and social system, and therefore, as being less dependent on the approval of the authorities per se. Finally, the developmentally most advanced conceptualization of rights bases them on principles or universals which have an abstract meaning transcending social or legal sanction.

In the present context, the preconventional understanding of a right would not seem to be a sufficient perspective for the person who is deciding whether or not to waive the right to silence. Such a view assumes that the right is being extended by authority and can as easily be revoked at some future time if it suits the purposes of authority. A conventional level of development, on the other hand, at least demonstrates a sense of rights as being part of the legal and social order by which all citizens, including legal authorities, are bound to abide. Thus, it provides an adequate conceptual framework within which to consider whether or not to waive rights.

Melton (1979) operationalized the Kohlberg stages in an empirical study of children's conceptualization of rights. He found that the concept of a right was not generally known to children below third grade, but that most seventh grade children (about age 13–14) possess a conventional view of a right as being relatively independent of the whims of persons in authority. In contrast, we have noted in our CMV results in Chapter 4 that only about one-quarter of our sample of 10–16-year-olds included in their definitions of a right the idea that it was protected: that is, that it was more than merely something one is allowed to do. The discrepancy between our results and those of Melton might be due to differences in method. We asked juveniles to define the word "right"; but Melton's data consisted of juveniles' responses to hypothetical conflict situations, a method which may have better facilitated juveniles' expressions of their sense of a right. Given this possibility, we expected that the FRI might reveal a more adequate level of understanding of the protectedness of a right than was found using the CMV, since the FRI assesses understanding in the context of hypothetical situations rather than in the abstract.

Indirectly related to juveniles' perceptions of the right to silence is their perception of the power of legal authorities. Torney (1977) found that younger juveniles (in a sample range of ages 8–14) tended to perceive policemen as both law enforcers and lawmakers, suggesting that juveniles at earlier stages of development might perceive policemen as being in a position to create or revoke laws and rights. Grisso and Vierling (1978) reviewed developmental research suggesting that the early adolescent years are a time of increased awareness of the power of authority; one might assume that juveniles at this age would tend to view a judge's power as extending beyond the strictures of legal rights, even when rights are viewed as protections in the conventional sense. Two of the five items in the third FRI subscale were designed to directly examine this possibility.

Results

The mean score on Subscale III for juveniles (see Table 20) was markedly lower than that of both adult samples. Two-way analyses of variance (age and IQ), one involving juveniles and adult offenders and another involving juveniles and adult nonoffenders, indicated that both age and IQ score were significantly related to FRI Subscale III scores.[8]

[8]In a two-way analysis of variance of FRI Subscale III scores for juveniles and adult offenders: age, $F = 10.42$, $df = 10/350$, $p<.0001$; IQ, $F = 12.459$, $df = 4/350$, $p<.0001$. In a two-way analysis of variance of FRI Subscale III scores for juveniles and adult nonoffenders: age, $F = 3.20$, $df = 10/210$, $p<.001$; IQ, F 7.82, $df = 4/210$, $p<.0001$.

TABLE 20. RESULTS ON FRI SUBSCALE III: RIGHT TO SILENCE

Variable	Juveniles	Adult offenders	Adult nonoffenders
Mean score and *S.D.* (in parentheses), range 0–10	5.52 (2.51)	7.48 (2.07)	6.84 (2.36)
Percent of adequate (2-point) responses on items			
11. (Use of confession)	65.8	65.5	71.9
12. (Freedom from pressure)	45.2	81.8	77.2
13. (Right is irrevocable regarding police)	63.3	93.6	86.0
14. (No penalty for asserting right)	33.2	71.9	63.2
15. (Right is irrevocable regarding judge)	44.7	55.2	29.8
Percent of inadequate (0-point) responses on items			
11. (Use of confession)	22.6	25.1	22.8
12. (Freedom from pressure)	39.2	9.4	15.8
13. (Right is irrevocable regarding police)	21.1	5.4	14.0
14. (No penalty for asserting right)	61.8	21.7	35.1
15. (Right is irrevocable regarding judge)	55.3	42.9	70.2

Multiple range tests showed that all age groups of 15 years and below had significantly lower Subscale III scores than did all age groups of 17 years and above, and that 16-year-olds' scores were significantly lower than those of any age group above 19 years. Subscale scores were unrelated to race in all three samples, and were unrelated to number of prior felony referrals in the juvenile and adult offender samples. Adult nonoffenders performed significantly more poorly on this subscale than did adult offenders.[9]

The results suggest, then, that at each age group below 16, there is in general a less adequate understanding of the nature or significance of the right to silence than at ages 17 and above, and less adequate understanding among 16-year-olds than among adults 20 and above. The percent of adequate and inadequate responses (Table 20) indicates that juveniles demonstrated poor understanding in this area not only relative to adults, but also in an absolute sense. For example, on item 12, only 45% of the juveniles (compared to 81% and 77% of the adults) recog-

[9]In a two-way analysis of variance of FRI Subscale III scores for adult offenders versus adult nonoffenders: offenders versus nonoffenders, $F = 3.98$, $df = 1/256$, $p<.04$; race, $F = 2.61$, $df = 1/256$, *N.S.*

nized that if a suspect refuses to talk to police, the police are supposed to cease questioning and apply no further pressure. Similarly, the inability of the police to legally revoke the right to silence (item 13) was understood by fewer juveniles (albeit a two-thirds majority) than adults. Differences between juveniles and adults on both of these items were statistically significant ($p<.01$).

Two of the items, 14 and 15, require special attention. On item 14, only about one-third of the juveniles, compared to about two-thirds of the adults ($p<.01$), recognized the legal inappropriateness of judicial penalties in response to a person's assertion of the right to silence. Several of the juveniles indicated that a judge could attempt to force a person to "talk" if the person had previously decided to remain silent. Item 15 asked the question directly: if a defendant has chosen to remain silent, will he or she have to talk about any involvement in an alleged offense if the judge orders it? A majority of the juveniles said yes, as did a majority of the adult nonoffenders and nearly a majority of the adult offenders, for which reason the difference between juveniles and adults was not statistically significant. In all three samples, responses to this question were unrelated to age, IQ, or race, and were unrelated to number of prior felony referrals among juveniles and adult offenders.

Subjects' reasoning about the necessity to comply with a court order to "talk" is enlightening. Some juveniles and adults explained that the judge makes the law and has the power to assess penalties against those who do not comply with it. Several juveniles felt that the sole purpose of a court hearing was to obtain a juvenile's confession, for which reason asserting the right to silence in court would be legally disallowed. Many juveniles and adults believed that refusal to talk about one's illegal involvements when questioned by a judge would amount to perjury. As one juvenile put it, "If I'm in court, I have to tell the truth, the whole truth, and nothing but the truth. So when the judge asks you what you done, you got to tell him even if you don't want to."

We noted in Chapters 4 and 5 that almost all subjects understood that they had a right to remain silent, meaning that they did not have to talk to anyone about charges against them. The present results, however, question whether many juveniles and adults comprehend the meaning or significance of this right. For those who responded inadequately to item 15, either they did not understand that the right to silence is controlled by constitutional law, or they believed that the powers of a judge are so awesome that they transcend the law. In either case, a developmental perspective would characterize the majority's perceptions of the right to silence as preconventional: that is, that the right can be given and taken away by the authorities. This view does not prepare a suspect to make a knowing, intelligent, and voluntary decision about the right to silence at the time of interrogation. The significance of the right is greatly diminished if a suspect believes that ultimately a judge can require a personal statement about charges even against the suspect's will.

FRI TOTAL SCORES

The mean FRI total scores for the three samples are shown in Table 21. In a series of two-way analyses of variance of FRI total scores, adult offenders obtained significantly higher FRI scores than did adult nonoffenders when the comparisons were statistically controlled for any differences between the samples in age, race, or IQ.[10] It would appear that adults with greater experience with the police and courts are somewhat more familiar with the function and significance of the rights to counsel and silence than are those with less experience.

A two-way analysis of variance involving juveniles and adult offenders showed the FRI total scores were significantly related to both age and IQ score.[11] The age effect is clearly visible in the mean FRI scores for each age, as shown in Table 21. A multiple range test produced the following results regarding FRI total scores at various ages: (1) scores at ages 13 and below were significantly lower than at ages 15 and above; (2) scores at age 14 were significantly below those at ages 16 and above; (3) scores at age 15 were significantly below those at ages 17 and above; (4) scores at age 16 were significantly below those at age 20 and above; (5) there were no significant differences in scores between any categories of ages 17 and above. In summary, all juvenile age groups (10 and 11 through 16) demonstrated significantly poorer understanding of FRI content than did adults who were 20 years old or older.

Very similar results were obtained in an analysis of FRI total scores involving juveniles and adult nonoffenders.[12] Therefore, the juveniles' inferior understanding in relation to the adult offenders is not merely a

[10]For example, in a two-way analysis of variance of FRI total scores by group (offender and nonoffender) and IQ: offender–nonoffender, $F = 6.11$, $df = 1/250$, $p<.01$; IQ, $F = 4.26$, $df = 4/250$, $p<.002$.

[11]In a two-way analysis of variance of FRI total scores by age and IQ (including all juveniles and adult offenders): age, $F = 14.50$, $df = 10/350$, $p<.0001$; IQ, $F = 15.27$, $df = 4/350$, $p<.0001$; age and IQ interaction, $F = 1.75$, $df = 37/350$, $p<.05$.

[12]In a two-way analysis of variance of FRI total scores by age and IQ (including all juveniles and adult nonoffenders): age, $F = 4.18$, $df = 10/210$, $p<.0001$; IQ, $F = 9.11$, $df = 4/210$, $p<.0001$; age and IQ interaction, $F = 1.68$, $df = 3/210$, $p<.02$.

TABLE 21. MEAN FRI TOTAL SCORES FOR THE THREE SAMPLES, BY DEMOGRAPHIC GROUPS

Variable		Juveniles	Adult offenders	Adult nonoffenders
Total samples				
Mean		23.13	26.31	25.52
Standard deviation		3.80	3.26	3.27
Age (*F*,*p* within samples)		(2.77, .02)	(1.54, *N.S.*)	(1.71, *N.S.*)
Juveniles	Adults			
10–11	17–19	20.25	25.70	25.00
12	20–22	21.33	26.64	26.50
13	23–26	22.13	26.03	25.60
14	27–31	22.84	26.71	26.75
15	32+	23.72	27.16	25.73
16		24.36		
Sex (*F*,*p* within samples)		(0.02, *N.S.*)	(0.01, *N.S.*)	(0.10, *N.S.*)
Male		23.11	26.52	25.20
Female		23.19	26.21	25.78
Race (*F*,*p* within samples)		(4.86, .01)	(1.48, *N.S.*)	(2.61, .10)
White		23.62	26.72	26.31
Black		22.00	26.26	25.21
IQ (*F*,*p* within samples)		(7.36, .005)	(5.55, .0003)	(2.31, .05)
70 and below		20.77	25.22	[a]
71–80		22.63	25.93	25.00
81–90		22.40	25.71	25.64
91–100		24.32	27.05	25.26
101+		25.03	27.72	26.33
SES (*F*,*p* within samples)		(1.97, *N.S.*)	(1.15, *N.S.*)	(0.77, *N.S.*)
High-middle		24.56	28.00	[a]
Middle		22.90	26.13	24.25
Low-middle		22.83	26.33	25.77
Low		22.42	26.10	25.41
Number of prior felonies (*F*,*p* within samples)		(2.00, *N.S.*)	(0.04, *N.S.*)	Not applicable
Juveniles	Adults[b]			
0	0	22.76	26.35	
1	1–2	23.86	26.16	
2	3–4	23.74	26.83	
3+	5+	25.57	26.90	

[a] $N = 1$ in this cell; data unreliable and therefore no cell mean is reported.
[b] Number of prior felonies for adults refers to the number of felony arrests subsequent to age 16, since juvenile records were not available on adult offenders.

reflection of the adult offenders' more extensive experience with police and courts. Instead, the difference reflects a deficiency in understanding of FRI content compared to both experienced and nonexperienced adults of similar intelligence to the juveniles themselves.

The two foregoing analyses also revealed significant age and IQ interaction effects (see footnotes 11 and 12). That is, the quality of IQ scores made a greater difference in FRI scores at younger ages than at older ages. Put another way, at higher levels of IQ, the FRI differences between juveniles and adults were not as remarkable as in the case of low IQ juveniles and adults. For example, in the mean scores for each IQ group in Table 21, a 5-point difference in FRI means separates juveniles from adults at the IQ level of 70 and below, compared to about a 2-point difference between juveniles and adults at IQ's of 101+.

Table 21 indicated a significant race effect within the juvenile sample. It will be recalled, however, that there was a mean IQ difference between the black and white juvenile subsamples; consequently, the race effect was found not to be statistically significant in analyses which controlled for IQ differences between the subsamples.[13]

Table 21 indicates no simple relationship between the number of prior felony referrals and FRI scores in the juvenile sample. Again, it was known that the high-felony subsample had a lower mean IQ than the low-felony subsample. When IQ was controlled in a two-way analysis of variance, we discovered that a higher number of prior felony referrals was significantly related to higher FRI scores.[14] In contrast to the findings with other *Miranda* measures in Chapter 4, then, juveniles' understanding of the nature of the attorney–client relationship and the significance of the right to silence may be increased by more exposure to court processes and the juvenile legal system.

Finally, Table 22 displays the intercorrelations between FRI total score, FRI subscale scores, and *Miranda* comprehension measures used in the studies in Chapters 4 and 5. The fact that correlations between FRI subscales were low suggests that the FRI does not measure a unitary substance of knowledge or beliefs. That is, the accuracy or inaccuracy of a person's perceptions in any one of the three areas is not predictive of the quality of perceptions in any other area. The low correlations between FRI scores and other *Miranda* comprehension scores suggests that perceptions of the function of rights in the context of interrogation are relatively independent of one's level of comprehension of the *Miranda* warnings themselves. It would not be surprising, then, to find juveniles who clearly understood the *Miranda* warnings, but who lacked knowledge of their significance, or who understood matters of police, attorneys, and the right to silence, but who could not grasp the message of the *Miranda* warning statements themselves.

[13]In a three-way analysis of variance of FRI total scores for juveniles: age, $F = 5.13$, $p<.001$; race, $F = 0.69$, *N.S.*; IQ, $F = 7.96$, $p<.001$.

[14]In a two-way analysis of variance of FRI total scores for juveniles: IQ, $F = 8.83$, $p<.001$; number of prior felony referrals, $F = 4.06$, $p<.008$.

TABLE 22. TOTAL FRI, FRI SUBSCALES, AND OTHER *Miranda* COMPREHENSION SCORES: INTERCORRELATIONS FOR JUVENILE SAMPLE AND ADULT SAMPLE (IN PARENTHESES)

Variable	Subscale I	Subscale II	Subscale III	Total FRI score
FRI subscale I		.08	.20	.48
FRI subscale II	(.12)		.24	.63
FRI subscale III	(.03)	(.17)		.83
FRI total score	(.36)	(.59)	(.83)	
CMR	.24 (.19)	.13 (.14)	.19 (.21)	.26 (.28)
CMV	.17 (.14)	.18 (.20)	.21 (.22)	.27 (.29)
CMR-TF	.12 (.11)	.11 (.27)	.05 (.23)	.12 (.32)

CONCLUSION

The results of this study indicate that the courts have been correct in their concern about juveniles' possible misunderstanding of the function and significance of the *Miranda* rights. On the whole, juveniles were significantly less aware of the significance of the rights in the context of legal process than were adults, whether they were compared to adults with very little experience or adults with a great deal of experience in police and court matters.

Our results indicate that this conclusion is applicable to all juveniles through age 16, not merely to those in their early adolescent years, and it is especially true for juveniles with IQ scores below 90. That is, adults with IQ scores below 90 were far more knowledgeable of the attorney–client relationship and the function of the right to silence than were juveniles at this IQ level. This is especially important, since the majority of juveniles referred to the courts manifest this subaverage level of intellectual functioning. Using adults as the standard, then, our results indicate that juveniles' competence to waive their rights to silence and counsel is seriously diminished by their inferior understanding of the function and significance of those rights.

The one exception to this conclusion is the juvenile with a great deal of experience with court processes: that is, juveniles who have been referred for felony charges three or more times in the past. As a group, these juveniles manifested a level of understanding of FRI content which equaled that of the average adult nonoffender in our study.

Certain specific results in this study should receive close attention by juvenile courts and defense attorneys, and should be the subject of more definitive social science research.

First, we would urge courts to consider our finding that nearly one-third of the juveniles with few or no prior felony referrals believed that defense attorneys defend the interests of the innocent but not the guilty. Waiver of the right to counsel by a juvenile with this belief clearly does not satisfy the standard for valid waiver. It would be consistent with the intent of due process for courts to require that when an inexperienced juvenile is to be interrogated concerning a delinquency charge, he or she should be provided with a brief, clear explanation of the services which a public defender should provide in the context of interrogation proceedings. It would be best if public defenders themselves were allowed to provide this information prior to interrogation. On the other hand, this procedure would seem to be of less importance in those juveniles courts where the public defender's role is that of an assistant to the court in the fact-finding and disposition process.

Defense attorneys themselves are greatly in need of more information than this study has provided concerning juveniles' perceptions of the lawyer–client relationship. What types of juveniles are more or less likely to understand and respond to the confidential nature of the relationship? What are the most frequent and most important misconceptions which juveniles hold concerning the defense attorney, and how are these best dealt with by the attorney? What do juveniles perceive to be the defense attorney's relationships with other court personnel, and what specific functions do they attribute to the attorney? These would seem to be important directions for future psychological research.

The second specific finding which deserves special attention is juveniles' failure to sense the legal protection behind the right to silence. Many juveniles believed that police were allowed to try to dissuade a person from a decision to remain silent, and the majority of them believed that a judge could revoke a person's right to silence. The significance of the right at the time of interrogation is certainly diminished by either of these beliefs.

Juveniles' ideas that a judge can require one to answer for one's behaviors are quite understandable, given a circumstance which is peculiar to juvenile law. A common interpretation of *Gault* holds that the Supreme Court extended the *Miranda* rights to juveniles only in cases which might lead to delinquency adjudication—that is, when misdemeanor or felony charges were involved—and not when the court referral is for a status offense such as runaway, truancy, or incorrigibility. Thus, it might be common for juvenile court judges or referees to forego the statement of *Miranda* rights in hearings on status offenses, and to require juveniles to make an account of their behavior leading to the court referral. Juveniles who have had this experience in the past are likely to expect the same to be true in the future, whatever the level of seriousness of their next referral. Thus, experience might teach some juveniles to believe that judges can require that one "talk," the "right" to silence notwithstanding.

What is more startling is the very large percentage of adults—nearly three-quarters of the adult nonoffenders—who believed that the right to silence can be revoked by a judge. Perhaps this is a testimony to the awesome powers which we attribute to judges in our society, or a confused misinterpretation of the law against perjury in the courtroom. Whatever its explanation, it is an unexpected finding in this study, which suggests the need for further research on adults' perceptions of the nature of a legal right.

Viewing a right as an allowance which is bestowed by and can therefore be revoked by the authorities—the view taken by the majority in this study—is typical of a developmental level of reasoning referred to as preconventional. This level of reasoning about the concept of rights is typical among children below the ages of 10–12. Beyond about 12 years, an increasing number of people are capable of a conventional level of legal reasoning; law, rule, and rights are seen as methods agreed on by a society to provide social order, not tools developed and modified by the authorities merely to maintain control. It is not reasonable to assume that the majority of adults in our study, or even the majority of the juveniles, have remained at a preconventional stage of legal reasoning (Tapp & Levine, 1974). It is more likely that most of the subjects would manifest the more advanced, conventional level of reasoning about laws and rights in general, but that their perceptions of judicial power may in certain specific matters reduce their views to a preconventional level. Research on these questions might have important implications for our knowledge of the capabilities of "average" adult citizens to understand the legal system and the rights which affect their lives.

It is not clear what can be done at the time of interrogation to correct juveniles' misperceptions of the nature of their right to silence. It is a more difficult concept to explain to juveniles than is the function of legal counsel, and the moments between arrest and interrogation are not conducive to educating a suspect concerning the nature of a right. As in our earlier studies, the results generally point to a level of misunderstanding which warrants some special form of protection for juveniles which is not provided to either juveniles or adults in the present legal system. We will return to this question after describing another of our studies, this one dealing with juveniles' expectancies about the consequences of rights waiver.

7

Juveniles' Reasoning about the Waiver Decision

In the studies reported in the previous chapters, we examined juveniles' abilities to understand the *Miranda* warnings and to comprehend their function and significance in the context of interrogation and subsequent court proceedings. Courts which have addressed the issue of juveniles' competence to waive rights have focused primarily on these matters of comprehension. But a little reflection will suggest that there are other personal characteristics which juveniles bring to the arrest and interrogation event which might also influence their decisions to waive or assert their rights. Specifically, there are considerable differences among children in the ability to reason or to engage in problem-solving tasks of the type presented by the waiver decision. Thus, in addition to individual differences in what they understand, there might also be differences in how they go about the process of deciding how to respond under the circumstance of an arrest, a police accusation, and a potential interrogation.

The present chapter reports on an investigation of some elements involved in juveniles' reasoning about the *Miranda* rights waiver decision. When deciding on our approach to this study, it became apparent that it would be quite different conceptually from the studies of juveniles' comprehension of elements of the *Miranda* warnings and rights. The major differences were two.

First, the earlier studies were designed to compare juveniles' performance to set standards in order to evaluate the adequacy of their comprehension. This was possible because the law had defined what a person must know in order to make a competent waiver of rights and because legal consultants to the research project were able to reach a consensus on measurement criteria which would satisfy the legal definition.

But as one approaches the question of how juveniles make a waiver decision, one finds almost nothing in case law to suggest what judges perceive as suggesting an adequate level of reasoning or problem-solving ability. Many of the court opinions cited in Chapter 4 do indicate courts' concerns about juveniles' abilities to reason, to weigh the elements involved, or to process the information which they might have in arriving at a decision. Going beyond the matter of juveniles' cognitive capacities for reasoning, the Supreme Court in *Gault* commented on children's affective characteristics—their "fantasy, fright or despair" in interrogation—which might influence this reasoning process. In spite of this concern, nowhere have courts offered standards or opinions which could be translated into measurable indexes of legally relevant reasoning capacities. Indeed, so complex are the psychological questions about children's thought processes that it is difficult to imagine how judges could specify the level of cognitive complexity or problem-solving facility which they would require of a juvenile in order for a waiver of rights to be seen as competently provided.[1]

In light of these circumstances, we decided to explore and describe certain elements of juveniles' reasoning about the waiver decision, but not to attempt to evaluate juveniles' abilities against a standard of adequacy as we did in the earlier studies.

A second distinction between this study and the earlier ones is with regard to method. In order to explore the ways in which juveniles arrive at a waiver decision, it seemed necessary to use a method which allowed us to follow juveniles' thinking through several elements of the decision-making process. The emphasis would be less on measurement than on allowing juveniles to describe to us their thinking at various stages in that process. The method suggested by these considerations was an interview format, in contrast to the "testing" format of the earlier studies.

[1]This problem has been addressed by Roth, Meisel, and Lidz (1977) in the area of patients' competence to provide informed consent for psychological and medical procedures. Roth reviewed five standards which have arisen, one of them being the patient's ability to reason about the proposed medical procedures and alternatives. This standard has generally been passed over by courts and physicians in favor of more easily defined standards (e.g., understanding of the risks and benefits of a medical procedure, as presented by a physician), since there has been no clear way to evaluate the reasoning process.

Previous research on children's problem-solving abilities suggested a structure for our exploration. Earlier studies of children's reasoning also offered interview methods after which we patterned our own research procedure. A brief review of these studies will help to explain our own procedure, after which we will describe the subject sample and offer the results of our exploration of juveniles' reasoning about the waiver decision.

INTERPERSONAL PROBLEM-SOLVING SKILLS

The process of deciding whether to waive or assert rights in response to police requests for information is an interpersonal problem-solving task. In contrast to decisions about such things as how to solve an unfamiliar mathematics problem or how to arrive at a particular destination on the other side of a city, the waiver decision involves thinking about how to respond to other people and, in turn, how the other people will respond to that decision.

Problem-solving skills in social situations have recently been described in studies by several researchers (D'Zurilla & Goldfried, 1971; Shantz, 1975; Spivack & Shure, 1974; Weinstein, 1969). Having reviewed these works, Spivack, Platt, and Shure (1976) provided an outline of problem-solving skills which is generally in accord with the current views of others in this field of study. They describe five elements contributing to the quality of interpersonal problem-solving: (1) sensitivity to the existence of an interpersonal problem; (2) the ability to imagine alternative responses or a number of potential solutions to a problem; (3) perceiving the series of steps leading from one's intention to the desired end; (4) considering the social consequences which one's alternative solutions or decisions might have; and (5) understanding the reciprocal, interpersonal influences concerning one's feelings and actions in the social problem-solving situation. Reflecting on the waiver decision as an interpersonal problem-solving situation, we selected two of these skill areas for exploration, on the basis of their probable relevance for understanding how juveniles think about their responses to *Miranda* warnings. These two areas are one's awareness of alternative responses and one's consideration of the potential consequences of alternative responses. Let us describe these skills in more detail.

In general, the person who can imagine only one or two available options in response to a problem has less satisfactory skills in alternative thinking and will have a lesser chance for success than does the person who can imagine more alternatives (Spivack *et al.*, 1976). This is because the person with a more narrow perception of options is somewhat less likely to have the most fruitful decision within his or her repertoire of planned responses and is likely to respond more rigidly (and therefore less effectively) to the broad range of social situations which might be encountered. For example, studies of alternative thinking in middle school and adolescent children (Platt, Spivack, Altman, Altman, & Peizer, 1974; Spivack & Swift, 1966) have shown that children who are more effective in adapting to and resolving interpersonal problems exhibit a greater capacity to generate alternative solutions to real-life problems than do children with observable behavior problems.

It follows that one index of a juvenile's capacity to reflect meaningfully on the waiver decision is his or her ability to consider some range of optional responses to the problem at hand. The juvenile who considers only two options (e.g., to remain silent or to present one's alibi) will probably engage in the decision-making process with less effectiveness than a juvenile who can consider additional options (e.g., confessing, asking for an attorney, requesting information about the consequences of potential waiver decisions, requesting to make a phone call to parents, and so forth). The propensity or ability to imagine more options would not in and of itself guarantee that the juvenile's eventual decision would be the most adaptive one given the particular circumstances of the case. But it would suggest in theory that the decision was the product of a more meaningful decision-making process. It is this capacity, not the nature of a juvenile's final decision, which judges must weigh when addressing the validity of that juvenile's waiver of rights.

The second problem-solving skill area, that of considering the consequences of alternative responses, involves the ability to attend to the fact that one's responses do have interpersonal consequences, as well as the ability to think about more than one consequence which might follow from one's actions. In general, the ability to conceptualize a greater range of potential consequences will also be related to more effective social problem solving. Social learning theories of behavior (Rotter, Chance, & Phares, 1972) suggest that the consequences which one anticipates play an especially important role in directing one's behavior and decisions. According to this view, behavior is a function of one's expectancies regarding the potential outcomes of one's anticipated behavior, in combination with the values one places on those consequences.

We conceptualize a juvenile's reasoning about the *Miranda* rights decision, then, as more likely to represent a competent cognitive process if he or she can generate a wider range of possible consequences to alternative responses to the waiver situation. For example, a more careful weighing of the consequences of waiving one's right to silence would include a consideration of the immediate potential consequences (e.g., the possible responses of police officers) as well as more long-range possibilities (e.g., a judge's possible response to one's decision). For juveniles, certain consequences outside the realm of the legal system might also be relevant (e.g., parents' potential reactions to one's decision).

Alternative thinking and consequence thinking are not to be viewed as personality traits (Spivack *et al.*, 1976). Nor are they merely a function of intellectual ability. When children perform at a less adequate level on tasks measuring these abilities, it may be related to lower intellectual capacity, or merely to insufficient exposure to (and thus a lack of familiarity with) the social situation to which they are asked to respond, or to their personal, emotional reaction to the particular social situation represented by the problem-solving task, or a combination of all of these variables. Spivack *et al.* (1976) and Shantz (1975) report many studies relating experimental measures of children's social problem-solving skills to their effectiveness in actual classroom and peer situations. But most studies have found no systematic relationship between measures of social problem-solving skills and IQ, socioeconomic class, or language ability (Jennings, 1975; Muuss, 1960; Shure & Spivack, 1975; Turnure, 1975). Spivack *et al.* (1976) have further pointed out that children might demonstrate greater or lesser social problem-solving abilities in different types of social situations.

Therefore, when examining juveniles' thinking of alternatives and consequences in relation to the *Miranda* waiver situation, we should not assume that we are assessing any single trait or intellectual capacity. The past research suggests that we might be assessing, at least in part, something called social intelligence or social problem-solving potential. But even so, some juveniles might perform worse in this situation than in other more common interpersonal events because of unfamiliarity with the legal system, while others might perform better in this situation than in their daily interpersonal relations if their past experience (for example, frequent court contact) has produced a familiarity with the events and consequences of juvenile court processes.

In summary, our exploration of juveniles' reasoning about the *Miranda* waiver decision focused on their perceptions of the alternative responses available to them and their expectancies regarding the probable consequences of the available alternative responses. We wanted to assess the degree to which they could generate a range of alternatives and consequences, and we sought to describe the content of the alternatives and consequences to which they attended when making the decision to waive or assert *Miranda* rights. Finally, since juveniles' responses might in part be dependent on the particular circumstances of any single arrest, we wished to examine their responses to a variety of arrest situations.

THE WAIVER EXPECTANCY INTERVIEW

A semistructured interview procedure was chosen as the method for exploring juveniles' reasoning and problem solving in regard to the waiver decision. Interview formats have been used successfully in several major studies of children's cognitive development: notably, investigations of children's social problem-solving skills (Spivack *et al.*, 1976), moral development (Kohlberg, 1964; Selman & Damon, 1975), and development of legal reasoning (Tapp & Kohlberg, 1971; Tapp & Levine, 1974).

When developing the format for such interviews, one must strike a balance between standardizing the administration and allowing interviewees to respond freely (Kahn & Connell, 1957; Merton, Fisk, & Kendall, 1956; Selltiz, Wrightsman, & Cook, 1976). The more structured the interview process, the more standardized can be the administration, and consequently the greater is one's confidence in the reliability of comparisons of results between persons who have been interviewed by different interviewers. On the other hand, exploration of relatively uncharted areas of cognition or attitude requires an interview which is sufficiently open-ended to allow latitude for individual expression. Selltiz *et al.* (1976) recommend movement from relatively open-ended questions to more restrictive and specific ones in the course of the interview. Thus, the interviewee's own frame of reference or fund of knowledge can be explored before his or her responses are biased by the examiner's preconceived ideas or concerns regarding the topic area.

The Waiver Expectancy Interview, reproduced in Appendix E, is a structured interview to the extent that each interviewee receives the same questions focused on the particular areas of inquiry around which the study was built—that is, perceived alternatives and their consequences in the *Miranda* waiver situation.[2] This amount of structure

[2]Training of the three interviewers who collected data for the present study involved an intensive two-month process. It consisted of tape recorded role-playing of the interview and practice interviews with juveniles, all of which were reviewed and discussed by the research team at twice-weekly training meetings. The objective was to achieve a relative uniformity of administration among the interviewers by strict adherence to the wording and sequence of the interview questions, while at the same time producing interviews

seemed reasonable in light of our prior conceptualization of important dimensions based on earlier social problem-solving studies as well as a number of very open-ended pilot interviews which we had conducted with juveniles and juvenile court personnel. But the questions themselves are relatively open-ended, allowing for considerable freedom of choice and expression, with questions which restrict and focus the interviewee's thinking being reserved until the later portions of the interview. In overall structure, the interview follows a model set forth by Galtung (1967) involving four major stages: introduction to the task, questions relating to the main goal of the interview, a phase of interviewee reflection on the foregoing process, and a closing phase in the interviewer–interviewee relationship.

In constructing the interview, we were especially concerned that juveniles' responses might sometimes be the product of unwanted mediating variables—that is, of juveniles' perceptions of the interviewers and of the task itself as a research procedure. For example, it was likely that some juveniles in detention might perceive us as representatives of the court, as persons who might influence their own present situations or who, for any other reason, should be responded to in a way which would manage a "good" impression.

Therefore, the interview incorporated several features to reduce the influence of unwanted mediating variables. First, the introduction emphasized the interviewer's university affiliation and research objectives, reaffirmed confidentiality and separateness from court activities, and attempted to establish a nonjudgmental atmosphere. Second, the situations to which interviewees were asked to respond were framed in the third person, as recommended by Weiss (1975) and Kahn and Connell (1957); that is, interviewees were asked to explore a hypothetical third person's options, choices, and consequences in *Miranda* waiver situations. It was hoped that this depersonalization of the process, in which interviewees would not be asked to reflect on their own potential responses to the situations, would allow them to respond more freely. Third, interviewees were assured that a wide range of responses were acceptable and endorsed by other people: that is, that there were no wrong or right answers. Finally, in accordance with procedures outlined by Schontz (1965), the interview ended with a structured examination of

---

which were conversational in tone rather than mechanical in delivery. Since all interviews used in the study were tape recorded, periodic checks were possible during the study in order to compare interviewers for uniformity of administration and to correct for unwanted "drift" toward individualized styles of administration in the course of data collection.

interviewees' retrospections on their own emotional or cognitive states during the foregoing experimental procedure. This series of questions focused especially on interviewees' expectancies regarding the examiner's identity, objectives, and eventual use of the research data. When interviewees demonstrated misperceptions or skepticism concerning the examiners' identities or purposes, their data were not used in the analysis of study results. (Only five subjects met this criterion for exclusion in the course of the study. For details, see Appendix G.)

The *content* of the main part of the interview includes the presentation of three hypothetical offense and arrest situations. An examination of the interview in Appendix E shows that each of the hypothetical situations is followed by a series of questions following a standard sequence: (1) the interviewee's view of the alternative responses which a juvenile could make to the situation; (2) how the interviewee recommends that the hypothetical juvenile respond to the *Miranda* waiver situation; (3) an exploration of the consequences of the choice and of other options which were not chosen; and (4) the introduction of new information to examine the effects of particular social circumstances in the hypothetical situation on interviewees' reasoning about choices or consequences.

The three hypothetical situations are all similar in that they describe a juvenile (age 14–15) as having engaged in some illegal act, as having been arrested by police on suspicion and transported to a detention center, and as having been informed of his rights. The situations were constructed after pilot interviews with juveniles and juvenile court personnel revealed two major dimensions along which to structure differences between the situations: seriousness of the crime and the amount of direct evidence available to police regarding the person's involvement in the crime. Interviewees' responses in relation to other situational variations were examined in questions posed to them in later stages of the inquiry about each hypothetical situation—for example, whether a juvenile's innocence or culpability regarding the crime would suggest to the interviewees different "best" responses to the question of waiving or asserting rights.

Concerning the major questions, interviewees were uniformly encouraged to generate as many possible alternatives as they could imagine regarding the juvenile's optional responses in the *Miranda* waiver situation. Interviewees were then asked to "recommend" one of these alternatives to the juvenile in the situation ("Which of these would be best for the boy in this story to do?"). We did not assume that these choices would necessarily reflect the ways in which our interviewees would have responded in actual waiver situations. But it was felt that asking interviewees to make a choice would provide a logical progression to the discussion of expected consequences of this choice as well as the consequences of alternatives which were rejected.

Asking interviewees to reflect on the potential consequences of waiving or refusing to waive rights constituted our main exploration of their reasoning about the *Miranda* waiver decision. Consistent with our adoption of a social learning theory perspective of decision making, we assumed that the choices which interviewees recommended would be a function of their anticipations regarding the positive or negative consequences which they believed would follow if the choice were put into action (Rotter, 1954). Thus, our "reasoning" questions always asked "*What would happen* if the boy did this," never "*Why* should he or should he not do this." Not only was this form of question consistent with our use of social learning theory concepts to guide the interview, but it also allowed for more classifiable and quantifiable responses than would have followed from the more open-ended question. In addition, we found that juvenile interviewees had a much easier time responding to this slightly structured form of questioning in contrast to the vague and somewhat judgmental "Why."

Finally, we developed a highly objective system for coding and classifying various elements of juveniles' responses to the interview. Details of the various elements of the coding of interview responses will be provided as they arise in the later discussion of the results. In general, alternative responses (that is, the interviewee's perceptions of the options available to a juvenile in the *Miranda* waiver situation) were coded for the number and types mentioned by each interviewee. An interviewee's perceptions of the consequences of each alternative were coded for the number of different consequences which he or she could imagine, for specific content in a system employing ten content categories, for degree of attention to short-range and long-range consequences, and for the positive or negative value of each consequence (that is, whether it represented a desirable or undesirable outcome for the juveniles). In addition to providing the means to describe juveniles' reasoning about the waiver situation, the coding system also allowed us to explore how juveniles' thinking about the *Miranda* waiver situation might be related to their demographic characteristics and to the variations in circumstances provided by the three hypothetical situations.

SUBJECTS AND PROCEDURE

The interviewees were 183 juveniles who were residents of the same three settings from which samples were drawn in the earlier studies (detention center, boys school, boys town). The demographic description of these subjects (see Appendix A, Table A.5) indicates that as a group they were not remarkably different demographically from our earlier samples. Subjects interviewed in detention included virtually all juveniles who, during the period of the study, remained in detention more than 24 hours and who were not being detained on a felony allegation.[3]

The interview session for each subject began with a review of the voluntary nature of participation and obtaining of consent, and then proceeded to a description of the interview and the administration of the interview procedure (as shown in Appendix E). All subjects received all three of the hypothetical situations described in Appendix E. The session ended with administration of the three Wechsler subtests (IQ) which were used in our earlier studies. The sessions were tape-recorded in their entirety, since later coding of interview data required an accurate record and since taping of sessions freed the interviewers to attend completely to managing a standardized interview and maintaining rapport with the juveniles. The remaining sections in this chapter describe the various results derived from this interview procedure.

ALTERNATIVE THINKING

The interviewees' abilities to imagine alternative responses to police requests for information were examined with a single question, which followed the examiner's description on the hypothetical situation A. This situation described a boy who had committed a crime of moderate seriousness (breaking and entering, theft). He had been arrested by police officers and taken to a detention center for questioning, although the police officers were not sure that he had committed the offense. He is described as having been told that he did not have to answer questions. Other than this comment, the hypothetical situation did not provide our interviewees with more specific cues regarding options available to the hypothetical juvenile, since we wished to allow for maximum variability of response when they were asked to imagine all of the possible ways in which the juvenile could respond to the police officers' request to question him.

When interviewees were asked to imagine all of the possible things the boy could do, the alternatives mentioned by our interviewees could be categorized into four main responses, except for a small number of

[3]As explained in Chapter 4, the exclusion from the study of juveniles detained on felony charges was a precaution agreed on by the juvenile court and the research project personnel. Nevertheless, 26.8% of the present sample had at least one prior referral to the court for an alleged felony.

highly idiosyncratic ones. Almost all juveniles (91.9%) mentioned that one could answer the policemen's questions truthfully, which in this situation would have been a confession of guilt. A large number (77.6%) also included the option to answer officers' questions but to deny the allegations, which in this situation would have amounted to lying (because the juvenile was described as culpable). The frequency with which juveniles' mentioned these two alternatives did not differ in relationship to any of the demographic variables used in the study.[4]

Refusal to answer questions (remaining silent) was offered as a possible alternative by 59.6% of the interviewees. This percentage is somewhat lower than one might expect, in that the situational description had made reference to the right to silence. Its mention was even less frequent among blacks (47.6%) than whites (65.8%), and among juveniles with IQ scores of 80 or below (48.4%) than for those with IQ scores over 90 (68.8%). (These differences did not achieve statistical significance.) This option apparently was rejected by some juveniles as a true alternative even though it was cued in the situational description.

Apparently, the alternative to request an attorney is not an option which would occur spontaneously to most juveniles—that is, without specific cuing concerning the availability of counsel—since only 15.8% of the interviewees mentioned it as an option. The frequency of mention of this alternative was not related in a statistically significant way to the demographic characteristics of interviewees. But it occurred less frequently among juveniles of ages 13 or younger (9.7%) than at ages 15 and 16 (18.2%), and less often among those with IQs of 80 or below (14.0%) than among those with IQs over 90 (22.9%).

There was considerable variability in the number of alternatives imagined by the interviewees, with 6.9% offering only one option, 35.5% offering two, 38.3% three, and 20.2% four or more. Thus, about 40% of the interviewees were operating on a very limited number of assumed alternatives, usually to confess or to deny any illegal involvement.

Statistical analyses revealed a significant relationship between the number of alternatives mentioned and an IQ–race interaction.[5] That is,

[4]Throughout this study, all dependent variable data were analyzed in relation to a standard set of demographic variables: age, sex, race, IQ score, socioeconomic index, number of prior referrals to the court, number of prior felony referrals, and residence (detention, boys school, boys town).

[5]A two-way analysis of variance of number of alternatives by race and IQ revealed a nonsignificant IQ effect ($F = 1.93$, $p < .10$) and a nonsignificant race effect ($F = 0.69$, *N.S.*), but showed a significant IQ × race interaction effect ($F = 4.04$, $p < .004$). Mean alternatives for blacks at each of five levels of IQ were between 2.4 and 2.6, while means for whites increased linearly from 2.5 at lower IQ levels to 3.2 at IQs of 101 or more.

the mean number of alternatives for blacks was identical at all levels of IQ. For whites, the means of alternatives at lower IQ levels were similar to those of blacks, but the mean alternative scores increased linearly for whites at each successive higher IQ level.

Discussion

Effective problem-solving begins with the imagining of alternative responses to a problem. In the present waiver situation, most juveniles considered options involving what they could tell police about the allegations. But the option to say nothing occurred to only slightly more than half, even when it was offered to them in the preceding description of the problem. We would hypothesize that many juveniles, even though having been told of the option to refuse to talk, dismiss it as an alternative altogether. For example, they might be so constricted in their view of responses to requested information by legal authorities that refusal to give information is not considered. The evidence for constriction in alternative thinking, and thus for potentially less meaningful decision making in waiver situations, was more marked for juveniles with lower IQ scores and for average IQ blacks as compared to average IQ whites.

CHOICES

After each of the three hypothetical situations, interviewees were asked, "What would you tell the boy to do," in response to police requests for information about the youth's involvement in an offense. Situations B and C included a description of the juvenile's right to obtain legal counsel prior to interrogation, while Situation A did not. The three situations were otherwise similar in describing juveniles' culpability and police officers' uncertainty regarding the involvement; but the offense in Situation C (armed robbery and assault) was more serious than those in A and B (see Appendix E for situation descriptions).

Table 23 shows the percentage of interviewees making the various choices in response to the above question. Confession (talk/truth) was far more common in Situation A than in B or C, with the recommendation for legal counsel chosen far more often in Situations B and C (which explicitly described the availability of legal counsel) than in Situation A. Refusal to talk was infrequently chosen in any case, although it might have been implied by interviewees who mentioned getting a lawyer.

Later in the series of questions following each hypothetical situa-

TABLE 23. PERCENTAGE OF SUBJECTS CHOOSING EACH RESPONSE TO INTERROGATION, BY SITUATION

	Situations		
Choice	A	B	C
Initial response			
Talk/truth	65.6	25.1	24.6
Talk/deny	17.8	11.5	9.3
Silence	10.4	6.0	4.9
Lawyer	6.0[a]	57.4	61.2
"Should he get a lawyer?" (affirmative responses)	67.2	80.9	84.2

[a] Right to attorney had not been mentioned in the hypothetical Situation A prior to subject's choice of a response.

tion, interviewees were asked specifically whether or not the youth in the stories should ask for a lawyer before the interrogation. Those results (Table 23) show a high rate of endorsement for this choice across all three situations.

"MEANINGFUL" WAIVER OF RIGHTS

We noted earlier that when interviewees were asked to imagine all of the possible alternative ways to respond to the waiver situation, approximately 40% did not mention the option to remain silent even when they had been informed of the option in the foregoing hypothetical situation. A decision by any of these juveniles to "talk" (whether this be a confession or a denial of guilt) would seem not to constitute a meaningful waiver of the right to silence, since they apparently had not perceived silence as an alternative from which to choose.

We wished to see how many juveniles "meaningfully" recommended rights waiver. We defined rights waiver as the choice (in Situation A) to talk, whether that be to confess (tell the truth) or to deny the allegations. We defined a juvenile's recommended rights waiver as having been provided "meaningfully," if the juvenile had indicated earlier that remaining silent and/or obtaining a lawyer were among the alternatives from which he or she could choose.

Taking as a group all juveniles who recommended rights waiver in Situation A (83.4% of the interviewees), Table 24 shows by demographic groups the percentage of these juveniles who met our definitional requirements for a "meaningful" waiver of rights. It can be seen that the criteria were met by a much greater percentage of older juveniles (age

TABLE 24. PERCENTAGES OF SUBJECTS CHOOSING WAIVER OF RIGHTS WHO RECOGNIZED SILENCE OR LAWYER AS OPTIONS

Variable	Percentage
Age	
13 or less	42.7
14	57.0
15	52.6
16	70.4
Sex	
Male	52.7
Female	61.9
Race	
White	63.9
Black	42.1
IQ	
70 or below	42.8
71–80	48.6
81–90	56.5
91–100	68.3
101+	68.0
Number of prior felonies	
0	58.5
1	45.0
2+	66.5

16) than of younger juveniles (age 13 or below), more often by whites than by blacks, and more often by juveniles with IQ scores above 91 than by those with scores below 81. Separate analyses of variance for each of these variables indicated that these effects were statistically significant, while the effects of sex and number of prior felonies were not. In other words, rights waiver by the majority of younger juveniles, black juveniles, and juveniles with less satisfactory intelligence test performance occurred without their acknowledgment that rights assertion was even an alternative to be considered.

CHOICES IN DIFFERENT CIRCUMSTANCES

One of our main interests was to explore whether interviewees' choices were related to their demographic characteristics and to different circumstances within the hypothetical situations. We arbitrarily set a criterion of a 20 percentage point difference as suggesting meaningful trends. We examined first the interviewees' choices in response to Situations B and C, because they represented very similar circumstances except for seriousness of offense. Situation B presented a somewhat less serious offense (hotwiring a car) than did Situation C (armed robbery and assault with a weapon).

Concerning differences by demographic characteristics, the percentages recommending confession of guilt ranged from 18.0% (Situation B) and 21.3% (Situation C) for juveniles with IQ scores of 91 and above, to as high as 47.8% (Situation B) for juveniles with two or more prior felony offenses. The percentages recommending silence ranged narrowly from 2–10%, while those recommending a lawyer ranged from 45.3% (Situation B, IQ below 81) to 72.7% (Situation B, five or more prior court referrals). The only systematic differences meeting our 20 percentage point criterion occurred in relation to race, IQ, and number of prior felonies.

Concerning race, black juveniles more often recommended confession (B, 38.1%; C, 33.3%) than did white juveniles (B, 18.3%; C, 20.2%). This might have been related to white juveniles' somewhat greater tendency to recommend obtaining a lawyer (B, 63.3%; C, 65.0%) than was found for blacks (B, 46.0%; C, 54.0%). Concerning IQ, juveniles with scores above 90 were more likely to recommend a lawyer (B, 65.5%; C, 65.5%) than were juveniles with IQ scores below 81 (B, 45.3%; C, 53.1%).

A rather distinctive pattern of choices emerged in examining Situation B and C choices in relation to interviewees' number of prior felony arrests. Juveniles with two or more prior felonies recommended confession to the lesser offense (47.8%) much more often than they did to the more serious offense (17.4%). In contrast, juveniles with no prior felonies less often recommended confession to the lesser offense (22.4%), and they maintained this opinion regarding the more serious offense (26.2%). In the more serious offense, many juveniles with more prior felonies preferred denying the allegations (26.1%), a choice which none of them (0.0%) had recommended in regard to the lesser offense. Juveniles with no prior felonies rarely recommended denial of allegations (6.7%) in the more serious offense situation. Maintaining silence remained in the area of 4–6% for both groups on both situations. It appears, then, that juveniles with more prior experience with police arrests have a different perspective on what is the best response to interrogations than do less experienced juveniles, and they might be more responsive to circumstantial variables in deciding their responses.

We wondered whether juveniles' choices might be influenced by their perceptions of how much evidence the police officers had concerning the culpability of the hypothetical juvenile. Thus, one of the final questions following Situation A asked interviewees whether they would recommend a different choice if they knew that the police officers had proof (prior to the interrogation) that the hypothetical juvenile had committed the offense. The figures in Table 25 show that juveniles did not change their choices appreciably in response to this added information. There was a tendency to recommend silence more often when police already had "proof," and a decreased tendency to recommend denying the allegations with alibis or arguments. But there was no increase in the choice to talk and tell the truth (confess), a strategy which we thought juveniles might consider to be wise when police already had incriminating evidence.

Finally, since all suspects in the situations had been described as culpable, we asked juveniles in the later questioning following Situation C whether their recommendations would be different if the juvenile in the story were innocent of the alleged offense. Table 25 shows that compared to their original choices, they more often recommended that the juvenile tell the truth (e.g., about his whereabouts at the time of the crime), or simply deny that he had any involvement in the crime. It is interesting that juveniles seemed to focus more strongly on verbally asserting one's true innocence than on the potential benefits of a lawyer's presence; their primary recommendation in the original circumstances (guilt of suspect) was to obtain legal counsel, but only about 20% recommended this to the innocent juvenile. This finding was paralleled in responses to our direct question, in Situation B, concerning whether the suspect should obtain a lawyer if he is innocent. While the primary recommendation to the guilty youth in the original story (B) had been to obtain a lawyer (57.4%), 44.3% of the total interviewees changed their recommendations about getting a lawyer, given the circumstance of the youth's innocence. Of these changes, 70% were in the direction of

TABLE 25. SUBJECTS' CHOICES IN RESPONSE TO CHANGES IN HYPOTHETICAL CIRCUMSTANCES

Situation and question	Percentage of subjects making choice			
	Talk/truth	Talk/deny	Silence	Lawyer
Situation A				
Original choice	65.6	17.8	10.4	6.0
Choice when police have evidence	61.9	6.6	22.2	9.3
Situation C				
Original choice	24.6	9.3	4.9	61.2
Choice when suspect is innocent	46.4	21.5	12.2	19.9

negating the need for a lawyer if one was innocent, while 30% affirmed a greater need for legal counsel for the innocent than for the guilty.

Discussion

The results concerning interviewees' choices of response to the hypothetical interrogation situations should not be used to infer specifically how they would respond in actual interrogations. The experimental session is too far removed—emotionally, interpersonally, and in terms of precise circumstances—from that which would be experienced by juveniles in the event of their own arrest. The most one can do with any particular result in this section is to evaluate it relative to other results within the same experimental situation, or in comparison to what is known about juveniles' choices in actual interrogations. When this is done, one can derive some general suggestions regarding how juveniles think about their choices.

For example, when asked directly if youths in trouble should ask for attorneys prior to interrogation, the vast majority of juveniles answered affirmatively, whatever their age, race, or amount of prior experience with arrests and subsequent court contact. This is in striking contrast to the near absence of requests for attorneys in actual juvenile interrogations, a fact which was documented in our study in Chapter 2 and in a study we will present in Chapter 8. If it is true that most juveniles believe they ought to request attorneys, but that they do not do so in actual situations, the reason might be that they are too inhibited by the interpersonal and emotional characteristics of police interrogation to do what they would otherwise believe to be in their best interest. This possibility is not far-fetched; social psychological researchers have found situations in which adults, when faced with real life exigencies, engage in behavior which they would at other times view as improbable or contrary to their values (Asch, 1956; Milgram, 1963).

A "knowing, intelligent, and voluntary" waiver implies choicefulness, and choicefulness involves one's consideration of the major alternatives offered in the *Miranda* warnings. Some results in this section suggest that a substantial percentage of juveniles might not be able to produce this type of "choiceful" waiver. After being reminded of the right to remain silent, about 40% of the juveniles did not mention this as even an alternative when we asked them to review their options. Further, "unchoiceful waiver"—that is, choosing to talk to police in the absence of any sign that silence had been considered as an option—occurred more frequently in this study among younger juveniles, black juveniles, and those with scores indicating diminished intellectual functioning. The degree to which juveniles' choices in this research setting reflect choices they would make in actual interrogations cannot be known; but it is unlikely that juveniles' thinking would be more adaptive and flexible—that is, that they would by more aware of available options—under the pressures of police interrogations.

Finally, circumstances regarding seriousness of offense or amount of evidence available to police had no general effect on juveniles' choices in the waiver situation. This does not rule out the possibility that such effects do exist in actual interrogations, but they were discovered here only within certain types of juveniles—for example, those with more experience of felony arrests. In contrast, there was strong evidence that juveniles perceive a greater need for a lawyer when one is culpable than when one is innocent.

CONSEQUENCES

Fifteen times during the interview, we asked interviewees "What do you think would happen if...?"[6] Five of these times the question referred to the option to "talk and tell the truth" (confess), five times to "talk and say he didn't do the crime" (deny), and five times for "refused to talk or asked for a lawyer." Interviewees were allowed to describe as many expected outcomes as they wished for each alternative, and their responses were tape recorded. Each expected outcome an interviewee mentioned was called a consequence response.

After completing the interviews with about half of the juveniles in the sample, we used a random sample of these interview responses to assist in the process of defining categories into which we could code three aspects of consequence responses: content, value, and time perspective. Subsequently, each consequence response of an interviewee was coded for each of the three variables.

The ten consequence content categories are shown in Appendix E, Table E-1. They cover a range of potential reactions by police, as well as more long-range consequences related to judicial decisions about case disposition.[7]

[6]These fifteen questions appear in the interview (Appendix E) as items 3, 4, and 5 in Situation A and as items 2, 3, and 4 in Situations B and C. In Situation C, each of the three items actually contain three questions, bringing the total consequence-related questions to fifteen.

[7]Because the interview and coding system were viewed as exploratory in purpose, we did not perform tests of intercoder reliability in the use of the content, value, or time perspective systems. Possible coder differences in use of the systems were controlled, however, by having every interview coded by two coders independently, followed by research team discussion and consensus to resolve differences in the coding on each interview.

Consequence value refers to the positive or negative quality of the consequence (see Appendix E, Table E-2). This system allowed any consequence response, regardless of its content, to be coded as representing a more favorable or less favorable outcome for the suspect.

Consequence time perspective involved coding each consequence response as representing a short-range or long-range consequence. Short-range consequences, examples of which appear in Appendix E, Table E-3, were defined as relatively immediate reactions of police officers or other consequences which would follow the interrogation situation within a few minutes or hours. Long-range consequences referred to later court events, including judicial decisions. Time perspective will be discussed in a later section.

Content Frequency

The first question we wished to address was simply which categories of consequence content received the greatest and which the least attention from interviewees across all alternatives. That is, what outcomes do juveniles think about most and least when considering whether or not to waive *Miranda* rights?

Table 26 shows the results of three methods for rank ordering the frequency with which each content category was referred to by interviewees. The methods of calculation are briefly described below the table.[8] Since the three methods of calculation produced relatively similar rankings, we shall discuss the results by category rather than by method of calculation.

The effects of one's waiver decision on the likelihood of immediate incarceration (detention) and on the eventual case disposition were mentioned by almost every juvenile at least once in the course of the fifteen relevant interview questions (Method I). Mention of these was

[8]Three methods were used to rank order the ten consequence content categories by frequency of reference. Method I in Table 26 was a calculation of the percentage of subjects who made reference to a given category at least once in the fifteen consequence items. The categories were then ranked on the basis of these percentage figures. Method II involved nine consequence items: that is, the three open-ended consequence questions in each of the three interview situations (A, 3–5; B, 2–4; C, 2a, 3a, 4a), omitting the six "leading" consequence items in Situation C (2b & c, 3b & c, 4b & c). Figures in this method were calculations of the percentage of the total consequence responses ($N = 2643$) to the nine questions which fell in each content category. (An interviewee could provide more than one consequence response to any consequence question in the interview.) For example, 24.3% of all consequence responses referred to whether or not juveniles would be detained if they waived or asserted rights. Method III involved determining the percentage of juveniles for whom each content category was the one to which they most frequently referred, across all fifteen consequence items.

TABLE 26. THREE METHODS FOR RANK ORDERING CONTENT CATEGORIES BY FREQUENCY OF USE

Consequence content	Method I[a] Subjects (%)	Method I[a] Rank	Method II[b] Responses (%)	Method II[b] Rank	Method III[c] Subjects with first rank (%)	Method III[c] Rank	Mean rank
Freedom/detainment	93.4	2	24.3	1	46.4	1	1.3
Disposition	97.8	1	19.2	2	30.1	2	1.6
Investigation	88.0	3	14.1	3	15.3	3	3.0
Initiate proceedings	80.3	4	12.3	4	7.1	5	4.3
Leniency/harshness	71.5	6	10.1	5	8.7	4	5.0
Counsel	73.8	5	7.5	6	5.5	6	5.6
Assume innocence or guilt	67.8	7	5.8	7	1.6	8	7.3
Questioning	57.9	8	4.3	8	2.7	7	7.6
Anger	37.7	9	1.3	9	0.5	9	9.0
Other	9.1	10	1.0	10	0.0	10	10.0

[a]Percent of subjects referring to category at least once during fifteen consequence items.
[b]Percent of total responses during nine open-ended consequence items.
[c]Percent of subjects for whom a content category was the most frequently used. Total exceeds 100% because some subjects used two categories with equally high frequency; in these cases, a rank of 1 was given to both categories.

more frequent than mention of any other types of consequences. But of these two content areas, the matter of detention accounted for the greater percentage of the total responses (Method II) and was the most frequently mentioned consequence for a greater percentage of juveniles (Method III). It would appear that when juveniles are deciding how to respond to the *Miranda* warnings, their primary concern is with the most immediate question: "Will I spend the night in jail (detention), or will the police release me to return home?" The possible effects of their decision on the more long-range matter of court decisions about case disposition are of frequent concern as well, but secondary to the more immediate issue of temporary detention.

The two areas next in frequency of reference both involved formal police functions: investigation of the offense and the power of police to decide whether or not to initiate legal proceedings. Concerns about police investigations tended to focus on whether or not the police would acquire incriminating evidence in ways other than interrogation, for example, after one had denied the charge or refused to talk. Concerns about the initiation of legal proceedings centered on how one's decision to waive or assert rights might influence police officers' decisions to refer the case to the juvenile court for intake and a possible judicial hearing.

The "lenient/harsh" category, next in order of frequency, refers to any consequence responses which focused generally on "easier" or "harder" outcomes, but in which the specific outcome area (e.g., detention, disposition) was not clearly stated and could not be clarified by interviewer inquiries. "Counsel" refers to any mention of the provision or withholding of attorney services as a consequence of one's decision.

At least once during the interview questions, two-thirds of the juveniles mentioned the effects which one's statements or refusal to talk might have on others' assumptions regarding one's guilt or innocence. Police officers' and judges' assumptions were most frequently mentioned in this category.

Finally, the two least frequently mentioned concerns both involved the very immediate, interpersonal interactions between suspects and interrogators. About half of the juveniles made some reference to whether or not police would pursue questioning more vigorously, usually in relation to a suspect's option to deny or to refuse to talk about the offense. But this content area accounted for only a small percentage of total responses and was the primary concern for very few juveniles. Of even less concern was whether or not police officers would respond to one's decision with angry words, gestures, or physical abuse. This possibility occurred to about one-third of the juveniles at least once during the interview, but it accounted for a very small percentage (1.3%) of the total responses. It is possible that juveniles' concerns about these two areas of potential police pressure might be more pronounced when they are faced with "real" events, in contrast to hypothetical situations in the context of a research interview. On the other hand, their responses in the interview might reflect their own experiences with police officers, which in most cases probably did not involve overt pressure or threat (President's Commission on Law Enforcement, 1967).

There were no statistically significant differences between juveniles by age, race, IQ score, or number of felony arrests, with regard to rank orders of frequency of reference to any of the ten consequence content categories.[9] But the juveniles at the boys town did manifest a very different pattern of concerns than did juveniles at the boys school or those in detention. Boys town subjects made significantly less frequent reference to the matter of temporary detention than did juveniles in the other two settings, and they made significantly more frequent reference to categories involving other, immediate police reactions—their ability to investigate and discover evidence by means other than interrogation, the possibility of persistent questioning, and the possibility of angry reactions by police. The boys town subjects did not differ remarkably from other juveniles in the sample by way of major demographic characteristics. But it was our impression during contact with these subjects that they seemed more dependent as a group; such unmeasured personality differences might have been related to the aforementioned differences in consequence concerns between them and youths in the other two settings.

Consequences in Relation to Alternatives

Tables 27, 28, and 29 will assist us in addressing a question which was at the heart of our exploration of juveniles' reasoning when deciding how to respond to waiver situations. That is, what consequences do they tend to associate with each of the major alternatives? Each table presents the results for one of the three alternatives: Table 27, for talking

[9]For these analyses, the frequencies of a juvenile's reference to the ten content categories were rank ordered. Then, for each content category, analyses of variance of juveniles' rank scores for that category were performed, with separate analyses for each of the independent variables of age, race, IQ category, number or prior felony arrests, and the three detention or rehabilitation settings. As described in the text, significant differences were found only in relation to setting, with the boys town youths referring less frequently to the detention category ($F = 43.29$, $p < .001$), and with significantly greater frequency to the investigation category ($F = 9.15$, $p < .001$), the questioning pursued category ($F = 22.67$, $p < .001$), and the anger category ($F = 3.11$, $p < .05$).

TABLE 27. "WHAT WOULD HAPPEN IF HE TALKED AND TOLD THE TRUTH/CONFESSED?" PERCENTAGE OF SUBJECTS MAKING REFERENCE TO EACH CONTENT CATEGORY, BY POSITIVE AND NEGATIVE VALUES, AND BY SITUATIONS (A, B, C)

Consequence content	Positive value			Negative value		
	A	B	C	A	B	C
Freedom/detainment	11.5	7.1	2.7	37.1	38.8	24.0
Disposition	16.4	7.1	3.3	26.2	44.8	62.8
Investigation	0.0	0.0	0.0	2.2	3.3	2.2
Initiate proceedings	2.2	1.6	0.0	22.4	31.7	20.7
Leniency/harshness	28.4	13.1	18.0	0.5	3.2	4.9
Counsel	3.3	8.2	3.8	0.0	0.0	0.0
Assume innocence or guilt	0.0	0.0	0.5	1.1	1.6	0.5
Questioning	2.2	0.0	0.5	0.5	2.2	0.5
Anger	0.5	0.5	0.5	1.6	1.1	1.1

and telling the truth (which in the hypothetical situations amounted to confession); Table 28, talking and denying involvement; and Table 29, refusing to waive rights, either by refusing to talk or by requesting legal counsel. In each table, data are provided separately for positive and negative values (desirable or undesirable outcomes) and for the three hypothetical situations with each consequence content category. Each figure is the percentage of juveniles who made reference to the positive

TABLE 28. "WHAT WOULD HAPPEN IF HE TALKED AND SAID HE DID NOT COMMIT THE CRIME?" PERCENTAGE OF SUBJECTS MAKING REFERENCE TO EACH CONTENT CATEGORY, BY POSITIVE AND NEGATIVE VALUES, AND BY SITUATIONS (A, B, C)

Consequence content	Positive value			Negative value		
	A	B	C	A	B	C
Freedom/detainment	33.3	21.8	17.5	18.0	21.3	18.0
Disposition	2.2	2.2	2.2	9.8	12.5	23.5
Investigation	1.1	4.3	1.1	37.1	46.9	45.9
Initiate proceedings	1.6	1.1	0.5	19.6	20.2	18.0
Leniency/harshness	0.0	0.0	0.0	15.8	13.6	19.1
Counsel	0.0	3.2	6.0	0.0	0.5	0.5
Assume innocence or guilt	0.0	2.2	1.1	10.0	9.8	7.6
Questioning	5.4	0.0	0.0	7.6	6.5	9.2
Anger	1.1	0.5	0.0	1.6	1.6	0.5

TABLE 29. "WHAT WOULD HAPPEN IF HE REFUSED TO TALK/ASKED FOR A LAWYER?" PERCENTAGE OF SUBJECTS MAKING REFERENCE TO EACH CONTENT CATEGORY, BY POSITIVE AND NEGATIVE VALUES, AND BY SITUATIONS (A, B, C)

Consequence content	Positive value			Negative value		
	A	B	C	A	B	C
Freedom/detainment	13.1	12.0	6.5	35.5	16.9	15.8
Disposition	3.2	10.9	7.1	10.4	15.3	24.0
Investigation	0.0	1.6	1.1	24.0	19.1	13.1
Initiate proceedings	0.0	1.6	0.5	16.4	17.4	16.4
Leniency/harshness	1.6	7.6	7.1	6.0	2.2	4.3
Counsel	9.2	33.3	37.7	1.1	0.5	0.5
Assume innocence or guilt	0.0	0.0	1.1	28.4	19.2	18.2
Questioning	1.1	0.5	0.5	10.4	7.6	7.1
Anger	0.0	0.0	0.0	4.3	0.0	3.8

or negative consequence content in a given situation.[10] The narrative which follows offers general observations based on these data.

Perceived Consequences of Confession

In general, juveniles perceived negative consequences of confession as more likely than positive consequences (Table 27). Immediate detention, referral of the case to the court (initiate proceedings), and an unpleasant disposition were all seen as likely outcomes by substantial numbers of youths.[11] The more serious the offense (least to most serious are, respectively, Situations A, B, and C), the more often a negative dispositional consequence was mentioned.

When positive consequences were mentioned, they were with re-

[10]Only nine of the fifteen interview questions about consequences were used in calculating these percentages. The reason for this was that Situation C contained six "leading" consequence questions in addition to the three open-ended consequence questions which appeared in Situations A and B. To use the six additional Situation C questions would have produced figures which could not be meaningfully compared to figures from the other two situations. Thus we used only the three questions in Situation C (items 2a, 3a, and 4a as noted in Appendix E) which were worded in an open-ended way similar to the three items in Situations A and B.

[11]The negligible percentage of juveniles noting that confession would lead to an assumption of guilt probably reflects merely their failure to specifically refer to what was an all too obvious consequence.

gard to greater leniency by the court, a less unpleasant disposition, or avoidance of detention as a consequence of confessing. But these rewards for cooperating with police were viewed as unlikely except with regard to Situation A, the least serious of the offenses. From the juveniles' perspectives, then, the probability of escaping negative consequences by confessing to charges would not come close to the probability of suffering an unpleasant outcome except, perhaps, in the case of offenses less serious than auto theft and armed assault.

Perceived Consequences of Denying Allegations

The juveniles appeared to believe that if there is a benefit to be gained by denying one's involvement in an offense, it is the avoidance of immediate detention, especially when the offense is not of great seriousness (see Table 28). But they recognized a wide range of negative consequences which would be risked by attempting to secure immediate freedom through denial or fabricated alibis.

For example, they were frequently concerned that police officers would respond by instigating a formal investigation and would thereby acquire evidence to contradict the suspect's denial or alibi (see investigation, negative, in Table 28). This was often paired with the expectancy that once the investigation had produced incriminating evidence, it would result in harsher treatment because the juvenile had denied involvement (see leniency/harshness, negative).

References to negative dispositional outcomes were less frequent here than in relation to confession. But this probably should not be read as conveying a belief that denial of charges is less likely to lead to negative dispositions than is confession. It is likely that juveniles who noted that police investigations would turn up incriminating evidence were implying negative dispositional outcomes as well, even though they did not follow through verbally to express these expectancies. Finally, referral of the case to the court (initiate proceedings, negative) was noted with about the same frequency as was seen in reference to confessions. Thus, juveniles did not seem to view denial of charges as a way to avoid becoming the subject of court involvement.

Perceived Consequences of Asserting Rights

We should explain first that the sizable percentage figures of positive responses in the counsel category (Table 29) do not allow for inferences about whether juveniles perceived legal counsel as valuable.

Positive responses in the counsel category were simply those in which juveniles indicated that in response to a request for an attorney, police officers would set in motion the process for obtaining one.

Apart from the positive counsel responses, juveniles' references to negative consequences of assertion of rights far outweighed the frequency with which they referred to positive consequences. The imbalance in this regard is greater than for either of the other two alternative responses, both of which involved waiving rights.

The attention to negative consequences was generally dispersed across several content areas. There was no appreciable tendency to attend to any particular negative consequence more or less often in relation to varying seriousness of offenses, except that attention shifted from immediate detention in the least serious offense (Situation A) to negative long-range dispositions in the more serious offense situations (B and C).

Here, more than in the other two alternatives, interviewees noted that police officers or judges would assume that the juveniles in the hypothetical situations were guilty. That is, they believed that refusal to talk or asking for a lawyer would suggest to legal authorities that the juvenile had something to hide.

Consequence Indexes of Problem-Solving Abilities

A time perspective (TP) score was calculated for each subject, consisting of a weighted ratio of the short-range and long-range consequences provided by the subject.[12] A series of analyses of variance revealed no simple relationships between TP scores and any single demographic variable. But a series of two-way analyses of variance revealed a significant interaction between age and IQ: at higher IQ levels, TP mean scores were relatively similar at each age, while at lower IQ levels, TP mean scores increased with age.[13] These results suggest that younger (ages 12–14), less intelligent (IQ less than 80) juveniles were more likely to focus one-sidedly on short-range consequences of waiver decisions than were other juveniles in the study.

A range of consequences (RC) score was also calculated for each subject. The RC formula credits subjects not only for the number of

[12]The formula used to calculate TP scores was: [sum S + (sum $L \times 2$)]/(sum S + sum L), where S = short-range consequence and L = long-range consequence. TP scores ranged from 1.00 to 2.00, with higher scores indicating a greater proportion of long-range consequences in a subject's total consequence responses.

[13]The two-way analysis of variance of TP scores yielded a significant age × IQ interaction: $F = 2.10$, $df = 12/163$, $p < .02$.

different consequence content categories they used across the fifteen interview items, but also gives extra credit to subjects whose responses do not focus mainly on any one or two of the several content areas which they employ.[14] In other words, a higher RC score will be obtained by the subject who uses four content areas than by the subject who uses only two. But of two subjects who both use four content areas, the one whose responses are more evenly distributed across the four content areas will receive a higher RC score than the one whose responses stay mainly with two of the four areas. In essence, the RC score was intended as an index of subjects' flexibility in their attention to possible consequences, a characteristic which has been noted as an important part of adaptive problem solving (Spivack *et al.*, 1976).

A series of analyses of variance revealed only one weak, but still statistically significant, relationship—that between RC scores and race.[15] Black subjects had a lower RC mean score than white subjects, suggesting that the black youths as a group were somewhat more constricted in their range of considerations when reviewing the consequences of waiver decisions.

We were not surprised that these indexes of problem-solving ability did not relate strongly to many of the demographic or intelligence measures. As was mentioned in our earlier review of past research, most studies have found no systematic relationships between social problem-solving variables and such characteristics as measured intelligence, socioeconomic class, or language ability. We suspect that time perspective and flexibility of thinking in the context of the waiver decision might relate more closely to certain personality differences among juveniles than to demographic or intellectual differences per se.

DISCUSSION

Rather than summarizing the full range of results in this exploratory study, let us focus on those findings which suggested differences between various types of juveniles in their decision making in waiver situations.

Several results pointed to less effective thinking within certain de-

[14]The RC formula was: [sum $(f \times R)$ $c_1 \ldots c_n$]/F, where f = the number of times a content category was used by a subject, R = the rank of the content category when the categories which the subject used were ranked in order of frequency of use, $c_1 \ldots c_n$ = the categories used by the subject, and F = the total number of consequence responses across the fifteen items.

[15]The analysis of variance of RC scores by race yielded: $F = 3.96$, $df = 1/181$, $p < .05$.

mographic groups: black youths, juveniles with IQ scores below 80, and juveniles below age 14. Generally, the thinking of these groups could be described as more constricted; the results suggested that one or more of these groups tended to consider fewer alternatives, a more limited range of possible consequences, and more immediate consequences in contrast to long-range consequences. As noted in our earlier discussion of social problem-solving theory, these tendencies may be unrelated to the intellectual abilities of these groups per se. That is, they might result from some interaction between personality characteristics and the demands of situations involving legal authorities.

One possibility is that these groups—black or younger youths—tend to perceive themselves as exceptionally powerless in relation to legal authorities, and thus less capable of having an influence on the outcome of the interrogation event. Several studies (Davis & Phares, 1967; Lefcourt & Wine, 1969; Seeman & Evans, 1962) have shown that when people perceive their own potential to influence social events as negligible, they do not attend as closely to information with which they are provided or options which are at their disposal. This might explain why the aforementioned groups tended not to list the "silence" alternative as among their options, even when they had been informed of this option by the interviewer.

Concerning the interviewees' reasoning about the consequences of the three major options, it is clear that they viewed a wide range of negative consequences in relation to any of the alternatives. Positive consequences were perceived as fewer and, if they were sought, would therefore require that one take considerable risks. An examination of the "risk–benefit" inferences in interviewees' thinking about the options allows for some speculations about the types of juveniles who would choose to confess, to deny charges, or to assert their rights.

First, interviewees tended to believe that confession can result in more lenient treatment, even though they felt it would almost inevitably result in some form of undesirable consequences such as detainment, referral to the juvenile court and—especially for more serious offenses—some form of undesirable disposition. Confession, then, represents a willingness to take the risk of allowing legal authorities to decide one's fate, in the hopes that one's own cooperation will soften the penalties which authorities determine. For this, one gives up any immediate benefits which might be provided by other, more assertive alternative responses to the interrogation situation. This option is more likely to be chosen, then, by dependent or frightened youths, or by youths who feel guilt. Some of our data suggest that more "sophisticated" youths might also see confession as the most viable option when offenses are not very serious, perhaps because they view these situations as offering better odds for leniency than is the case with major felonies.

Of the three major alternatives, denying the charges was seen generally as offering the most immediate positive consequences; there was a tendency to believe that there is some chance of avoiding immediate detention because, presumably, police will have insufficient evidence to support detainment. But it is also the most risky option. Police might proceed to investigate the case by other means and discover incriminating evidence, in which case harsh penalties can be expected because one has forfeited any chance of leniency by lying or failing to cooperate. Because the risks are great, denying the charges would seem to be an option which would be chosen by juveniles who are focused one-sidedly on immediate gains, or by juveniles who are sufficiently aggressive to play with dangerous odds. In addition, some data suggested that this high-risk option becomes more attractive to some juveniles (generally, more "sophisticated" youths) when the alleged offense is a very serious one, probably because the long-range negative consequences of confession (e.g., training school) were seen as markedly greater for these offenses.

When thinking about the alternative of asserting their rights, juveniles appear to perceive as many negative potential consequences as with any other alternative. Since asserting one's rights means forfeiting the chance for leniency by way of confession, the decision to assert rights might depend on one's expectancies about the value of obtaining a lawyer—that is, whether or not a lawyer might obtain the same benefits of leniency. (Juveniles appeared to see no positive consequences of merely refusing to talk, since the only positive consequence which they associated with assertion of rights was obtaining a lawyer.) Juveniles also perceived rights assertion as a forfeiture of the potential to avoid detention, which was the main benefit of waiving rights and denying the charges. One would expect that the option to assert their rights, then, would be chosen primarily by juveniles who are able to delay the immediate gratification which might be offered by denying charges and avoiding detention. Also, because one risks the full adversarial power of the court, one would not be likely to choose this option without having considerable self-confidence or confidence in the power of legal counsel.

In closing, it is worth repeating that although nearly two-thirds of the interviewees recommended obtaining legal counsel, this finding suggests only that these interviewees perceived some value in obtaining an attorney, not that they would necessarily request one in an actual interrogation situation. In fact, we observed in an earlier study that such a choice was exceedingly rare in a sample of actual interrogation cases. Together, the results of these two studies suggest that many youths, when faced with actual interrogation situations, do not make the choice which in less emotion-filled hypothetical situations they perceive as being in their own best interest. This discrepancy may be the result of the "fantasy, fright, or despair" of adolescents about which the Supreme Court in *Gault* expressed concern.

8

The Presence of Parents at Juveniles' Interrogations

What law or legal process could best protect juveniles from making uninformed or involuntary decisions about their rights in interrogation? Courts have addressed three general approaches to this problem.

First, a few courts have been asked to rule that juveniles' confessions are never valid. That is, juveniles' attorneys have sometimes argued that the right to silence should be nonwaivable in all juvenile cases, or at least that confessions should not be admitted as evidence in delinquency proceedings. This argument for blanket exclusion has met with no success, the courts having pointed to society's competing interest in resolving cases where the alleged offenses represented serious danger.[1] Such decisions, however, do not necessarily rule out the future possibility of *per se* exclusion of confessions in cases involving juveniles of some specifiable classes, and we will explore this option in the concluding chapter.

Second, some courts have suggested that disadvantages related to suspects' ages, backgrounds, or intelligence might be reduced if they were provided explanations of their rights in simpler, more understand-

[1]For example, in *In the Interest of Thompson,* 241 N.W.2d 2 (1976), the court noted: "It is apparent that courts, required to deal pragmatically with an evermounting crime wave in which minors play a disproportionate role, have considered society's self-preservation interest in rejecting a blanket exclusion for juvenile confessions" (at 5). See also *Cotton* v. *United States,* 446 F.2d 107 (1971) and *United States* v. *Ramsey,* 367 F.Supp. 1307 (1973), in which blanket exclusion was rejected.

able terminology than is used in the standard *Miranda* warnings.[2] About this approach, too, we will have more to say later. It is sufficient for now to note that few courts have ever considered the complexities of deciding what instructions will suffice for what types of juveniles, the practical difficulties of expecting police to "educate" juveniles in the context of police investigations, or whether any efforts of this type, no matter how extensive or how carefully implemented, would be likely to have any appreciable effect on juveniles' understanding of their rights or their capacities to make valid decisions about their rights.

Finally, the most frequent safeguard supported by the courts has been to provide juveniles with the presence of an adult advocate at the time of the waiver decision. The assumed importance of an adult advocate for juveniles has figured prominently in cases concerning the validity of juveniles' confessions since *Haley* v. *Ohio*, 332 U.S. 596 (1948) and *Gallegos* v. *Colorado*, 370 U.S. 49 (1962); judges in these cases decried the absence of any advice and support from a "friendly adult" when these juveniles were faced with the authoritative presence of police and the necessity of making decisions concerning rights waiver under trying conditions. The Supreme Court in *In re Gault*, 387 U.S. 1 (1967) clearly reaffirmed a juvenile's need for the advice of an advocate, although not specifically with reference to pretrial proceedings. Then, in *West* v. *United States*, 399 F.2d 467 (1968), the Court's prescription of circumstances to be weighed in evaluating the validity of juvenile waiver at pretrial interrogations specifically included "whether the accused is held incommunicado or allowed to consult with relatives, friends, or an attorney" (at 469).

Recommendations to make juveniles' right to counsel nonwaivable—that is, to require the presence of an advocate attorney for a valid confession—have issued from many major sources in recent years (Institute of Judicial Administration and American Bar Association, 1977; Paulsen & Whitebread, 1974; Piersma, Ganousis, & Kramer, 1975; Piersma *et al.*, 1977; President's Commission on Law Enforcement, 1967). But at this writing, only Connecticut (by statute) and Texas (by case law, *In re R.E.J.*, 511 S.W.2d 347 (1974) require that an attorney for

[2]In *Coyote* v. *United States*, 380 F.2d 305 (1967), it was noted that the *Miranda* requirement is "not a ritual of words" and must include advice in a language which the suspect can understand. The "*Coyote* test" is "whether the words in the context used, considering the age, background, and intelligence of the individual being interrogated, impart a clear, understandable warning of all of his rights" (at 308). The defendant was an adult and the test has not been the basis for any appellate decisions concerning juveniles.

the juvenile be present for a juvenile's confession to be valid.[3] Other courts have noted that it would have been advisable for juveniles to have had the benefit of advice from legal counsel, but they have ruled on the basis of absence of any competent adult advocate rather than because of the absence of legal counsel *per se.*

Far more in evidence is a trend toward requiring the presence of parents or guardians as advisors and protectors for juveniles in custodial interrogation. This trend, and the question of the extent of protection which parents can provide, will be the subject of this chapter. It is important to note that in considering the role of parents at juveniles' interrogations, courts have had to address a much wider range of questions, many of them involving the delicate balance between the interests of society, the newly accorded rights of juveniles, and the time-honored authority of parents to control their children.[4] For example, consider the following range of questions about the parent's role in interrogation, all of which have come before courts:

- Must a parent (or guardian) be present in order for a juvenile's waiver of rights to be valid?
- Is it necessary for the parent to agree with a juvenile's decision to waive rights in order for the waiver to be valid?
- Can a parent validly waive a juvenile's rights? If so, for which juveniles? Under what circumstances?
- Do a parent's persence and communications with a juvenile necessarily constitute due process protections, or might they sometimes produce a negative or coercive effect?
- Is a juvenile's confession admissable when given to police without *Miranda* warnings if the juvenile has been voluntarily brought to police officers by the parents, who then force the juvenile to confess?[5]

[3]Minnesota does not allow counsel to be waived in interrogation of "serious" cases (Minnesota Rules for Juvenile Proceedings, Rule 1–5). A few other states make the right to counsel nonwaivable at certain other stages of the juvenile court process.

[4]The same general questions have been the basis for difficult cases in other areas of law during the past decade: for example, *Wisconsin* v. *Yoder,* 406 U.S. 205 (1972); *Planned Parenthood* v. *Danforth,* 428 U.S. 52 (1976); *Kremens* v. *Bartley,* 431 U.S. 119 (1977); *J.L. and J.R.* v. *Parham,* 431 U.S. 936 (1977); and *Secretary of Public Welfare of Pennsylvania* v. *Institutionalized Juveniles,* 47 U.S.L.W. 4754 (1979).

[5]Another difficult question would be raised when a juvenile objected to making a statement after the parents effectively waived the juvenile's rights. But to our knowledge this question has not been brought to any appellate courts.

It is little wonder that a judge faced with one of the latter questions began the report of the court's decision with the complaint, "Oh, for the wisdom of Solomon!" [*K.E.S.* v. *State,* 216 S.E.2d 670, at 671 (1975)].

We will not be concerned here with certain questions which, although essential to judicial decisions, are beyond the reach of empirical methods of study.[6] Whether or not parents have an absolute authority to govern their children's behaviors in these matters—that is, to advise or decide for their child regarding their rights—is in large part a philosophical and moral question requiring a weighing of doctrine concerning the family and the state's interest in protecting the rights of children.[7] That is a different question from the one addressed here.

Specifically, we will focus on law and legal assumptions about the protective value of parents' presence at juveniles' interrogations—that is, the extent to which parents' presence has been required, the protections for juveniles which the requirement is believed to provide, and counterarguments that the requirement might not fulfill its intended protective purpose. Then we will present two studies which were designed to provide empirical information about the adequacy of protections for juveniles which parents might be expected to afford in custodial interrogations. Whatever the results, they can only serve as one of many factors to be considered when addressing questions about the appropriate legal relationship between a parent's authority and a juvenile's rights and interests.

THE LAW'S VIEW OF PARENTS' PRESENCE

Since *West*'s inclusion of the presence of a "friendly adult" as a relevant circumstance to be weighed, many courts have required the presence of parent, guardian, or counsel for a juvenile's waiver to be valid.[8] Perhaps the strongest statement was voiced in *Commonwealth* v. *Markle,* 380 A.2d 346 (1977): "When the juvenile has not been given this

[6]For a brief examination of legal precedent and theory concerning the full range of questions about parents' roles in juvenile interrogations, see Davis (1974) and Piersma *et al.,* (1977).

[7]See Teitelbaum and Ellis (1978) for a discussion of this issue in relation to a wider range of current questions in family law and mental health law affecting juveniles.

[8]For example, see: *In re D.,* 290 N.Y.S.2d 935 (1968); *Lewis* v. *State,* 288 N.E.2d 138 (Ind. 1972); *State* v. *White,* 494 S.W.2d 687 (Mo. Ct. App. 1973); *In re K.W.S.,* 500 S.W.2d 275 (Mo. Ct. App. 1973); *Commonwealth* v. *Starkes,* 335 A.2d 698 (Pa. 1975); *Matter of F.,* 386 N.Y.S.2d 185 (1976); *Commonwealth* v. *Gaskins,* 369 A.2d 1285 (Pa. 1977); *Commonwealth* v. *Smith,* 372 A.2d 797 (Pa. 1977).

opportunity for consultation, we need not look to the totality of the circumstances to determine the voluntariness of the confession. The confession must be suppressed" (at 348). Fairly recent changes in some state statutes have made the presence of parents mandatory for valid waiver by juveniles (e.g., in Connecticut, Missouri, New Mexico, Oklahoma). Finally, other courts, which have refused to adopt a per se rule that parents must be present, have nevertheless emphasized in strong terms the importance of parents' presence when weighing the totality of circumstances in each case.[9]

In spite of this growing body of case and statutory law, authoritative sources (Davis, 1974; Piersma *et al.*, 1977) have characterized the attention to parents' presence as a trend rather than common practice nationally. As we have seen in Chapter 4, many courts have considered juveniles to be competent to waive rights without the assistance of a friendly adult. In addition, the fact that a substantial number of cases in which parents were absent have found their way to the appellate courts (nearly all of the cases in Chapter 4, and notes 8 and 9 in this chapter) suggests that interrogation of juveniles without the presence of parents continues to be more the rule than the exception when viewed from a national perspective.

Where a parent's presence is required, the parent's role in the decision concerning the juvenile's waiver of rights generally is not specified by case law or statute. While some local jurisdictions require that both the juvenile and a parent sign a waiver form, others require only that the juvenile sign, the mere fact of the presence of the parent acting as evidence that there was no objection. Almost all state statutes are silent on the question of a parent's authority to waive the right to silence for the juvenile. In theory, it is assumed that parents may do so, by the same tradition that they have had the authority to consent to their child's medical treatment or mental hospital admission apart from the child's wishes. But recently some states have recognized a juvenile's independent claim to the rights to silence and counsel.[10]

[9]See *In re Carlo,* 225 A.2d 110 (N.J. 1966); *State* v. *Melanson,* 259 So.2d 609 (La. 1972); *Commonwealth* v. *Cain,* 279 N.E.2d 706 (Mass. 1972); *Theriault* v. *State,* 223 N.W.2d 850 (Wisc. 1974); *Tennell* v. *State,* 348 So.2d 937 (Fla. App. 1977); *Matter of S.H.S.*, 574 P.2d 1077 (Okla. Crim. App. 1978).

[10]For example, a Montana statute provides that a parent may waive the juvenile's rights when the juvenile is under 12 years of age. If the juvenile is 12 or older, however, both juvenile and parent must agree to the waiver. If they do not, waiver may be permitted only with the advice of counsel: §10-1218(1) (b) (i–iii). See also Virginia, §16.1-266, and Minnesota, JCR1-5(3). In contrast, Kentucky has legislated that a parent can never waive any right belonging to the accused child: §208:060(3) (e).

Parent as Protector: Legal Assumptions

A review of cases which have either required or strongly urged the presence of parents at interrogations of juveniles (see notes 8 and 9) reveals that courts have assumed that two broad types of benefits will accrue: (1) the reduction of the juvenile's sense of pressure, threat, or fear; and (2) the provision of advice about matters which the juvenile may not be able to comprehend.

The first of these has been the more frequent of the two rationales. The argument has been that a parent's presence will be a mitigating force to reduce the likelihood of abusive coercion by officers or will reduce the pressures which are inherent in the status and power differences between the juvenile suspect and police officers. For example, in *In re K.W.B.*, 500 S.W.2d 275 (1973) the court reasoned that a parent's presence would "lessen the atmosphere of coercion and fear which inheres in any such setting" (at 282). Likewise, "where an informed adult is present, the inequality of the position of the accused and police is to some extent neutralized" [*Commonwealth* v. *Starkes*, 335 A.2d 698, at 703 (1975)]. The emphasis in this rationale, then, is on parents' abilities to diminish the likelihood that a juvenile's decision concerning rights waiver will be merely acquiescent or deferent to authority.

The second rationale has focused on parents' abilities to provide advice or to assist juveniles' in reasoning about matters which might be beyond their own comprehension. For example, courts have remarked that an adult can assist a juvenile "to make the kind of judgment to intelligently, knowingly, and understandingly waive constitutional rights" [*State* v. *White*, 494 S.W.2d 687, at 691 (1973)] or "to fully understand the effect and results growing out of such waiver" [*Story* v. *State*, 452 P.2d 822 (1969)]. These courts, then, have focused on parents' abilities to explain the rights to the juvenile or to help the juvenile to weigh the options and consequences at hand.

These two reasons supporting the presence of parents at juveniles' interrogations are based on two general assumptions: (1) that there is an identity of interests existing between parent and child, such that parents will mitigate the inequality in the confrontation between officers and the juvenile suspect; and (2) that a parent will have a sufficient understanding and appreciation of a juvenile's rights and the consequences of their waiver, and therefore can supply the explanation and reasoning which the juvenile alone might lack. While these assumptions might be borne out in many cases, courts and legal commentators have frequently questioned their generality. In fact, Paulsen and Whitebread's (1974) assessment of the issue led them to suggest that "it cannot be assumed that parents in large numbers of cases will play a protective role" (p. 93). Let us examine the reasons why they and others have registered this concern.

First, the troublesome consequences of a juvenile's past misbehavior, or the inconvenience and embarrassment caused by their child's arrest and questioning by police officers, can result in parental attitudes toward their children ranging from apathy to anger and resentment (Paulsen & Whitebread, 1974). Thus, one juvenile court judge was led to comment on the frequency with which parents are "so worn out by the child's behavior that [their] attitude is 'Just take him, get him out of here'" (McMillian & McMurtry, 1967–1970, p. 570). This attitude can result not only in parents' disinterest in protecting or carefully advising their child, but sometimes can augment the pressure on the child to confess (Comment, 1972-1973; Piersma *et al.*, 1975). Such was found to be the case in *K.E.S.* v. *State,* 216 S.E.2d 670 (1975), for example, wherein the mother, who was the complainant, waived the rights of her daughter and pressed for a confession. In another case, two girls were confronted by the police, their parents, and their family's minister; police described the parents and minister as having "insisted on the girls giving the information—yelling at the girls," who became so upset that the police had considerable difficulty in controlling the situation [*In re Carter,* 318 A.2d 269, at 272 (1974)]. Other parental self-interests, such as avoiding the potential cost of attorney's fees, may produce pressure for juveniles to waive rights to counsel [I.J.A., 1977; also see *In re Ricky H.,* 468 P.2d 204 (1970)].

Some parents' angry insistence that their children waive the right to silence could derive from a well-meaning concern that their child receive treatment or expectation that the child will learn certain responsibilities by confessing to alleged wrongdoings. While advice based on such motives would seem to ignore the type of advocacy of rights which *Gault* intended, at least one court did not agree. In a case involving a 15-year-old boy whose mother repeatedly told him to "tell the truth (or) she would clobber him," the judge commented: "The moral upbringing of a child to be a useful citizen necessarily encompasses advice by a parent for the child to be truthful. The motherly concern for the basic precepts of morality are to be commended. We find no element of a threat or coercion on the part of the mother" [*Anglin* v. *State,* 259 So.2d 752 (1972)].[11]

[11]The potential for conflict of interest between parent and child has led several states to require separate counsel for the parent and child where a conflict is found to exist (e.g., Arizona, Minnesota, North Dakota, Ohio, Vermont, Tennessee, California, Missouri, and Pennsylvania). However, these requirements were developed in response to situations other than pretrial interrogations, and their effectiveness in dealing with the issue at the time of a juvenile's arrest is questionable.

A second point of concern has been the doubt that many parents have a sufficient understanding or appreciation of the juvenile's rights or of the consequences of waiver, to be able to provide meaningful advice (Paulsen & Whitebread, 1974). McMillian and McMurtry (1969–1970) observed that "often the parents are, at best, only equal in capacity to the child and therefore poorly equipped to comprehend the complexities confronting them" (p. 570). Several courts have, in fact, concluded that parents in the cases in question were incapable of providing meaningful advice to their children at the time of rights waiver because of their passivity or lack of understanding of the situation.[12] The issue in most of these cases was not the intellectual incompetence of the parents, but either the failure of the police to fully inform parents or the parents' failure to demonstrate an appreciation of the circumstances.

Directions for Study

Our review of this issue led us to develop several questions for research which might shed some empirical light on the matter of parents' capacities to provide meaningful protection for their children in interrogation circumstances.

First, *do parents generally perceive juveniles as having a legitimate claim to silence and counsel when suspected of legal wrongdoing?* Our question was not directed toward discovering whether or not parents understood the law in this regard. Instead, we wished to determine their attitudes toward the idea of noncompliance with police officers' requests for information regarding a juvenile's possible involvement in a crime. If parents believe that juveniles ought never to be allowed to withhold information from the police, then it might be inferred that they would not be inclined to weigh the pros and cons of the choice to waive or assert the right to silence: one weighs and chooses only when one accepts that there are optional responses. Without attitudes supportive of such a choice for juveniles, it is not likely that parents could provide the advice and protection which the Supreme Court in *Gault* believed were due to juveniles.

Such attitudes might vary as a function of the demographic characteristics of parents, as well as the characteristics of the juveniles in question. For example, Rogers and Rogers (1979) have demonstrated that people may have different attitudes toward children's rights in reference to older versus younger adolescents, with a tendency to favor greater

[12]See *Ezell* v. *State*, 489 P.2d 781 (1971); *Bridges* v. *State*, 299 N.E.2d 616 (1973); *McBride* v. *Jacobs*, 247 F.2d 595 (1957).

self-determination and autonomy (and therefore possibly to endorse noncompliance in adversarial pretrial proceedings) in the case of older adolescents. Intuitively, one might also expect "delinquent" juveniles—that is, juveniles with a history of repeated law violations—to be perceived by the public (and therefore parents) as having less of a legitimate claim to legal protections than nondelinquent juveniles, in that they might be perceived as being less worthy as a result of having behaved "irresponsibly." Tests of these hypotheses were objectives for empirical study.

Second, *when parents are asked to weigh the waiver choice and make a decision concerning what to advise their child, what reasoning or rationale do they employ for their decision?* For the same reasons which we described in Chapter 6, any decision about a juvenile's rights in interrogation (whether the final choice is to waive or to claim the rights) should at least consider the very serious consequences of adjudication and the consequent need for extra caution on the part of the suspect in accusatory and adversarial legal proceedings pursuant to possible adjudication [*In re Gault*, 387 U.S. 1 (1967)]. When a parent's reasoning about a child's waiver decision contains no reference to such precautionary thinking, it is questionable whether the parent has an adequate appreciation of the circumstances facing the child.

Third, *what do parents actually do when faced with the opportunity to advise their children concerning decisions about their rights in interrogation?* Knowledge of parents' attitudes toward children's rights, or their explanations of the reasoning behind decisions they might have to make, may provide some insight into the issue before us; but the truly critical test would involve observations of their behavior in actual interrogation situations. Do parents provide advice to their children, or do they passively observe? If they offer advice or admonitions, what is the nature of these communications? In Chapter 2 we discovered that the frequency with which juveniles waived rights in interrogation was no different when their parents' presence was required than when interrogations did not include parents. These results might suggest that parents play less of a role, protective or otherwise, in juveniles' interrogations than existing case law and legal commentators have implied.

The first of the two studies that follow investigated the first two questions by way of a questionnaire administered to a large sample of parents who were contacted through St. Louis area schools. The second study involved observation and documentation of the communications between parents and their children during actual preparation of juveniles for police questioning in St. Louis County. The latter study was performed by the St. Louis County Juvenile Court. The court has provided its permission for us to include this study in our report, which we have chosen to do because of its relevance in the interpretation of the results of our own studies.

PARENTS' ATTITUDES TOWARD JUVENILES' RIGHTS IN INTERROGATION

In this study, we examined parents' attitudes about juveniles' rights to withhold information from police and to obtain legal counsel, as well as their explanations or justifications for the advice which they claimed they would give to their own children in a hypothetical interrogation situation.

The Parents

The 753 parents who participated were those attending parent–teacher organization meetings at a high school (Sample I, $N = 408$) and junior high school (Sample II, $N = 345$) in the St. Louis metropolitan area. Because the meetings were the first in the school year for these organizations, attendance was very high; Sample I from a Catholic school represented about 90% of the families with children at the school, and Sample II from a public school represented approximately 60–70% of the families associated with that school. Table A-6 (Appendix A) shows the demographic composition of both samples, from information given by parents on the questionnaire used in the study. A range of ages was represented, as were both sexes. But it is important to note that certain demographic groups which are found in most broad metropolitan populations are almost entirely absent from these samples. Almost all of the parents were white and a disproportionately high percentage reported having occupations which we classified in the skilled, managerial, or professional categories. Almost all parents who volunteered their family income (about one-half) reported incomes above $12,000. Therefore, both samples must be construed as middle-class and upper-middle-class, with virtually no representation of low socioeconomic classes or of black parents. We must urge caution, then, against generalization of the results of the study to those segments of the population which were not represented.[13]

Table A-6 shows that the two samples were not remarkably dif-

[13]A considerable effort was made to obtain samples of other racial and socioeconomic composition. Of approximately forty schools which were contacted, the greatest barrier to similar research in urban and central-metropolitan schools was the nearly universal absence of any formal parent groups. This problem was encountered to a significant degree

ferent from each other demographically, except that parents of ages 40 or younger constituted 50% of Sample II (the junior high school) and 24% of Sample I (a senior high school). Finally, 21% of the parents in Sample I and 15% of the parents in Sample II reported that they had a child who had been "in trouble with the police" (more than a traffic violation) one or more times. These percentages are relatively consistent with past reports of prevalence rates for police investigations of violations by juveniles (more serious than traffic violations) in the general United States population (Gordon, 1976).[14]

The Research Form

Meeting in large groups, the parents were asked to volunteer to complete (anonymously) a research form. In addition to questions about demographic information, the form had two major sections. The first

in suburban schools as well. But an additional limitation frequently encountered in suburban school systems was a blanket policy prohibiting research by "outsiders" with students or parents. No schools had objections to our research method, after our demonstration of special care to matters of voluntariness and confidentiality and our offer to present group-analyzed results at subsequent parent meetings. But some school principals felt that the research topic was "too controversial." Our success in enlisting the two schools which participated was due in one case to the principal's special concern for the rights of children and the responsibilities of parents; in the other school, the principal left the decision to the parent–teacher council members, who were extremely interested and cooperative. Project personnel returned to both schools at a later date as featured speakers at a parent–teacher meeting, to provide "feedback" of results and (with an attorney in juvenile law) to answer questions about parent–child legal issues asked by the parents themselves.

[14]A direct comparison between our parents' reports of their children's police contact and past prevalence studies in the general adolescent population is very difficult, due to the fact that each past study has used somewhat different criteria (police record, court record, different severity of offenses, different age ranges). Gordon (1976) has summarized the studies, and his "Level 2" category represents the most appropriate index for our study; Level 2 included evidence from police, court, or probation files of a record including minor offenses (e.g., destruction of property, drinking, traffic escapades at high speeds, curfew violation) or any more serious offenses. Using these criteria, Hathaway and Monachesi (1963) reported that in Minnesota, about 25% of the male and about 7% of the female adolescent populations had at least a "Level 2" record by age 18. Havinghurst, Bowman, Liddle, Matthews, and Pierce (1962) reported 19% (males) and 2% (female) prevalence rates, for similar criteria in a medium-sized midwestern city. Most recently, Wolfgang, Figlio, and Sellin (1972) reported that about 28% of white males in Philadelphia had a written and filed police report by age 18. Given that a majority of our parents had children who were not yet 18, and that some had daughters but no sons (female prevalence rates are much lower than those of males), our parents' reported prevalence rates of 21% (high school sample) and 15% (junior high school sample) are comparable to past findings and might indicate that the parents were being relatively open about reporting such facts under the conditions of anonymity which we provided.

section included 30 items drawn from the Children's Rights Attitude (CRA) Scale developed by Rogers and Wrightsman (1978; also Wrightsman, Rogers, & Percy, 1976). Each parent received one of four randomly assigned instructional sets for answering the items, which we will describe shortly. The other section of the form presented a hypothetical situation involving the arrest of a juvenile, presentation of *Miranda* rights, a police request for waiver of rights to conduct investigative questioning of the juvenile, questions regarding what the parent subject would advise his or her child to do in response to such a police request, and the reasons for that advice.[15]

The CRA

This measure was originally developed to assess attitudes toward children's rights on ten subscales, each containing ten items (Wrightsman *et al.*, 1976). The ten subscales were formed by defining two broad classes of children's rights—nurturance rights and self-determination rights—across five content areas wherein children's rights have been discussed in the literature.

Nurturance rights have to do with "giving children what's good for them"—goods, services, or experiences which they could not obtain on their own because of their dependent and immature status. A strong positive attitude toward nurturance rights for children would be consistent with a benevolent, paternalistic orientation. In contrast, *self-determination rights* emphasize a child's personal control over his or her environment and situation, including decision making and some degree of autonomy. Attitudes toward these two types of rights for children are not to be thought of as two ends of a single dimension, but as two separate dimensions. That is, the results of the test developers' initial studies indicated that a person's supportive attitude with regard to nur-

[15]Between the CRA task and the hypothetical situation, the parents were asked to write their definitions of the meanings of each of the four standard *Miranda* warnings, which were printed on the questionnaire form. This had two purposes: (1) we wanted parents to have been exposed to these warnings before responding to the hypothetical situation; (2) we hoped that we might be able to score their explanations of the warnings, using the scoring criteria for the Comprehension of *Miranda* Rights measure (see Chap. 4). The procedure proved to be inadequate for the second purpose. It will be recalled that scoring of the CMR often requires that an "inquiry" be made about subjects' initial responses, so that their verbatim use of some words in the *Miranda* warnings can be reduced or vague responses can be clarified. This was not possible in the written response format of this group administration, and many parents did use some verbatim words and phrases. Thus, standardized scoring of the adequacy of parents' understanding of the warnings could not be accomplished.

turance rights may coexist with either a supportive or nonsupportive attitude concerning self-determination rights.

The ten subscales of the CRA were formed by constructing items related to five content areas in both of the major areas of children's rights. The five content areas of children's rights are health, safety and care, education, economic, and legal-judicial rights. Thus, for example, the CRA contains two subscales addressing the rights of children in legal-judicial contexts, one focusing on nurturance rights in these contexts and the other focusing on self-determination rights in legal contexts.[16]

The present study used only three of the ten CRA subscales developed by Wrightsman, Rogers, and Percy, requiring only 30 questionnaire items. The three CRA subscales used were legal, self-determination (LS), legal, nurturance (LN), and education, self-determination (ES). Our main interest was in the LS subscale, dealing with juveniles' rights to make decisions in legal-judicial circumstances affecting their own welfare. We deleted two items from the original LS subscale and added two new items dealing with whether or not children should be allowed to withhold information from police officers or court personnel.[17] The LS subscale already contained items concerning whether juveniles ought to be allowed to decide on their need for a lawyer.[18] We included the original 10 items from the ES subscale, to determine whether attitudes toward the critical LS items might be related to a general (across-contexts) attitude toward self-determination rights for children. The LN subscale focused on children's rights in such areas as legal

[16]Wrightsman *et al.* (1976) used adult, college, and high school samples in their initial development of the scale and reduction of the item pool. Internal consistency among items within any given subscale was relatively high (.78–.91). Yet there were only moderate correlations between subscales indicating some support for the logic behind the construction of separate scales for separate content areas, as well as the conceptualization of two broad types of rights.

[17]"Children should not be allowed to withhold information from police, when the police suspect that they have been involved in a crime." "When children are seen by a juvenile court because they are suspected of a crime, they should not have to give information about whether or not they were involved in a crime." We realized that deletion of two original LS items and addition of two new ones might alter the basic properties of the subscale for which the test developers had established internal validity. It will be seen later, however, that the two new items correlated substantially with the LS subscale score, suggesting that this alteration did not damage the meaning of the original LS subscale.

[18]"Children should have the right to decide whether they need a lawyer." "When these children are being tried in court, they should be granted the same rights granted to adults." Other items in the LS subscale addressed children's rights to sue, to get married, and to act as their own lawyer in trial.

protection from abuse and legal representation in custody disputes. By comparing LN to LS scores, we hoped to be able to clarify the meaning of the LS scores in our samples. For example, if some parents are very nonsupportive about allowing children to withhold information from police (one of the LS items), does this necessarily signify a lack of benevolent or paternalistic "concern" (LN scores) on the part of parents? The thirty items were presented in a randomized order on the questionnaire form and the response format required parents to indicate agreement or disagreement with each item on a six-point continuum.

To examine differences in parents' attitudes in reference to children of different ages and delinquency experience, the parents were randomly assigned one of four printed instructions on their questionnaire copies. One-half of the parents were instructed to complete the CRA with boys of ages 10–13 in mind and one-half with boys of ages 15–17 in mind. In addition, half of the parents with the younger age set and half with the older age set were asked to consider boys who had been in trouble with police often (delinquent set) and the other half of each age set received instructions to consider boys who had never been in trouble with police (nondelinquent set).[19] The instructions created a two-by-two (younger/older by nondelinquent/delinquent) design for purposes of data analysis. Random assignment of instructional sets was successful, in that there were no significant differences between groups receiving the four instructional sets with regard to parents' age, sex, or occupational classification.

The Hypothetical Situation

Another part of the research form offered the following description of an arrest situation:

> For a moment, imagine that a teenage son of yours has been arrested by the police, and you are called to go to the police station right away. When you arrive, the police inform you that they believe that your child might have broken into a house and stolen some money, and they wish to ask your child some questions. You and your child are read the four statements (rights)

[19]The decision not to construct instructional sets regarding girls was based on our earlier finding (see Chapter 2) that juvenile females accounted for a very small percentage of juvenile interrogations (see also Gordon, 1976). Furthermore, the addition of the gender variable would have reduced the size of each of the existing four experimental cells by one-half, which would have ruled out some analyses using parent demographic characteristics as additional independent variables. Thus, on balance, it was felt that less would be lost by sacrificing the gender variable.

which you have just read on the previous page. The police ask your child now if he will answer some questions. In a sentence or two, please answer the following three questions.

The form then allowed space for answering these questions: (1) What do you believe would be the thing for your child to do at this point? (2) What advice do you think you would give to your child at that point? (3) *Why* do you believe that this would be the thing for your child to do? Questions 1 and 2 proved to be redundant in almost every case; thus, the second question was used as the indication of what the parent might advise in such a situation. (We made no assumptions that these responses would reflect, or be predictive of, what the parents might have advised had they been faced with the actual situation.) Parents' reasons for their advice (Question 3) were categorized on an intuitive basis after all responses were collected, since this portion of the study was exploratory in nature.

Results of CRA Questionnaire

Rights to Silence and Counsel

Our primary interest was in parents' attitudes toward the rights related specifically to the *Miranda* warnings. Table 30 shows parents' responses on critical questionnaire items related to these rights. For ease of interpretation, parents' responses on each six-point continuum have been converted in such a way that support of the right or privilege in question is signified by higher scores (5 or 6, labeled "Agree") and nonsupport by lower scores (1 or 2, labeled "Disagree"). There were no significant differences between the two samples (I and II) in responses to any of these items.

Table 30 shows that 66–74% of the parents believed that juveniles should have the same rights as adults in court proceedings. It seems clear, however, that parents were answering the question as a matter of general policy rather than from an absolute position, because only about 20% of the parents believed that juveniles should be allowed to withhold information from police officers or courts (right to silence) when suspected of a crime. In fact, over half of the parents expressly disagreed with the idea that juveniles should be allowed to avoid incriminating themselves by withholding information. The majority of the parents, then, did not support the protective privilege for juveniles which the Supreme Court ruled must be provided to juveniles and adults alike.

TABLE 30. RESULTS ON CRITICAL CRA ITEMS

			Percentage reporting		
Sample	Mean	*S.D.*	Disagree 1–2	Neutral 3–4	Agree 5–6
Should have the same rights as adults in court (LN).[a]					
I	5.01	1.49	10.2	15.5	74.3
II	4.73	1.71	16.8	16.6	66.6
Should be allowed to withhold information from police when suspected of crime (LS).					
I	2.72	1.79	53.6	25.5	20.9
II	2.63	1.76	55.0	25.8	19.2
Should not have to provide information to court about own involvement in a crime (LS).					
I	2.55	1.78	60.2	20.5	19.3
II	2.52	1.73	58.1	24.8	17.1
Society should make lawyer available if child arrested (LN).					
I	4.99	1.51	9.6	15.9	74.5
II	5.01	1.44	8.8	18.8	72.4
Should have right to decide whether needs a lawyer (LS).					
I	3.39	1.95	40.0	24.5	35.5
II	3.40	1.82	35.8	31.9	32.2
Should have right to choose own lawyer (LS).					
I	1.75	1.29	79.4	15.1	5.4
II	1.90	1.32	74.4	19.0	6.6

[a] Wordings of items in the table have been shortened and, where necessary, modified so that they are worded in a direction favorable to the rights in question.

Nearly three-quarters of the parents endorsed the need for society to make legal counsel available to arrested juveniles. But parents were divided in their opinions about allowing juveniles to decide whether or not they needed to avail themselves of legal counsel, and about three-quarters of the parents clearly disfavored allowing juveniles to choose their own lawyer. (It should be noted that none of these questionnaire items specified any particular stage in the legal process when addressing questions of legal counsel.)

Whether the parents were responding with reference to younger (ages 10–13) or older (ages 15–17) juveniles or with reference to non-delinquents or delinquents produced no consistent significant differences across both samples in parents' professed attitudes toward any

TABLE 31. PEARSON r CORRELATION COEFFICIENTS BETWEEN CRA SCALES AND FOUR CRITICAL ITEMS (SAMPLE I ABOVE DIAGONAL, SAMPLE II BELOW DIAGONAL)

	CRA scales			Critical items			
Scale or item	LN	LS	ES	A	B	C	D
LN		.05	.09	.01	.07	.07	.43[a]
LS	.04		.36[a]	.50[a]	.47[a]	.55[a]	.00
ES	.01	.34[a]		.13	.11	.24	−.10
A (Right to silence, police)	.07	.37[a]	.14		.36[a]	.17	.00
B (Right to silence, court)	.10	.37[a]	.18	.49[a]		.12	.09
C (Right to decide need lawyer)	.10	.38[a]	.16	.00	.03		−.06
D (Grant same rights as to adults)	.39[a]	.09	.19	.01	.16[a]	.04	

[a]$p<.001$.

of these allowances.[20] Age and occupation of parent and whether or not parents reported that their children had been in trouble with police also produced no significant differences in their responses. But fathers were significantly less negatively predisposed to allowing juveniles to withhold information (both items) than were mothers. Nevertheless, even fathers' mean scores on these items were in the negative direction (i.e., below 3.5).[21]

Parents' negative attitudes toward juveniles' rights to withhold information and to decide whether to seek legal counsel were consistent with their negative attitudes toward juveniles' self-determination rights in general in legal-judicial settings (LS scale) (see Table 31). But gener-

[20]Means on four of the critical items, for both samples and for each age-by-delinquent status instructional set, are presented in Appendix F, Table F-1, with results of statistical tests of significance in Appendix F, Table F-2. It can be seen that there was a tendency in both samples, and on all four critical items, for parents to be more supportive of rights to silence and counsel for older than for younger juveniles, and more supportive in reference to nondelinquent than delinquent juveniles. In some cases these differences were significant in either one of the samples only. We considered any such differences to be unreliable since they were not obtained from both of the samples.

[21]Right to withhold information from police: I, means = 3.01 (fathers) and 2.47 (mothers), $F = 11.72$, $p < .01$; II, means = 3.02 (fathers) and 2.38 (mothers), $F = 10.89$, $p < .01$. Right to withhold information from court: I, means = 2.83 (fathers) and 2.38 (mothers), $F = 5.92$, $p < .01$; II, means = 2.97 (fathers) and 2.24 (mothers), $F = 14.89$, $p < .01$.

ally their opinions on these items were unrelated to their views on nurturance rights in such contexts (LN scale): that is, the general nonsupport for the right to silence for juveniles was related to neither benevolent nor nonbenevolent attitudes toward satisfying the nurturance needs of children. Their attitudes toward juveniles' right to silence were also not related to their general attitudes toward self-determination by juveniles in educational settings (ES scale) (see Table 31). Thus, parents' nonsupportive view of the right to silence for juveniles would appear to be relatively specific to their views of the social roles of juveniles in their dealings with legal or judicial authority, and might not be related to the general degree of autonomy or decision making which they allow juveniles in other social contexts.

General Attitudes toward Juveniles' Rights

Let us look now at parents' general attitudes toward self-determination by juveniles, as well as their view of providing protection by way of nurturant, paternalistic safeguards in legal-judicial circumstances. The majority of parents clearly endorsed the need for protections of juveniles from abuse by parents and other authorities, and endorsed the importance of providing needed goods and services; this is indicated by the fact that the LN mean scores of the two samples (Table 32) were very near to 50 on a scale allowing scores to range from a low of 10 to a high of 60. It seems clear, then, that these parents' lack of support for juveniles' right to withhold information from police was not due to a lack of concern on their part for protecting or nurturing their children.

TABLE 32. MEAN SCALE SCORES ON LN, LS, AND ES SCALES, AND MEAN SCALE SCORES FOR AGE-BY-DELINQUENT CONDITIONS (STANDARD DEVIATIONS IN PARENTHESES)

Scales and samples	Total means	Age 10–13		Age 15–17	
		Nondelinquent	Delinquent	Nondelinquent	Delinquent
LN scores					
I	48.68 (6.41)	50.00 (5.90)	48.12 (6.19)	49.21 (5.85)	47.26 (7.38)
II	48.96 (5.71)	49.97 (5.84)	48.71 (5.42)	49.45 (5.35)	47.75 (6.00)
LS scores					
I	22.11 (7.52)	21.29 (7.32)	19.96 (7.28)	23.18 (7.56)	24.04 (7.33)
II	22.42 (7.52)	21.10 (6.65)	21.03 (7.25)	23.05 (8.03)	24.46 (7.68)
ES scores					
I	23.94 (6.50)	21.85 (6.32)	21.29 (6.05)	24.52 (6.84)	24.13 (6.54)
II	24.46 (7.23)	22.34 (5.75)	22.29 (6.90)	25.60 (7.09)	27.52 (7.72)

Parents were generally nonsupportive concerning juveniles' self-determination rights in both legal-judicial and educational contexts (see Table 32), judging from their mean scores near 20 on the scale ranging from 10 (low) to 60 (high). This is consistent with their views on the critical self-determination items discussed earlier.

Parents indicated a significantly greater concern regarding nurturance rights in legal contexts for nondelinquents than for delinquents.[22] But an examination of mean attitude scores in relation to these two types of juveniles (Table 32) reveals that the absolute differences are too small to be of practical significance. On both the LS and ES scales, younger juveniles were viewed as significantly less deserving of self-determination rights than were older juveniles, but there were no differences in self-determination attitudes regarding delinquent and nondelinquent juveniles.[23] Thus, it would appear that juveniles' past history of obedience or misbehavior was not a salient factor in determining parents' professed views of what should be allowed to juveniles by way of decision making and autonomy. Finally, there were no consistent differences in LN, LS, or ES scores between parents of different ages, sexes, or occupational categories, nor between parents who did or did not report that their children had prior experiences with police.[24]

CRA Summary

Most parents, then, claimed to have strong concerns for protecting children and providing for their needs. But the majority were reluctant to allow juveniles, either older or younger, to exercise self-determination in decisions affecting their welfare, in either educational or legal-judicial contexts. In fact, only about 20% of the parents believed that juveniles ought to be allowed to withhold information from police or court officers concerning their alleged involvement in a crime. To-

[22]In a two-way analysis of variance of LN scords for Sample I: age of juvenile, $F = 1.72$, $p < .18$; delinquent/nondelinquent, $F = 9.30$, $p < .003$. For Sample II: age of juvenile, $F = 1.47$, $p < .22$; delinquent/nondelinquent, $F = 5.85$, $p < .01$.

[23]The significant differences in attitudes demonstrated in LS and ES scores in reference to younger and older juveniles derived from two-way (younger/older by nondelinquent/delinquent) analyses of variance for the two samples separately. LS: Sample I, $F = 16.25$, $p < .001$; Sample II, $F = 12.36$, $p < .001$. ES: Sample I, $F = 18.51$ $p < .001$; Sample II, $F = 29.42$, $p < .001$. In these analyses, nondelinquent/delinquent differences were not significantly different. LS: Sample I, $F = 0.11$, *N.S.*; Sample II, $F = 0.11$, *N.S.* ES: Sample I, $F = 0.56$, *N.S.*; Sample II, $F = 2.05$, $p < .14$.

[24]In Sample I, older parents (ages 40 and above) had significantly more nonsupportive Views of juveniles' self-determination than did younger parents, in both the legal context ($F = 5.86$, $p < .02$) and the educational context ($F = 2.87$, $p < .05$). No such differences were found in Sample II.

gether, the results suggest that parents would not allow juveniles to decide about waiver or assertion of their rights to silence, and one might infer that at least 55–60% of the parents (those who were strongly negatively predisposed to allowing juveniles to withhold information) might decide that their child should cooperate with police questioning. With only a few exceptions, parents' attitudes toward juveniles' rights were no different for younger than older adolescents, for delinquent than nondelinquent adolescents, or for various demographic differences among the parents themselves.

Parents' Advice and Reasoning

In response to the hypothetical situation, 35% (Sample I) and 32% (Sample II) of the parents said that they would advise their children to provide police officers with any information about their possible involvement in a crime. Typical responses included, "He should tell the truth," "Tell him to tell the police whatever they want to know," and "If he's guilty, own up—if he's not, there's nothing to hide."

We were able to classify into three categories most of the reasons these parents gave for their advice to cooperate with police requests for information (see Table 33). "Moralistic" reasons emphasized that cooperating with law enforcement was the right or obedient thing to do, that it was important to be truthful in all matters, or that "honesty is the best policy." Reasoning of this type, focusing on conventional moral principles and without reference to any other aspects of the circumstances, was predominant among parents advising cooperation in the Catholic high school sample (40%), but received secondary (though not significantly less) emphasis among those who advised cooperation in

Table 33. Percent Giving Reasons for Advice in Hypothetical Arrest, by Type of Advice Given

	Confess/make statement		Remain silent and/or get lawyer	
Type of reason	Sample I	Sample II	Sample I	Sample II
Moralistic	40.5	27.8	0.0	0.0
Responsibility	18.3	21.1	0.0	0.0
Strategic	37.7	46.7	2.3	0.0
Confusion	0.0	0.0	37.7	41.0
Distrust	0.0	0.0	45.8	44.8
Other	3.2	3.3	14.0	9.3

the public junior high school samples (27%). Somewhat more common in the latter sample (46%), and found in a substantial percentage in the high school sample as well (37%), were reasons which we labeled "strategic." These were responses which emphasized that cooperation with police was likely to result in more lenient treatment or a less severe disposition of the juvenile's case. Finally, about 20% of parents in both samples who advised cooperation with police did so for reasons we called "responsibility." They explained that children must learn to face the consequences of their behavior and to accept punishment when it is due, or reasoned that confession would be a painful but important learning experience for the juvenile.

Advice not to talk to the police was given by 63% (Sample I) and 65% (Sample II) of the parents. Advice to obtain an attorney was mentioned by 57% (I) and 58% (II) of the parents; all parents who advised the presence of a lawyer were also among those who advised silence. Reasons for recommending silence were primarily of two types (see Table 33). One type, "confusion," emphasized that juveniles might give accounts of their behavior which would be distorted because of their emotional state, with the possibility that they might implicate themselves to a greater degree than was factual. "Distrust" responses emphasized the adversary nature of the interrogation and that police might purposefully or inadvertently distort information provided by the juvenile.

It is important to note that perhaps one-half of the parents who advised silence seemed to imply in their reasoning that silence was temporarily recommended, and that they would expect the juvenile to answer police officers' questions eventually. For example, several parents recommending silence explained that the juvenile should say nothing until both parents and/or attorney were present to monitor or witness the questioning; the objectives here were to reduce the juvenile's "confusion" or to keep police from distorting the juvenile's story. Other reasons for recommending silence could be construed as temporary, but their meaning was vague: for example, "Keep silent until things cool down a little." Thus, many parents who advised silence seemed to expect that the juvenile would make a statement to police after a period of "silence" which would produce more favorable circumstances within which the juvenile could tell his story. Unfortuantely, the ways in which such "temporary silence" was implied were too numerous and varied to allow for adequate classification.

There are some additional reasons to believe that some of the parents who recommended silence expected juveniles to make statements to the police eventually. It will be recalled that on the CRA questionnaire, nearly 60% of the parents believed that juveniles generally should not be allowed to withhold information from police. But since only 35% of the parents advised providing information to the police in the hypothetical session, some portion of the parents who recommended silence in the hypothetical situation apparently indicated on the earlier CRA questionnaire that juveniles should not withhold information. Thus they might have recommended silence only in a temporary sense. In addition, both for parents advising cooperation and for parents advising silence, we examined their responses to the two CRA items regarding a juvenile's right to withhold information from police and the court. The mean scores for parents advising silence were 3.0 or below on both of these items (1 = nonsupportive, 6 = supportive), suggesting that even these parents were not supportive of juveniles' withholding of information.

Whatever their reasoning, there is some evidence that parents' advice to juveniles in the hypothetical situation was related to their attitudes toward juveniles' nurturance and self-determination rights. Parents advising confession were significantly less supportive of juveniles' nurturance rights in legal-judicial contexts, and were significantly stronger in their denial of the right to withhold information from police and courts, than were parents who recommended silence. (See Appendix F, Table F-2 for analyses of these data.)

In summary, about two-thirds of the parents recognized the need for asserting the right to silence for juveniles in the hypothetical situation. About one-third of the parents believed that juveniles ought to answer police officers' questions. Further, there was some evidence that a substantial portion of the parents recommending silence intended this to be temporary, and that they might believe that juveniles eventually ought to make statements to police. Types of reasoning for recommending cooperation or confession included moral principles and matters of responsibility, as well as a concern for obtaining lenient decisions by police. When silence was urged, it was primarily out of fear that juveniles might become confused in telling their story or that the police might distort the information obtained. Parents' advice was related to their attitudes toward nurturance and self-determination rights of juveniles in a consistent manner.

PARENT–CHILD COMMUNICATION IN INTERROGATION

There are several reasons that certain results of the study we have just reviewed are difficult to interpret, or offer only limited answers to our original questions. For one, the samples are not representative of a broad spectrum of the population of any city. In addition, there is no way to determine how our sample of parents might differ demographically from parents whose children make up the population of juveniles who are in fact interrogated by police officers. Most important are the limitations on what can be inferred from questionnaire responses and parents' reactions to hypothetical interrogation situations while seated in the relative comfort of a school auditorium. Parents' behaviors and advice in actual interrogations may or may not correspond to what they profess on paper.

More relevant data would be provided by a study in which the participants were parents whose children were being questioned by police. Especially useful would be direct observations of the advice and other communications which occur in the parent–child interaction within actual interrogations. This type of data would come closest to addressing the assumptions noted earlier in this chapter concerning the degree of protection which parents provide for juveniles in interrogation.

The study to be discussed in this section obtained this type of data. The juvenile court wherein our own earlier studies were accomplished developed an independent interest in documenting the role played by parents in juveniles' interrogations after the results of the previous project study had been discussed with court personnel. A study to obtain this information was subsequently designed by the court's administration and legal staff, and data collection was done by court personnel. Our research project staff had no hand in the design or implementation of the study apart from some assistance in statistical analysis of the results. In fact, it is very unlikely that the court could have authorized us to perform the study, because our presence at juveniles' interrogations might raise difficult questions of interference with legal process as well as privacy for juveniles and their parents. Although the study has some methodological difficulties, we requested and obtained permission to report the results of the court's study, since the importance of the observations and the lack of any similar type of data in the literature clearly justify its description.

Method and Sample

During the brief period in 1978 in which data collection was done for this study, court administrators required that juvenile court officers who monitor all police interrogations of juveniles complete a brief checklist form immediately following each interrogation. Policy in this jurisdiction holds court officers responsible for monitoring police interrogation of juveniles, whom the police must bring to a police station or the court's detention center for questioning. The court officer contacts the juvenile's parents, presents the *Miranda* rights warnings to the juvenile and the parents after the parents have arrived, and monitors and records their decisions concerning the rights before the juvenile or parents can be questioned by police.

The checklist developed by court administrators and legal staff included a variety of demographic and offense information, questions concerning location of the interrogation and who was present, and a number of checklist items concerning whether or not various types of communications had transpired between the parents, the juvenile, the court officer, and the police up to the time that a decision about rights waiver or assertion was made.[25]

Court administrators estimated that the 390 interrogations on which forms were completed probably represented nearly all of the in-custody interrogations during the period when data collection was in effect, judging from the usual frequency of interrogations per month. From ten to twenty juvenile court officers appeared to have been involved in the data collection process, involving interrogations across a wide range of police precincts within the county. Of the 390 cases, 53% occurred at the detention center, 40% at police stations, and 7% at other locations. These percentages were very similar to those obtained in our random sample of juvenile court files in 1976 (see Chapter 2), which indicated that 49% of interrogations occurred at the detention center, 38% at police stations, and 13% at other locations. These comparisons provide some evidence that the court's data collection process did not produce an inordinate bias in terms of the representativeness of the sample. In addition, the checklist forms indicated that rights were waived in all but 7.9% of the cases, a figure which is very similar to the rate of refusal to waive rights (6–9%) discovered in our random sample of juveniles' files in the study in Chapter 2.

A majority of the interrogations (57%) involved juveniles of ages 15–17, with 27% of ages 13–14, and 19% of ages 12 or younger (for 7% age was not recorded). Males were interrogated in 76% of the cases, females in 10%, with sex not recorded in the remainder of cases. Felony charges accounted for 71% of the cases and misdemeanors for 12%, the remainder being traffic and status offenses.[26] The presence of one

[25]One unfortunate omission was information on race of juveniles.

[26]There were no differences between ages in types of offense being investigated, except that when 11- and 12-year-olds were involved, it was more likely to be for a misdemeanor charge (60%) than was true for the overall sample. Half of the females were questioned in relation to felony charges, compared to 72% of the males. Status offenses accounted for 21% of the cases in which females were questioned, compared to 2% of the male interrogation cases.

policeman was noted in 75% of the cases, two policemen in 18%, and three or more in 7% of the cases.

Both parents were present in 23% of the cases, father only in 27%, mother only in 45%, other unspecified (but we assume "friendly") adult in 3%, and no notation of any "friendly" adult present in 2% of the cases. It is not surprising to find that parents were present in almost all cases; Missouri law requires that parents must be present, and court officers were well aware that the juvenile court would accept no confessions evolving from situations wherein the presence of parents could not be proved. Whether one or both parents were present was relatively constant across ages, except that mothers alone were present in 83% of the cases involving juveniles of ages 11 or younger. Both parents tended to be present more frequently in status offense cases (46%) than in felony (24%) or misdemeanor (20%) cases.

Communications Results

Table 34 shows the frequencies with which various types of parent–child communications in interrogation were observed and recorded on the checklist by the court officers. We need not detail those results here, since the table is quite clear. The vast majority of parents apparently offered no advice to their children and sought no information from the court officer, and very few juveniles sought the advice of their

Table 34. Parent–Child Communications in Interrogation

Variable	Number of cases	Percentage
Total cases	390	100.0
Regarding right to silence, parents told juvenile:		
Nothing	278	71.3
To talk (waive right)	65	16.7
Not to talk (assert right)	22	5.6
Make up own mind	25	6.4
Regarding attorney, parents told juvenile:		
Nothing	317	81.3
Not to get attorney (waive right)	44	11.3
Get attorney (assert right)	9	2.3
Make up own mind	20	5.1
Cases involving no communication from parent to child	258	66.2
Parents asked court officer:		
For general information	72	18.5
For private conference with juvenile	17	4.4
Juvenile asked parents for advice	34	8.7

parents. When parents did advise their children, it was usually to tell them to waive rather than to assert their rights. But in general, the figures would suggest that most parents play neither a verbally coercive role nor a helpful one. One might say that they play no role at all, except that a study of this type cannot reveal the beneficial effects or subtle pressures which might result from the silence and the mere presence of the parents.[27]

Analysis of these results in relation to age and sex of juvenile, types of offenses investigated, who was present, and site of interrogation revealed only a few differences which were statistically significant ($p < .05$). Concerning age of juvenile, parents instructed juveniles to answer police officers' questions in 50% of the cases of juveniles of age 11 or younger, compared to about 17% of the total sample. Parents sought general information more often in the cases of 16-year-olds (32%) and 11-year-olds or younger (50%) than for 12–15-year-olds (13%). Certain other results which did not achieve statistical significance represented interesting trends. For example, when juveniles asked parents for advice, generally they were older (16, 11%; 14, 7%; 12, 0%). Concerning parents, 31% of the two-parent cases resulted in parents asking court officers for information, compared to 20% of father-only cases and 23% of mother-only cases. Finally, juveniles were told by their parents to answer police officers' questions in 22% of the father-only cases and 12% of the mother-only cases. None of the communication variables manifested any relationships with sex of juvenile, type of offense investigated, or site of interrogation.

DOES PARENTS' PRESENCE SATISFY LEGAL CONCERNS REGARDING SAFEGUARDS IN JUVENILE CASES?

We have presented information with which to evaluate the adequacy of protection which would be afforded to juveniles by parents' presence at interrogations. As we move now to apply this information to concerns which have been expressed in law, it is important to acknowledge that there have been various legal opinions concerning the amount of protection which should be required in juvenile cases. Let us examine the relevance of our information for each of the three positions in turn.

First, juvenile and family law has traditionally viewed children as the property of the parent. When considering questions of waiver of

[27]Although we were startled by these results, a few court officers with whom we talked predicted this outcome prior to their knowledge of the results for the total sample.

juveniles' rights, then, this view would find no more reason to question a parent's will in relation to the juvenile's welfare than to question the parent's will in relation to his or her own welfare. Further, the competence of adult suspects to waive *Miranda* rights has not often been questioned; similarly, it can be argued that parents' competence must be presumed in accordance with the assumptions of rationality and free will which undergird our system of law.

If one takes this traditional position, then the mere presence of a parent is enough to satisfy the law's obligation to juvenile suspects, and the data from our studies will be considered to be irrelevant. Parents' attitudes, choices, or reasoning are no more applicable to this standard of protection than they would be if parents themselves were the suspects who were deciding about their own need to be silent or to obtain counsel. The critical issue in this view is merely whether or not the parents were provided every opportunity to protect their interest, which in theory subsumes the juvenile as chattel. But this traditional position in juvenile and family law is giving way to an increased recognition of juveniles' interests independent of the interests of their parents, as we have noted in earlier chapters.

Second, many defense attorneys and other juvenile advocates would claim that the only adequate protection for juveniles in interrogation would be a nonwaivable right to silence and to legal counsel. This position would argue that legal counsel is essential because neither juveniles nor parents can be expected to understand the consequences of confession for later adjudicatory or dispositional decisions about juveniles.

Short of arguing for nonwaivable rights for juveniles, this position would suggest that the only adequate protection which parents could afford juveniles would be their assertion of the rights to silence and to legal counsel. Any parental advice providing less protection than this would be seen as placing the juvenile at the mercy of a court system which has the potential to punish, and which as yet does not provide the due process protections which are found at the trial and dispositional stages of adult criminal proceedings.

The juvenile court study which we have just described suggests that most parents do not provide the protection which this extreme position would require. Most parents gave no direct advice to their children regarding the waiver decision, and those that did offer advice almost always urged their children to waive rights. In fact, less than 10% of the parents in this study would meet the aforementioned criterion for adequate protection.

The similarity between this percentage figure and the rate of rights assertion which we discovered in our earlier random sample of juveniles' court files (Chapter 2) suggests that this is a valid estimate of the percentage of cases in which parents provide protection which is "adequate" as defined above. The questionnaire study, in which approximately one-half of the parents said they would recommend obtaining legal counsel, might indicate that parents of the demographic type included in this study would provide this higher level of protection more frequently than did the parents in the court's study. But one cannot assume that these parents' questionnaire responses accurately reflect what their behavior would be if they were faced with actual interrogation situations.

The third view is that adequate protection is afforded by the presence of a "competent parent": that is, a parent who understands the juvenile's rights, appreciates the nature of the decision and its consequences, can weigh the issues without interference by conflicts with the child, and then advises the child. This view of adequate protection is different from the first we described, in that the general competence of parents is not automatically presumed. It is different from the second view in that the adequacy of protection is not judged on the basis of the actual advice which the parent gives, but rather on the basis of the evidence that the parent can provide advice which is the product of a careful and rational decision-making process. Thus, the Supreme Court in *Gault,* 387 U.S. 1 (1967) warned that not only the presence of parents, but also their competence, is an important consideration in weighing the validity of juveniles' confessions (at 55). This position is evident in several other cases we have cited earlier (see note 12).

The results of the two studies we have reported are applicable to this standard of adequacy of protection in several respects. In the questionnaire study, a substantial majority of the parents felt that juveniles should never be allowed to withhold from police any information about their alleged involvement in a crime. In order for parents to weigh the issues concerning a juvenile's waiver of the right to silence, it would seem to be necessary for them first to approach the decision with at least an open mind about silence as an option. The categorical denial of this constitutionally protected option by such a large proportion of our parents strongly suggests that such an open-minded approach to the waiver decision would not occur in most cases.

Our examination of parents' reasoning for the advice they claimed that they would give their children generally supports the aforementioned conclusion. Even many of the parents who would advise their children to remain silent appeared to approach the decision as though it were a matter of when the juvenile was going to make a statement rather than whether or not a statement would be made. The analysis of parents' reasoning also demonstrated a remarkable lack of consideration for the potential effects of the juvenile's statement on adjudicatory and dispositional consequences. The "distrust" and "confusion" rationales, noted by over 80% of the parents who recommended silence, focused only on the accuracy of the statement the juvenile might make, not on the potential long-range consequences of the statement itself. About 35–45% of the parents who recommended waiver of the right to silence were concerned about obtaining a more lenient disposition (see "strategic," Table 33), but they showed no evidence of having weighed such benefits against the potential danger in making a statement. Thus, if a careful weighing of the major potential consequences of rights waiver is a necessary part of adequate protection for juveniles, our evidence suggests that most of our parents would not meet this standard.

It is important to note that our data allows one to characterize most of these parents as having the best of intentions and benevolent concern for the welfare of children. This is evident from two types of data. First, as a group these parents were clearly supportive of nurturance rights (LN scores, Table 32) for juveniles; that is, they were benevolent concerning the provision of necessary and growth-producing experiences and services for juveniles, even for those juveniles who were described to them as "delinquent." Second, their reasoning for advice about the waiver decision can be interpreted to reflect this benevolent concern. Many were worried about juveniles' welfare at the hands of police, either in the form of juveniles' confusion or the inadvertent or purposeful distortion of information by police. Others who recommended waiver of the right to silence provided reasons which reflect their adherence to conventional views of "good" child-rearing principles. The ideas that children should learn to accept the consequences of their acts ("responsibility") or should always be honest whatever the consequences ("moralistic") are widely accepted in our culture as principles which parents who care about their children will endeavor to teach them.

The study, therefore, suggests that a large proportion of parents do not manifest attitudes or perspectives which constitute adequate protection as defined by the "competent parent" standard. Whether this conclusion can be extended to parents with different racial and socioeconomic characteristics than our sample is not known. In addition, our results are most generalizable to parents who, like those in our sample, appear to have very benevolent attitudes toward the nurturance of their children. Yet, since even these parents do not inspire confidence in one's view of their ability to provide "adequate" protection, it is unlikely that parents with less benevolent attitudes toward their children's welfare would do better.

Finally, if the "competent parent" view of adequate protection includes the willingness or ability to provide advice to juveniles in interrogation, the court's study of interrogation events suggests that most parents of arrested juveniles fall short of this requirement. Whether or not juveniles would be better prepared to make waiver decisions if their parents were more active and communicative at the preinterrogaton stage is not at issue here. The simple fact that most parents provided no advice indicates that they were not assisting juveniles to weigh or understand the waiver decision in the active sense which many courts have seen as necessary in order to compensate for juveniles' deficiencies in understanding.

It does not follow from our examination of parents' attitudes and behavior that they should be excluded from the interrogation process, nor that their often passive role in the process makes their presence less important. Except where there is a clear conflict of interest between parent and child, a parent's mere presence might serve in most cases to provide some measure of protection against harsh treatment of the juvenile by some interrogators. We have noted, too, that there are other legal and philosophical reasons for including parents in matters which affect their children. But the weight of evidence from our studies supports the court's opinion in *K.E.S.* v. *State* that "we cannot equate physical presence of a parent with meaningful representation" [216 S.E.2d at 673 (1975)]. Judges, of course, must decide in each case whether parents have provided adequate protection. But as to the formation of general policy, our results suggest that the law must look beyond parents to seek the assistance which would allow a juvenile's waiver of rights to meet the "intelligent, knowing, and voluntary" standard.

9

Summary and Policy Recommendations

PROTECTING JUVENILES' RIGHTS

Our research results provide sound, empirical evidence of the need for special methods to safeguard juveniles' interrogation rights to silence and legal counsel. In this final chapter, we will examine several potential safeguards, using the research results and the reality of law and the legal process to evaluate these proposals. In addition, we will show how the results can be used as guidelines for legislative reform and judicial decision making regarding juveniles' waiver of rights. First, however, let us review the major conclusions from the studies in the foregoing chapters.

SUMMARY OF MAJOR FINDINGS

An examination of juvenile court records for a three-year period (Chap. 2) indicated that about three-quarters of juveniles who were referred to the court for alleged felonies had been questioned by police. This proportion was relatively similar for both older and younger adolescents. For the cases in which police pursued questioning of juveniles, less than 10% of the juveniles asserted their right to remain silent. Further, refusal to waive the right to silence (that is, assertion of that right by juveniles) was almost nonexistent below age 15. The rate of rights assertion is relatively low compared to the only figure (42%) available for adult suspects in an earlier study.

In Chapters 4 and 5 we saw in the study employing empirical measures of *Miranda* comprehension that about one-half of juveniles of ages 10–16 demonstrated inadequate understanding of at least one of the four *Miranda* warnings. Understanding of the *Miranda* warnings was significantly poorer among juveniles who were 14 years of age or younger than among 15–16-year-old juveniles or adult offenders and nonoffenders.

Comprehension of the *Miranda* warnings among 15–16-year-olds varied considerably in relation to general intellectual functioning (IQ). Juveniles at these ages whose IQ scores were in the average range or higher performed about as well as did adults on the whole. On the other hand, 15–16-year-old juveniles with IQ scores below 80 manifested no better understanding of the *Miranda* rights warnings than did the majority of younger juveniles (ages 14 and below.)

There were no straight-forward relationships between juveniles' understanding of the *Miranda* warnings and their race, socioeconomic status, or amount of prior experience with police and courts. Certain results did suggest, however, that black, lower socioeconomic class juveniles might be at a special disadvantage in comprehending *Miranda* warnings because of subculturally related linguistic factors.

Further deficiencies in juveniles' competence to waive rights were found in the study of their ability to understand the function and significance of the rights to silence and legal counsel (Chap. 6). Of special concern was that about one-third of the juveniles misperceived the intended nature of the attorney–client relationship. A majority also demonstrated faulty perceptions of the protection of the right to silence; for example, they believed that a judge could waive a defendant's right to silence. On the experimental measure of these perceptions, juveniles at ages 15 and below manifested significantly less satisfactory understanding than did adults (ages 17 and above); 16-year-olds generally performed as well as 17–19-year-olds, but were significantly below adults of ages 20 or above. Finally, juveniles with a relatively extensive history of serious offenses and a commensurate amount of juvenile court experience generally demonstrated an understanding of the significance and function of their rights at a level typical of the adult subjects.

In the exploratory study of juveniles' responses to hypothetical interrogation and waiver situations (Chap. 7), a majority of the juveniles recommended obtaining legal counsel. These results are in marked contrast to the finding (in Chap. 2) that almost no juveniles request legal counsel in actual interrogations. Together, the results suggest that the circumstances of actual interrogations tend to inhibit juveniles from making decisions which they would otherwise believe to be in their own best interest. In other words, the results question the voluntariness of rights waiver by many juveniles.

In general, the reasoning employed by juveniles when considering the waiver of rights in the hypothetical situations was markedly constricted for juveniles in the early adolescent years, for black juveniles as a group, and for juveniles with IQ scores below 80. These groups, for example, were less capable of considering as many optional responses to the waiver situation as were their older or brighter peers, could imagine only a more limited range of possible consequences of rights waiver, and tended more often to focus on immediate rather than long-range consequences.

Finally, Chapter 8 described studies of parents' attitudes and behavior, relevant to their children's rights in interrogation. These studies evaluated the proposition that parents who are present at interrogations will provide advice and protection for juveniles. In a sample of parents of middle school and high school students, questionnaire results verified the parents' benevolent concern for providing nurturance for their children. Yet, only 20% of the parents agreed that adolescents should be allowed to withhold information from police or courts when they are suspected of legal wrongdoing. About one-third claimed that they would advise their children to waive the right to silence; the remaining two-thirds were more cautious, but most of them appeared to expect their children to answer police officers' questions after proper protections against threat or misunderstanding were available. In a related study of actual interrogations (performed by the participating juvenile court), only about 20% of parents provided advice of any kind to their adolescent children during preinterrogation proceedings. The remaining 80% of the parents had virtually no communications with their children, leaving the children to make their waiver decisions unassisted.

Conclusions about Juveniles' Competence

The results of Chapters 4 through 7 pointed out specific ways in which various classes of juveniles manifested competence or incompetence to waive their rights to silence and legal counsel. In order to address matters of policy and recommendations, it is necessary to offer a synthesis of the results across the various measures of understanding and perception used in these studies. When all of the results are taken together the following general conclusions are supported:

1. As a class, juveniles of ages 14 and below demonstrate incompetence to waive their rights to silence and legal counsel. This conclusion is

generally supported across measures of both understanding and perception in our studies, and in relation to both absolute and relative (adult norm) standards.

2. As a class, juveniles of ages 15 and 16 who have IQ scores of 80 or below lack the requisite competence to waive their rights to silence and counsel.

3. About one-third to one-half of juveniles 15 and 16 years of age with IQ scores above 80 lack the requisite competence to waive their rights when competence is defined by absolute standards (that is, the satisfaction of scoring criteria for adequate understanding). As a class, however, this group demonstrates a level of understanding and perception similar to that of 17–21-year-old adults for whom the competence to waive rights is presumed in law.

4. Race is a relevant variable for consideration in weighing juveniles' competence to waive rights, for two reasons. First, a greater percentage of black juveniles than of white juveniles perform in the lower IQ range noted above. Second, black juveniles in lower socioeconomic classes may have greater difficulty translating the *Miranda* warnings than do whites in lower socioeconomic classes.

5. Indexes of the amount of prior court experience (for example, number of prior felony referrals) bear no direct relationship to the understanding of *Miranda* warnings *per se.* In fact, among juveniles with extensive court and police involvement, this greater degree of experience was related to better understanding if the juvenile was white, but poorer understanding if the juvenile was black. On the other hand, greater experience is related to more adequate understanding of matters such as the roles of police, attorney, and the judge, and their functions in juvenile cases.

The Meaning of "Competence"

When we say in the foregoing conclusions that a particular class of juveniles is incompetent to waive rights, we are using the term "incompetent" in a special way which must be distinguished from its other possible meanings in psychology and in law. This definitional matter has been discussed in Chapter 3. Before proceeding to consider policy implications of the foregoing conclusions, however, it would be well to repeat these definitions in the context of our results.

In a *psychological* sense, we mean nothing more by the word "incompetence" than that a juvenile *did not demonstrate a sufficient level of performance* on a criterion measure of understanding or perception of the rights. Specifically, we do not assume (even though it is possible) that a juvenile's inadequate performance is related to a trait, a maturational "given," an intellectual limitation, or any other unalterable characteristic. We refer merely to the juvenile's condition of deficient understanding or perception, both of which might be alterable regardless of the demographic or intellectual characteristics of the juvenile. Without modification, however, the juvenile's condition of understanding or perception does not meet the standard for competent waiver of rights.

Thus, when we say that most juveniles of ages 14 or below are incompetent to waive rights, we do not necessarily mean that they are too immature in a cognitive or psychological sense to ever grasp the meaning and significance of the rights. We mean simply that very few of them do, given the usual *Miranda* warnings and their present knowledge, perceptions, and beliefs.

In a *legal* sense, we must distinguish between the competence of a juvenile to waive rights and the validity of a juvenile's waiver of rights. Under prevailing law, the validity of a juvenile's waiver of *Miranda* rights is determined by judicial weighing of the "totality of circumstances" in a case. Our earlier review of case law showed that among the potentially relevant circumstances are the time and place of the interrogation, the demeanor of police officers, whether or not parents or legal counsel were present, and those characteristics of the juvenile which would address whether or not he or she was capable of providing a knowing, intelligent, and voluntary waiver. All of these matters, and conceivably other unique circumstances, can be relevant to the question of a waiver's validity. In contrast, only the final set of circumstances—the characteristics of the juvenile—refer to the competence of the juvenile *per se*.

The primary focus of our project was to examine the competence of juveniles, not to study directly the ultimate question of the validity of waiver. Indeed, it would have been impossible to anticipate and to study the effects of all the circumstances which juvenile court judges must weigh in these cases. We were content to assess only whether or not juveniles understand the matters which courts themselves have seen as necessary for meaningful decision making about one's waiver of rights. Thus, when we say that a class of juveniles is incompetent to waive rights, we mean that they do not meet the research definitions of the legal standard for knowing, intelligent, and voluntary participation in the waiver decision.

What is the relationship of our results, then, to the broader legal question of the validity of juvenile waiver of rights, which rests on a determination of the totality of circumstances? It will be recalled that we assessed juveniles' competencies under relatively "ideal" conditions. They demonstrated their understanding and resources to deal with the rights and decisions without the emotional or distracting circumstances which would pervade most interrogation circumstances. Most juveniles' degree of understanding of their rights would be expected to be no better in most interrogation circumstances—indeed, might well be poorer—than in the research situation. Since a juvenile's waiver cannot be valid if the juvenile is not competent (unless the totality of circumstances in some way compensates for the juvenile's inadequacies), the waiver of rights in actual interrogations by juveniles who demonstrated incompetence in the research situation would seem to be valid only if the circumstances of the interrogation included ameliorating circumstances over and above the conditions under which we assessed juveniles' competencies.

By the same token, we must caution that some juveniles who demonstrated competency to waive rights in our research sessions might produce invalid waivers of rights in actual interrogation cases. That is, our results do not reduce the need to weigh the totality of circumstances which might have diminished an otherwise competent juvenile's ability to provide a knowing, intelligent, and voluntary waiver.

These definitional matters have been discussed at length because they provide guidance for the following exploration of legal and social remedies for juveniles with diminished competence to waive their rights. They direct us to examine ways to increase juveniles' competence by increasing their understanding of the rights and their significance, and to examine whether the use of certain procedural circumstances in interrogations might compensate for juveniles' inadequacies.

EXPLORING LEGAL AND SOCIAL REMEDIES FOR JUVENILES' DIMINISHED COMPETENCE TO WAIVE RIGHTS

Having empirically demonstrated the types of juveniles who lack the competence to provide a meaningful waiver of *Miranda* rights, it is time to examine potential remedies for this legal issue. In this section we will review a number of options which have serious limitations, but which are worthy of review in order to understand what those limitations are. Then, in a subsequent section on recommendations, we will offer two options which appear to provide the most fruitful response to the problems documented by our research findings.

Revising the *Miranda* Warnings

One might propose that juveniles should receive an adequate explanation of their rights—one that they can clearly understand—prior to their rights-waiver decision. This proposal raises three questions: one empirical, one conceptual, and a third practical.

First, there have been two studies examining whether simplified wording of the *Miranda* warnings would increase juveniles' comprehension of the information contained in the warnings (Ferguson & Douglas, 1970; Manoogian, 1978). The study by Manoogian was especially well-controlled and employed the CMR as the experimental criterion for understanding. Neither study demonstrated a significant increase in juveniles' understanding of simplified wording compared to the standard wording of *Miranda* warnings. This does not mean, of course, that a more successful version of the warnings could not be developed. It would be surprising, however, if any single rewording of the warnings would suffice, given the wide range of cultural, linguistic, and educational backgrounds of juvenile suspects.

Second, even if a simplified version of *Miranda* warnings produced nearly optimal scores on the CMR measure of understanding, it would be conceptually incorrect to assume that juveniles who made these scores would be prepared to make a meaningful waiver decision. In Chapter 6 we cited the courts' concerns regarding juveniles' understanding of the *significance* of the rights, which goes beyond the matters explained by the *Miranda* warnings themselves. For example, our results indicated that while virtually all of the juveniles in our sample understood the warning about the right to silence ("I don't have to talk"), the majority did not grasp the sense of that right (that is, that a judge could not legally order them to "talk"). These results suggest that preinterrogation attempts to prepare juveniles to make a valid waiver would require more than a simplified wording of the *Miranda* warnings. The juveniles might also need to be informed, for example, about the nature of a legal right, the legally allowable response of police and court personnel to an assertion of that right, the various potential consequences of rights waiver, the nature of an attorney–client relationship, and the ways in which an attorney works for a client.

Finally, from a practical viewpoint, one could hardly expect police or court representatives to review all of these matters with juveniles prior to rights waiver. To do so would seem to be far overreaching the job of law enforcement in the investigative process. Even if some more extensive explanation were required in juvenile cases, the moments between arrest and interrogation are hardly conducive to educative efforts.

Therefore, while simplifying the explanation of rights in juvenile cases surely can do no harm, it offers no remedy for the problem of juveniles' frequently inadequate understanding of the *Miranda* rights and their significance.

Public Education

An alternative would be to teach juveniles their rights and the significance of those rights long before they are in the position of having to decide about waiving them. Some public schools are now providing courses in "street law" to middle school and high school students. Juveniles who master this material might in general be better prepared to deal with preinterrogation choices concerning rights waiver or assertion.[1]

While this is an appropriate social response to the problem of juveniles' competence to waive rights, it does not provide a solution to the legal difficulties facing judges and police officers. The mere fact that a juvenile's school system provides instruction regarding legal rights, or that the juvenile has attended such a course, does not indicate that the juvenile mastered the course material or was able to use past learning at the time of interrogation.

Assessing Understanding Prior to Rights Waiver

An objective assessment of a juvenile's degree of understanding at the time of rights waiver would assist police officers in knowing whether or not to pursue interrogation and would provide judges with empirical information on which to base their decisions about the validity of the juvenile's confession. There are certain difficulties, however, in proposing the use of our *Miranda* comprehension measures for this purpose.

One problem is that the measures could not be administered validly by police officers or court personnel who are not trained in test administration. Special assessment or screening personnel would be required. That in itself presents no insurmountable difficulty, so long as police officers would at least temporarily forego interrogation at the time that they take a juvenile into custody. Yet, delays in investigation would be produced by the fact that social service personnel, who would probably be needed to perform screening procedures, often are not available during nighttime hours when most arrests occur. A screening requirement, then, might interfere with police investigations in some cases, and it is arguable that society's welfare and protection would be jeopardized in those instances where immediate interrogation was needed to prevent some danger.

Furthermore, the experimental measures of *Miranda* comprehen-

[1]The content of the various experimental measures developed in the present project can be recommended as a way to structure the objectives and evaluation of classroom efforts to teach children the *Miranda* rights and their significance.

sion provide no way of determining whether a juvenile has intentionally performed poorly on the measures in order to gain some legal advantage. It is not known whether this would occur with any great frequency, but it is conceivable that certain "street-wise" juveniles might adjust to a screening procedure by using it to their advantage. The juveniles in our studies received clear explanations that they had nothing to gain by the quality of their performance on the measures; so our results provide no information relevant to juveniles' psychometric performances under different motivational conditions. The validity of the measures as preinterrogation screening devices, then, cannot be assumed.

Similarly, one cannot assume that the measures are appropriate in individual cases as postinterrogation indexes of *Miranda* comprehension. Some juveniles might understand the implications of their scores for the court's view of the validity of confessions which they have already made. Thus, a psychologist's postinterrogation assessment of a juvenile's competence to waive rights faces the same interpretive difficulties as would a preinterrogation screening.

Presence of Parents at Interrogation

In Chapter 8 we reviewed the legal precedents and statutes which, in many states, require that parents must be present at the time of a juvenile's decision to waive rights. The results of the studies reported in that chapter indicated that parents generally cannot be relied on to provide juveniles with explanations of the rights and their significance. In addition, a majority of the parents were negatively predisposed to juveniles' right to withhold information from police officers.

In the discussion of these results, we concluded that the weight of the evidence from our studies clearly supported the court's opinion in *K.E.S.* v. *State* that "we cannot equate physical presence of a parent with meaningful representation" [216 S.E.2d at 673 (1975)]. This conclusion has an important implication for judicial decisions concerning the validity of a juvenile's waiver of rights and the admissability of a subsequent confession as evidence. Judges should not be influenced in their decisions by the mere fact that parents were present. They should weigh, in addition, the evidence concerning the parents' role in the preinterrogation waiver proceedings and evidence suggesting that the parents were or were not capable of providing the advice and protection which many juveniles need. Included in this deliberation should be a consideration of the parents' probable understanding of the rights and their potential significance, their attitudes toward these rights in juvenile cases, the parents' emotional and motivational states during the waiver proceedings, and the nature of the relationship between the parents and their child.

The difficulty with this recommendation, of course, is that it requires that judges evaluate a variety of cognitive, emotional, and motivational characteristics of parents, without providing any clear guidelines for doing so. Therefore, this approach might lead to the same frustrations and inconsistencies which have characterized judicial decisions about the competencies of juveniles themselves.

Although laws requiring the presence of parents offer no panacea for the problem of juveniles' waiver of rights, nothing in our results suggests that these laws should not exist. As we noted in Chapter 8, the involvement of parents in matters relating to their children satisfies many social and philosophical imperatives. Their involvement might even provide protection for their children in some waiver cases. The results of our studies of parents, however, indicate that we must look elsewhere for a method to provide adequate protection for most juveniles.

Mandatory Provision of Legal Counsel

A requirement to automatically provide legal counsel to juveniles prior to the waiver decision would probably be one of the most direct and potentially effective remedies to the problem of juveniles' lack of competence to waive rights knowingly, intelligently, and voluntarily. This recommendation has been issued by many legal commentators and policy groups (IJA-ABA, 1977; Paulsen & Whitebread, 1974; Piersma *et al.*, 1975; President's Commission on Law Enforcement, 1967).

Even this remedy, though, is not without serious difficulties. One problem is that of providing competent legal counsel. The mere fact that a juvenile has been advised by an attorney does not indicate that the juvenile's interests were protected. In Chapter 6, we reviewed evidence from other studies that many defense attorneys perceive their role in juvenile cases as being that of adviser to the court, while others take a more vigorous defense and advocacy position in working for juveniles. At the time of pretrial interrogation, a defense attorney's advice to a juvenile concerning waiver or assertion of rights should be based on the attorney's duty (consistent with the opinion of the Court in *Gault*) to vigorously represent the interests of the juvenile as would be appropriate in an adversarial justice system. Advice given by those public defenders or other defense attorneys who perceive their main responsibility to be to the juvenile court rather than to the juvenile might not be based on the advocacy posture supported by the *Gault* Court. Therefore, a requirement that all juveniles must be advised by legal counsel prior to a rights waiver decision would be meaningful only to the extent that the proper advocacy position of defense attorneys would come to be viewed by juvenile courts as a true defense counsel for juveniles.

One major obstacle to implementing mandatory counsel is the concern of law enforcement and many juvenile courts about the effects which such a requirement would have on police investigation. It is often assumed that if suspects were automatically provided legal counsel, attorneys would routinely advise suspects to remain silent. Thus, a major obstacle to providing mandatory legal counsel for juveniles is the fear that police investigations would be severely hampered. This would be a less difficult obstacle to deal with in promoting automatic legal counsel for younger adolescents than for older ones. The greater social threat of more serious offenses and repeat offenders generally involve older adolescents. It is in the investigation of these cases that the courts have been resistant to making procedural requirements which might obstruct police officers' investigations.

Blanket Exclusion of Juvenile Confessions

If legal counsel for juveniles was required, and if attorneys routinely advised juveniles to remain silent, the effect would be the same as if interrogation of juveniles was not permitted by law. Blanket exclusion or invalidation of juvenile confessions would, of course, nullify the issue of juveniles' competence to waive rights, and would therefore offer one remedy to the problem which our studies addressed.

The concept of blanket exclusion, however, has received no support in the courts. The prevailing rule is that which was established in *People* v. *Lara,* 432 P.2d 202 (1967), to the effect that the mere fact of being a juvenile does not invalidate a waiver of *Miranda* rights. All challenges to this rule have been rejected on the grounds that "society's self-preservation interests" (*In re Thompson,* 241 N.W.2d at 5 (1976) would not be served by a rigid restriction against juveniles' interrogations (see note 1, Chap. 8).

Therefore, while blanket exclusion of confessions in all juvenile cases might provide a satisfactory resolution of the problems raised by our data on juveniles' diminished competence, this remedy will not be viewed by most courts as being practical, and therefore does not provide a fruitful direction for legal reform.

RECOMMENDATIONS FOR THE LEGAL PROCESS

We come now to alternatives which would seem to provide the most feasible and effective protection of juveniles' diminished competence to waive rights. One of these requires legislative reform and the other involves the use of our research results in the judicial decision process.

Differential Exclusion and Mandatory Counsel

As a group, juveniles who were 14 years of age or younger consistently fell short of the research definitions of the legal standards for competence to waive rights. This was true when they were compared to older juveniles or adults and also when their performance on experimental measures of *Miranda* comprehension were examined against the absolute criteria represented by the scoring systems. We believe that the results support the need for extraordinary protections for juveniles at ages 14 and below. Legislation to provide blanket exclusion of confessions, or to provide automatically for effective legal counsel to these juveniles prior to police questioning, would afford the type of protection which our results suggest that these juveniles need. The research results themselves should be helpful in supporting this type of legislation.

The traditional arguments against blanket exclusion might be easier to deal with when addressing policy for this specific age group than for juveniles as a whole. "Society's self-preservation interests" are less often at issue in cases involving younger adolescents because seriously dangerous or repetitive offenses are more common among older adolescents than among juveniles of ages 14 or below.

Ancient common law concepts of age-related abilities have established precedent for special legal considerations in matters involving children below 14 years of age. This, too, might work in favor of promoting the legislative reform which we are suggesting. It should be recognized, however, that the age of 14 traditionally has been employed in law as the upper end of an age range (7–14) in which various mental capacities or competencies have been considered to be "rebuttable" (Keasey & Sales, 1977). In contrast, our results indicate that with regard to competence to waive *Miranda* rights, age 14 should stand as the age below which incompetence should be presumed. These juveniles' waiver of rights should be considered valid only when made with the assistance of competent legal advice and advocacy at the time of rights waiver. The question of what constitutes competent legal advice and advocacy in juvenile cases must therefore be given increased attention by juvenile courts, legal scholars, and behavioral science researchers.

It is more difficult to use our results to argue for blanket exclusion of confessions or mandatory legal counsel for 15–16-year-olds. Juveniles in this age range with IQ scores of 80 or below were as much in need of these protections as were juveniles of ages 14 or below. Among 15–16-year-olds with IQ scores above 80, however, performance was not remarkably different from that of adults, who are not seen by the courts to be in need of these extreme protections. Yet, there would probably be legal objections to a proposal to provide automatic protections for one IQ class of 15–16-year-olds and not for others in the same age group. For example, it would be most difficult for police to determine at the time of interrogation whether or not a particular juvenile falls into the specified class.

One argument, then, would be to provide blanket exclusion or mandatory legal counsel to all 15–16-year-olds, in order to protect the substantial proportion which demonstrated a special need for these protections. The second argument, of course, would be to avoid these extreme protections for 15–16-year-olds, since some majority of them appear to be as competent to waive rights as are adults. Our results outline the nature of these options and some of the data relevant for weighing them; but the results cannot address the question of which of these views should prevail.

Promoting Rational Judicial Decisions

The aforementioned protections generally do not exist for any class of juveniles at present, so that there is a need for some more immediate protective measures in cases involving juveniles' waiver of rights. In fact, as we shall point out later, the recent history of the United States Supreme Court does not offer encouragement for realizing the aforementioned protections.

In lieu of the recommended reforms in juvenile law, then, judges can use our research results in weighing individual juvenile's competence to waive rights, as an important element in considering the totality of circumstances of the case. It has already been made clear that the great majority of juveniles who are 14 years of age or younger were seen in this project to lack the competence to waive rights to silence and counsel. The results also indicate that the competence of juveniles who are 15–16 years of age should be questioned when the juvenile is black and of lower socioeconomic status, or has had little contact with police in relation to felony charges, or might manifest intellectual functioning which is well below average on an intelligence test (that is, an IQ of less than 80).[2]

Once it has been established that a juvenile falls into one of these "high risk" groups, the research results obtained for that class of juvenile can be offered as a guide for judicial decision on the matter. The judge, of course, must weigh that evidence against other circumstances of the case or other unique characteristics of the juvenile. The availability of these empirical guidelines, however, can provide a more rational base for this decision-making process, and it may contribute to consistency and fairness in judicial decisions about waiver validity.

The potential impact and usefulness of the research results in judicial deliberations probably will depend on their use by defense attorneys, who can introduce the results as evidence relevant to their juvenile clients' circumstances. Many of the tables in this book, as well as statements in the conclusion and summary sections of many of the chapters, were designed specifically to assist the attorney in using the data in hearings and legal briefs. For example, if an attorney's 13-year-old client is known to have an IQ score in the 71–80 range, the attorney may use Tables 10 and 11 (Chap. 4) to determine the frequency with which juveniles of that type demonstrated adequate understanding of the *Miranda* warnings (in this case, only 25%). These facts can be used as an initial basis for establishing the low probability of competence in the case, and can potentially be buttressed by consideration of ways in which the juvenile does or does not fit into other classes of "high risk" juveniles as described in Chapters 4, 6 (understanding the significance of the rights), and 7 (expectancies about the consequences of waiver).[3]

At this writing, defense attorneys in various parts of the country have been requesting copies of the results of the present project for potential use in their representation of juveniles. It is difficult to determine to what extent the results already have been used in juvenile court

[2]Besides the specific characteristics of the juvenile, of course, there may be many other types of circumstances of interrogations which could raise the question of the validity of a juvenile's waiver, even though the juvenile fits one of the classes which demonstrated relatively competent understanding in our research studies.

[3]Defense attorneys are well aware that some judges will not be impressed by a mere recital of probabilities. The fact that a juvenile possesses the demographic characteristics of a class of juveniles who in general performed inadequately in our studies does not guarantee that this particular juvenile is not an exception to the rule. No matter how persuasive some of our results might seem, in individual legal cases they must be accompanied by observations and descriptions of the juvenile's behavior and the specific circumstances of the interrogation.

cases, although we know of such uses in the states of Washington and Missouri. In addition, the results were employed in a petition for a writ of certiorari to the United States Supreme Court (April 23, 1979) in a South Carolina case [*State* v. *Smith*, 234 S.E.2d 19 (1977); *State* v. *Smith*, 192 S.E.2d 870 (1972)]. In most instances, the results have been cited to support the general argument that juveniles are less likely to be competent to waive rights, and that greater care must therefore be taken in weighing the validity of waiver. Enlisting the results of our research to make this general argument in a case involving a specific juvenile does not represent the best use of the data from our studies. The application of the data in specific cases should address whether the juvenile in question was or was not likely to be competent to waive rights, based on the juvenile's age, IQ, or other demographic characteristics and on our results with juveniles possessing those characteristics. This more specific application of the data has not yet been tested in the courts.

RESEARCH RECOMMENDATIONS

Our data concerning *Miranda* comprehension and perceptions among juveniles can address the legal question of competence across a fairly wide range of demographic types of juveniles, as specified in the subject samples in our studies. Some jurisdictions, however, might frequently deal with types of juveniles who are not represented in our samples: for example, juveniles with hispanic or other non-English-language backgrounds. In these jurisdictions, psychologists working in juvenile courts might wish to establish local norms on these populations with our experimental measures, so that they can provide relevant information about *Miranda* comprehension in cases involving these special population characteristics.

Our studies suggested the need for several other types of research which are not directly related to the question of juveniles' competence to waive *Miranda* rights.

First, the study in Chapter 6 examined juveniles' perceptions of the relationship between juveniles and their attorneys. That study, however, did not examine the question in depth, because its purpose was merely to provide an index of juveniles' levels of understanding rather than to thoroughly explore their perceptions. Juvenile defense attorneys are greatly in need of more definitive information concerning how they are perceived by their juvenile clients, and what degree and type of participation they can expect from juveniles when they attempt to counsel with them. Studies designed to provide this information would have great significance even apart from their application to the question of juveniles' competence to waive the right to counsel.

Second, there are many other questions in juvenile law which are in need of the same type of empirical approach which was used in the present series of studies. As in decisions about juveniles' waiver of rights, judges must also weigh the behavioral, emotional, social, and intellectual characteristics of juveniles in relation to other legal decisions. Among these are the decision to detain juveniles in custody between the time of arrest and the adjudication hearing, the decision that a juvenile's character warrants a trial in an adult criminal court rather than being dealt with in the juvenile justice system, and decisions about the use of various treatment alternatives or placements in delinquent cases. As in the present project, the legal standards controlling these decisions could be analyzed, translated into psychological concepts, and then studied with the use of measures defining these concepts. The results might be the development of empirical guidelines for juvenile justice decision making such as those developed from the present studies.

Finally, at several points in the discussion of our results we have noted the relationships between our data and the results of earlier empirical research on the development of children's concepts of law, rules, and rights. A growing body of research (Grisso & Vierling, 1978; Keasey & Sales, 1977; Kohlber, 1964; Melton, 1979; Tapp & Kohlberg, 1971; Tapp & Levine, 1977; Torney, 1977) has employed developmental theories to conceptualize stages in children's thinking in relation to legal questions. Several of our findings conform well to what has been known generally about the cognitive capacities and problem-solving skills of children. Yet, some of our results were not consistent with that which would have been predicted by past theoretical conceptualizations of children's developing concepts of laws and rights. For example, the proportions of juveniles and adults who manifested a developmentally primitive (preconventional) conceptualization of rights were far greater in certain circumstances than would generally be expected at the ages involved on the basis of developmental theories or past research (see, for example, subjects' views of judges' powers to revoke rights, in Chap. 6). Put another way, while most juveniles at some specific age might manifest a conventional level of legal reasoning when considering rights in the abstract or in certain social situations, it may be hazardous to infer that they can do so in the full range of legal situations with which they might be faced in life. Our final recommendation, then, is for more empirical research to test the limits of developmental theories of legal reasoning to predict children's thinking about rights in a variety of situations requiring their understanding and decision making.

10

Epilogue

FARE V. *MICHAEL C.*

As the manuscript for this book was nearing completion, the United States Supreme Court reached a decision in the case of a 16-year-old boy's waiver of the right to silence [*Fare* v. *Michael C.*, 442 U.S. 707, 99 S.Ct. 2560 (1979)]. The Van Nuys, California, police took this boy into custody on suspicion of murder and advised him of his rights at a station house prior to interrogation. The boy was said to be emotional (crying) at the time of interrogation, even though he had been arrested some number of times before, was apparently familiar with the procedures, and was not obviously mistreated by the police officers.

At issue in this case was whether or not the juvenile's request to talk to his probation officer prior to interrogation was an invocation of his right to silence. The juvenile's attorney argued that when the police refused access to the probation officer and persisted in inquiring as to the juvenile's desire to waive his rights, the subsequent confession was obtained in violation of Fifth Amendment protections. The juvenile's request for his probation officer's assistance was based on his trust of the probation officer, and also on his mistrust of the police. He was apparently afraid that a request for an attorney might be a trap. In his own words to the police, "How I know you guys won't pull no police officer in and tell me he's an attorney?" (*Fare* v. *Michael C.*, 442 U.S. at 710).

The juvenile court from which the case originated had decided that the confession was properly obtained. On appeal, the California Supreme Court reversed [579 P.2d 7 (1978)]. The California court reasoned [as it had done earlier in *People* v. *Burton*, 491 P.2d 793 (1971)] that a juvenile who seeks assistance cannot always be expected to request an attorney, but naturally will call for the help of some other trusted adult whom he or she knows. Further, the court noted that probation officers are charged by statute to represent the interests of juveniles with whom they work, and that the request was therefore as much an invocation of the Fifth Amendment right as if the juvenile had requested to see his parents or an attorney.

In a close 5–4 decision, the United States Supreme Court reversed the California Supreme Court decision. The Court decided that a juvenile's request to speak to a probation officer does not constitute *per se* an invocatoin of Fifth Amendment rights.[1] Beyond that, the Court underscored the "mandate" for an inquiry into the totality of circumstances in such cases, including the circumstances of the interrogation and "an evaluation of the subject's age, experience, education, background and intelligence and into whether he has the capacity to understand the warnings given him, the nature of his Fifth Amendment rights and the consequences of waiving those rights" (442 U.S. at 725). This test, the Court said, would provide the "necessary flexibility" for future courts to decide whether or not specific juveniles' requests for probation officers or parents were ever invocations of the right to silence. Using this test in the present case, the majority believed the juvenile's confession to have been the result of a knowing, intelligent, and voluntary waiver of rights. The tape recording of his preinterrogation waiver was said to indicate that he did understand the *Miranda* warnings and his previous experience with police was cited as suggestive that he understood the consequences of waiving his rights.[2]

One aspect of the majority's decision in *Fare* v. *Michael C.* might actually serve to strengthen one type of due process protection for juveniles in interrogations. The majority (and also apparently Justice Powell, who dissented for other reasons) concluded that a probation officer is in no position to represent the interests of a juvenile in the manner intended in the *Miranda* decision. They placed heavy emphasis on the probation officer's obligation to the state which seeks to prosecute the juvenile, and on the position of the probation officer as a peace officer in an adversarial system of justice. Whatever the obligations of the probation officer to the juvenile, they reasoned, these obligations are in

[1]One of the dissenting judges (Justice Powell) was in agreement with the majority on this point, while the other three were not.

[2]The dissent of one judge (again, Justice Powell) was because of his disagreement with the majority on this point. That is, he believed that the totality of circumstances in the case cast doubt on this juvenile's ability to provide a valid waiver of rights. The remaining three dissenters did not address this point.

serious competition with his obligations to the state. Thus, probation officers generally cannot be expected to provide the advocacy and protection intended by the *Miranda* decision when it provided the availability of legal counsel. Three dissenting judges, on the other hand, argued that California statutes require that probation officers represent juveniles' interests, and that therefore the juvenile's request to see the probation officer should have been a signal to go no further with the questioning and to contact the probation officer.

In these two views, then, we come full circle to the contrasting conceptualizations of the juvenile justice system which we reviewed at the beginning of this book. On the one hand is the view that the juvenile court was designed to treat juveniles benevolently and that its employees can be expected to do so because it is so mandated. On the other hand is the reaffirmation of the message in *Gault:* that in fact the juvenile justice system must be construed in many ways as an adversarial system of justice in which juveniles require the same protections as do adults. As in *Gault,* the latter view was that of the majority of the Court.

In other ways, however, the majority's decision is a warning that the Supreme Court under Chief Justice Burger will not look favorably on proposals for special due process protections in the interrogation of juveniles.[3] First, the majority refused to interpret the juvenile's request to see his probation officer as an indication of his desire to obtain protection or advice in the interrogation process. While the juvenile's choice concerning who to consult might have been less than ideal, that he requested some form of assistance from an adult would seem to be sufficient grounds to require a halt in the interrogation process. This would follow from the precedents and arguments set forth in a large number of cases.[4] Yet the majority opinion in *Fare* v. *Michael C.* did not cite this considerable body of case law, nor did it even acknowledge the Court's observations in *Gault* concerning the need for special protections in the interrogation of juveniles.

The second way in which the decision bodes ill for future attempts to strengthen protection for juveniles is in the majority's rigid adherence to the totality of circumstances test. The record of the United States Supreme Court since 1971 reflects Chief Justice Burger's view that there are no circumstances which would justify automatically the exclusion of

[3]Although the author takes responsibility for the following interpretations of the Court's decision, thanks are due to Harry Swanger, David Howard, and David Lambert for their helpful comments on the case.

[4]See Chapter 8 for a review of cases concerning the presence of parents or other interested adult. Especially see *Commonwealth* v. *Markle,* 380 A.2d 346 (1977); *Lewis* v. *State,* 288 N.E.2d 138 (1972); *Hall* v. *State,* 346, N.E.2d 584 (1976).

an adult defendant's confession as evidence (Keefe, 1977). [5] The decision in *Fare* v. *Michael C.* extended this view to juvenile cases, always requiring a consideration of the totality of circumstances and judicial discretion concerning the question of exclusion in a particular case.

One must be pessimistic, then, concerning the response which the present Court might have toward our recommendation that the confessions of juveniles, or at least of juveniles 14 years of age or younger, should be automatically excluded unless made with the advice of legal counsel. It is true that the majority opinion in *Fare* v. *Michael C.* acknowledged that it was concerned in this case with avoiding the imposition of "rigid restraints on police and courts in dealing with an *experienced older* juvenile with an *extensive prior record*" (at 725; italics added). Yet the Chief Justice's aforementioned principle against automatic exclusions suggests that the Court might be no more responsive even in the case of younger, less experienced juveniles.

Finally, in spite of the fact that the juvenile in this case showed signs of emotional distress, was uneducated, and was said to be "immature" (see Justice Powell's dissent at 733), the majority perceived him as competent to provide a valid waiver of rights when they considered the totality of circumstances. In a final irony, on the same day that the Court announced this decision, they decided in another case that juveniles committed "voluntarily" to mental institutions by their parents were generally too immature and too unaware of consequences to make decisions affecting their hospitalization [*Parham* v. *J.L.*, 47 U.S.L.W. 4740 (1979) and *Secretary of Public Welfare of Pennsylvania* v. *Institutionalized Juveniles*, 47 U.S.L.W. 4754 (1979)].

In spite of these decisions, there is reason to believe that the results of our research project will be useful in promoting protections for juveniles of the types put forth in our recommendations. Several states are moving toward legislation which would mandate the provision of legal counsel automatically at various stages of juvenile court cases. Throughout this report we have cited advocacy groups whose recommendations and model legislations are promoting these safeguards. In the meantime, we hope that the results of our empirical studies will assist juvenile courts and defense attorneys who, employing the totality of circumstances test, must weigh the need for special protection of juveniles' rights in interrogation.

[5] Chief Justice Burger stated this explicitly in *Brewer* v. *Williams*, 430 U.S.387 (1977); this case, and all others reflecting this view, involved adult defendants.

Appendix A

Subject Sample Descriptions

TABLE A-1. SUBJECT SAMPLE FOR 1974 AND 1975[a]

Variable	Category codes	Mean	Percent in categories					
			0	1	2	3	4	5
Race/sex	1 = white male							
	2 = black male			73.4	18.1	6.8	1.7	
	3 = white female			*69.3*[a]	*22.4*	*5.5*	*2.8*	
	4 = black female							
Socioeconomic	1 = high							
status	2 = median			19.8	39.7	28.7	10.8	
	3 = low			*16.5*	*44.1*	*24.8*	*14.6*	
	4 = unknown							
Age	0 = 12 & under							
	1 = 13	14.62	9.3	10.5	15.2	26.2	35.9	3.0
	2 = 14	*14.72*	*9.3*	*6.7*	*13.8*	*24.8*	*40.9*	*3.5*
	3 = 15							
	4 = 16							
	5 = 17							
Number of prior	0 = 0	.76	62.9	19.0	8.9	9.2		
felonies	1 = 1	*1.07*	*57.9*	*20.1*	*8.7*	*13.5*		
	2 = 2							
	3 = 3 & over							
Number of prior	0 = 0	2.16	58.1	24.0	9.7	8.5	9.6	
referrals	1 = 1-2	*2.57*	*40.2*	*30.7*	*7.1*	*12.2*	*10.0*	
	2 = 3-4							
	3 = 5-7							
	4 = 8 & over							
Number of	1 = 1	1.34		77.2	13.5	5.5	3.7	
felonies	2 = 2	*1.48*		*77.2*	*12.6*	*3.5*	*6.7*	
during year	3 = 3							
per subject	4 = 4 & over							

[a]Percentages for 1975 are in italic.

TABLE A-2. EVENT SAMPLE FOR 1974 AND 1975[a]

			Percent in categories					
Variable	Category codes	Mean	0	1	2	3	4	5
Race/sex	1 = white male							
	2 = black male			71.8	21.5	5.5	1.2	
	3 = white female			*66.0*	*27.6*	*4.4*	*1.9*	
	4 = black female							
Socioeconomic status	1 = high							
	2 = median			17.3	39.7	33.6	9.3	
	3 = low			*13.8*	*44.3*	*31.3*	*10.6*	
	4 = unknown							
Age	0 = 12 & under							
	1 = 13	14.75	7.5	9.4	14.2	27.0	39.7	2.1
	2 = 14	*14.93*	*7.6*	*4.8*	*11.7*	*29.4*	*43.2*	*3.2*
	3 = 15							
	4 = 16							
	5 = 17							
Prior felonies	0 = 0							
	1 = 1	1.00	54.5	20.6	11.5	13.3		
	2 = 2	*1.46*	*48.5*	*21.0*	*10.6*	*18.9*		
	3 = 3 & over							
Prior referrals	0 = 0							
	1 = 1	2.85	37.3	24.8	13.1	12.0	12.5	
	2 = 2-4	*3.25*	*30.8*	*27.8*	*12.1*	*15.9*	*13.3*	
	3 = 5-7							
	4 = 8 & over							
Type of felony for which referral is made	1 = person offense			14.2	69.1	16.7		
				10.9	*73.2*	*15.4*		
	2 = property offense							
	3 = possession offense							

[a] Percentages for 1975 are in italic.

TABLE A-3. ADULT OFFENDER SAMPLE FOR CHAPTER 5: NUMBER OF SUBJECTS IN EACH DEMOGRAPHIC GROUP

Variable	Category codes	Mean and standard deviations[b]	Categories 0	1	2	3	4
Age	0 = 17–19 1 = 20–22 2 = 23–26 3 = 27–31 4 = 32 & over	25.54 *6.93*	27 (13.3)[a]	54 (26.6)	52 (25.6)	39 (19.2)	31 (15.3)
Race	0 = white 1 = black		85 (41.9)	118 (58.1)			
Socioeconomic status	0 = upper middle 1 = middle 2 = lower middle 3 = lower 4 = not classified		8 (3.9)	16 (7.9)	78 (38.4)	47 (23.2)	54 (26.6)
Sex	0 = male 1 = female		161 (79.3)	42 (20.7)			

IQ	0 = 70 or below 1 = 71–80 2 = 81–90 3 = 91–100 4 = 101+	89.35 *13.50*	18 (13.9)	33 (16.3)	57 (28.1)	58 (28.6)	37 (18.2)
Prior felony arrests	0 = 0 1 = 1–2 2 = 3–4 3 = 5–33 4 = unknown	2.39 *3.84*	70 (34.3)	59 (29.1)	30 (14.8)	31 (15.3)	13 (6.4)
Total prior arrests	0 = 0–1 1 = 2–3 2 = 4–7 3 = 8–37 4 = unknown	4.08 *5.54*	68 (33.5)	54 (26.6)	43 (21.2)	27 (13.3)	11 (5.4)

[a] Percentages in parentheses.
[b] S.d. are italic.

TABLE A-4. ADULT NONOFFENDER SAMPLE FOR CHAPTER 5: NUMBER OF SUBJECTS IN EACH DEMOGRAPHIC GROUP

Variable	Category codes	Mean and standard deviations[b]	Categories 0	1	2	3	4
Age	0 = 17–19 1 = 20–22 2 = 23–26 3 = 27–31 4 = 32 & over	27.09 *13.07*	27 (47.4)[a]	6 (10.5)	5 (8.8)	4 (7.0)	15 (26.3)
Race	0 = white 2 = black		16 (28.1)	41 (71.9)			
Socioeconomic status	0 = upper middle 1 = middle 2 = lower middle 3 = lower 4 = unclassified		1 (1.8)	4 (7.0)	31 (54.4)	17 (29.8)	4 (7.1)
Sex	0 = male 1 = female		25 (43.9)	32 (56.1)			
IQ	0 = 70 or below 1 = 71–80 2 = 81–90 3 = 91–100 4 = 101+	91.74 *10.92*	1 (1.8)	10 (17.5)	14 (24.6)	23 (40.4)	9 (15.8)

[a] Percentages in parentheses.

[b] S.d. are italic.

TABLE A-5. SAMPLE DESCRIPTION FOR JUVENILES IN CHAPTER 7: NUMBER OF SUBJECTS IN DEMOGRAPHIC GROUPS

Variable	Category code	Mean and standard deviations[b]	Categories					
			0	1	2	3	4	5
Age	0 = 10/11 1 = 12 2 = 13 3 = 14 4 = 15 5 = 16	14.61 *1.23*	3 (1.6)[a]	6 (3.3)	22 (12.0)	41 (22.4)	66 (36.1)	45 (24.6)
Sex	0 = male 1 = female		108 (59.0)	75 (41.0)				
Race	0 = white 1 = black		120 (65.6)	63 (34.4)				
Socioeconomic status	0 = upper middle 1 = middle 2 = lower middle 3 = lower 4 = not classified		17 (9.3)	54 (29.5)	48 (26.2)	15 (8.2)	49 (26.7)	

(*continued*)

TABLE A-5 (*continued*)

Variable	Category code	Mean and standard deviations[b]	Categories 0	1	2	3	4	5
IQ	0 = 70 or below	85.88	27	39	57	27	33	
	1 = 71–80	*16.30*	(14.8)	(21.3)	(31.1)	(14.8)	(18.0)	
	2 = 81–90							
	3 = 91–100							
	4 = 101+							
Total prior referrals	0 = 0	2.85	34	66	50	33		
	1 = 1–2	*3.03*	(18.6)	(36.1)	(27.3)	(18.0)		
	2 = 3–4							
	3 = 5+							
Total prior felony referrals	0 = 0	0.55	134	26	23			
	1 = 1	*1.39*	(73.2)	(14.2)	(12.6)			
	2 = 2+							

[a] Percentage in parentheses.

[b] S.d. are italic.

TABLE A-6. SAMPLE I AND SAMPLE II (IN ITALICS) FOR CHAPTER 8

Variable	Category codes		Categories 0	1	2	3	4	5	6
Age	1. Below 40			24.5	50.5	25.0			
	2. 40–49			*50.0*	*43.0*	*7.0*			
	3. 50 & above								
Race	1. White			100.0	0.0				
	2. Black			*95.7*	*4.3*				
Sex	1. Male			39.2	60.8				
	2. Female			*39.9*	*60.1*				
Occupation									
A. Self	0. % of total not responding	A.	9.1	15.4	21.0	11.6	9.4	0.8	41.8
	1. Professional		*12.1*	*22.2*	*17.9*	*17.9*	*9.6*	*1.7*	*30.8*
	2. Managerial								
B. Spouse	3. Skilled	B.	18.9	20.8	27.2	15.4	8.8	0.9	26.9
	4. Semiskilled		*24.7*	*24.7*	*23.6*	*20.8*	*5.0*	*0.8*	*25.1*
	5. Unskilled								
C. High status	6. Unemployed	C.	22.1	32.7	41.2	20.8	3.5	1.3	0.6
			29.9	*40.1*	*35.5*	*19.4*	*1.7*	*2.5*	*0.8*

(continued)

TABLE A-6 (*continued*)

Variable	Category codes	Categories 0	1	2	3	4	5	6
Income	0. % of total not responding							
	1. 6,900 & below	54.4	0.0[a]	0.0	11.3	23.1	65.6	
	2. 7,000–11,900	*50.6*	*0.6*	*4.1*	*18.8*	*34.1*	*42.4*	
	3. 12,000–16,900							
	4. 17,000–21,900							
	5. 22,000 & above							
Delinquency experience	0. Never	78.6	12.5	8.8				
	1. Once	*86.9*	*9.9*	*3.2*				
	2. More than once							
No. of children in family	1–5 = no. of children		3.3	10.6	21.4	16.1	21.4	17.3
	6 = 6 or more		*6.8*	*31.8*	*32.4*	*15.6*	*7.9*	*5.6*

[a] Percentages in Categories 1–5 were calculated as percentages of subjects responding to request for information on income.

Appendix B

Comprehension of *Miranda* Rights Measures

COMPREHENSION OF *MIRANDA* RIGHTS

The Comprehension of *Miranda* Rights (CMR) measure is an objective method for assessing an individual's understanding of the standard *Miranda* warnings. Thus, adequate response on the CMR is viewed as a necessary part of any definition of competence to waive rights. However, an individual may comprehend the *Miranda* warnings but nevertheless be incompetent to waive rights because of other deficiencies in comprehension. For example, the CMR may reveal that a given individual comprehends the right to have a lawyer before and during interrogation. However, the measure does not allow one to infer that the individual understands the role and function of a lawyer sufficiently to make a meaningful decision regarding waiver or assertion of the right. Such information is not presented in standard *Miranda* warnings and thus is not assessed by the CMR.

The research project also has produced other measures designed to address questions of understanding which go beyond the information presented in the *Miranda* warnings themselves. Further, other measures were also developed to assess understanding of the *Miranda* warnings themselves. One of these, the Comprehension of *Miranda* Vocabulary measure, employs six words from the *Miranda* warnings and requires the examinee to provide definitions. Another employs a true-or-false format that requires the examinee to indicate whether several simply-worded sentences do or do not express the same meaning as the

Miranda warnings. These measures offer alternative or complementary methods to the CMR for assessing *Miranda* understanding.

The CMR assesses understanding of *Miranda* warnings under relatively optimal conditions. A review of the following materials will reveal the general objectives of maximizing the clarity of presentation of stimuli and the opportunity of the examinees to manifest any understanding they might have. These objectives necessarily make the CMR experience quite different from that which might occur when *Miranda* warnings are received and cognitively processed by a suspect in the context of actual interrogation procedures. Given the alternative objectives of producing optimal conditions or approximating the more stressful conditions of interrogation, we decided on the former primarily for reasons of research ethics and concern for the well-being of those youths who participated in the research. These objectives do not weaken the value of the results obtained by the CMR, so long as it is understood that: (1) an individual who demonstrates adequate understanding on the CMR might not have the benefit of that level of understanding under more emotionally arousing circumstances; and (2) individuals who demonstrate inadequate understanding on the CMR are not likely to do better in other contexts which provide less opportunity for input and comprehension than does the CMR experience.

Administration of the CMR

The CMR is administered individually to examinees because it is usually necessary for the examiner to inquire about the examinee's responses during the administration. It is recommended that the testing session be tape-recorded, since many examinees give lengthy paraphrase responses. The use of a tape recorder also frees the examiner to be attentive to the examinee's responses so as to select and employ the correct inquiry questions. Administration requires from 5 to 15 minutes, and is best accomplished in a room free of distraction.

Procedure

The examiner begins by giving the following instructions to the examinee:

> I will be showing you some cards with some sentences on them. When I show you one, I will read the sentence to you. Then I want you to tell me what it says *in your own words*. Try to tell me just what it says, but in different words from those that appear in the sentence on the card. Now can you explain to me what it is I would like you to do?

If the examinee does not understand, repeat the instructions slowly or answer specific questions. When understanding seems to have been accomplished, the examiner hands to the examinee a card on which a practice sentence has been typed, and says:

> This first card is just for practice so you can get used to what I want you to do. Here is the card. It says, "I have volunteered to be in this study."[1] Now tell me in your own words what is said in that sentence.

The primary reason for the use of a practice sentence is to "teach" the examinee to avoid verbatim use of words or phrases appearing in the stimulus sentences. Thus, if the examinee uses the words "volunteer" and/or "study" verbatim in his or her original response, the examiner should ask: "What do you mean by (volunteered) (study)?"

The examiner proceeds to the next stimulus sentence after the examinee has expressed an understanding of the elements of this practice sentence.

The remainder of the administration procedure consists of presenting each of the four *Miranda* warnings in the above fashion. Each *Miranda* warning statement is presented on a separate card, and an examinee's response to one statement (as well as any necessary inquiry) is completed before proceeding to the next *Miranda* statement.

Inquiry

During each original response by the examinee, the examiner focuses on the need for any inquiry. The objective of inquiry is: (1) to maximize the examinee's chances of manifesting whatever understanding might exist, but without providing cues which might supplement the examinee's understanding; and (2) to allow the examiner to understand clearly what the examinee is attempting to express. The nature of the inquiry in the CMR is highly standardized and does not allow variation from one examiner to another.

In general, inquiry most often occurs when an examinee's original response is incomplete or demonstrates at least partial understanding. (In the scoring system, these are 1-point responses.) Thus, inquiry generally occurs:

1. When the examinee's paraphrased response includes words or phrases verbatim from the *Miranda* warning

[1]This practice sentence was appropriate for the research project, but may be inappropriate for purposes for which others might wish to use the CMR. It is suggested that other sentences not related to the *Miranda* warnings can be substituted without invalidating the measure, since the examinee's response to this item is not scored.

2. When nonspecific pronouns are used so that it is unclear to whom the examinee is referring (e.g., police, lawyer)
3. When the examinee's original response omits some elements of the *Miranda* warning
4. When the examinee's verbal confusion, double negatives, contradictions, grammatical inconsistencies, or street slang render the response confusing or difficult for the examiner to understand

Specific instructions for inquiry, which appear in the section immediately following, show for each *Miranda* item the types of responses for which inquiry should occur and the specific questions which may be asked. The examiner *must* make the designated inquiry when an examinee's original response is of a type which calls for inquiry in the rules. Further, the examiner *must not* inquire about original responses which are not designated for further inquiry in the rules, and *must not* ask questions other than the inquiry questions appearing below. Not only does this assure standardized administration, but it also allows examiners to avoid asking leading questions which may supplement an examinee's understanding.

We have found that the CMR should be administered by individuals who are thoroughly familiar with the scoring system. If one knows the scoring system and the issues encountered in assigning credits to responses, one is more likely to be aware of the need for inquiry clarification of confusing responses and therefore more likely to acquire a scorable protocol.

CMR Standardized Inquiry

For each of the four *Miranda* warning statements below, specific responses requiring inquiry are shown along with specific inquiry questions which may be used. For standardized administration, it is necessary not to inquiry except in the instances outlined below. It is equally important that inquiry does occur whenever responses of the types outlined below are given by an examinee.

In addition to the specific inquiries noted below, examiners are permitted to attempt clarification of an examinee's response when it contains verbal confusions or slang which make its meaning unclear. In such instances, questions which are permissable are "Can you explain that again," "What do you mean by ______," "Can you tell me more about that," or "Let me read the sentence again, and you can start again from the beginning."

Examiners have found it invaluable to have with them during administration a set of cards on which the inquiry rules are printed as they appear in the following outline.

EXAMINEE'S ORIGINAL RESPONSE	INQUIRY
I. You do not have to make a statement and have the right to remain silent.	
A. If any of the following phrases occur verbatim: —make a statement —have the right —remain silent	What does ______ mean?
B. That it is best not to talk.	Tell me what the sentence says in your own words. (Reread sentence.)
C. That one does not have to *do* anything they do not want to do.	What do you mean by "not do anything?"
II. Anything you say can and will be held against you in a court of law.	
A. If any of the following phrases occur verbatim: —used against you, use (it) against you, used (in court) against you —court of law	What does ______ mean?
B. General idea of negative consequences but no mention of court or of use of confessions as evidence.	Can you explain what you mean?
III. You are entitled to consult with an attorney before interrogation and to have an attorney present at the time of the interrogation.	
A. If any of the following occur verbatim: —entitled —consult (consulted) —interrogation (interrogated) (interrogating)	What does ______ mean?
B. When identity of whom one can consult is stated merely as "someone."	Who can be consulted? OR Who do you mean?

C. When no mention is made of who may be consulted. (e.g., "You can get help when you are questioned.")	Can you tell me more about that?
D. When the time that one can have an attorney is not stated or is unclear.	Does this sentence tell you a certain time when you can have a lawyer?
E. When "before court" is stated as the time.	When before court?

IV. If you cannot afford an attorney, one will be appointed for you.

A. If any of the following occur verbatim: —afford —appointed (appoint)	What does ______ mean?
B. When identity of who will be appointed is stated merely as "someone."	Who is it that you mean?
C. When neither *financial inability nor free counsel* are are mentioned.	Please explain more about that.

Scoring the CMR

Detailed criteria for scoring are given later. Here we will describe the general nature of the scoring system and the procedure to be used when employing it. Scoring criteria are relatively complex because of the range of contingencies which may occur. Nevertheless, experienced scorers have found that most CMR protocols can be scored in 2–3 minutes.

Responses on each *Miranda* item may be scored 2,1, or 0. In general, 2-point responses convey adequate understanding of the *Miranda* warning statement in question.

There are several types of 1-point responses: (1) the examinee has omitted, distorted, or inadequately expressed some portion of the item while having demonstrated adequate understanding of another portion of it; (2) the response is vague, so that one cannot clearly determine whether the examinee had adequate or inadequate understanding; (3) some surplus meaning is attached to an otherwise adequate response, spoiling it because its meaning has been changed; (4) the response contains one (but no more than one) verbatim use of a phrase in the *Miranda* warning statement in question.

No credit is assigned to: (1) responses which demonstrate clearly inaccurate understanding of the *Miranda* item; (2) situations in which the examinee can offer no interpretation of the *Miranda* item.[2]

An examinee's response receives only a single score, even though the response may contain the examinee's original paraphrase as well as his or her response to inquiry. If an examinee's original response is sufficient to receive a 2-point credit, no inquiry will have occurred and the credit may be assigned usually without difficulty.

If an examinee's original response is of a 1-point quality, inquiry probably will have occurred. (If no inquiry occurred in such a case, a 1-point credit would be assigned.) If response to inquiry compensates for the omissions or vagueness in the original response so that 2-point criteria have been met, the whole response receives the 2-point credit. If response to inquiry demonstrates no improvement in the original quality, then a 1-point credit is assigned. Occasionally the response to inquiry will demonstrate that the examinee's understanding is inadequate as determined by the 1-point criteria; in such cases, a 0-point credit is assigned to the whole response.

If the original response is of 0-point quality, inquiry probably will not have occurred. Thus, a 0-point credit will be assigned to the response usually without difficulty.

Procedure for Scoring

1. Read through the whole response before attempting to match it with any scoring criteria.

2. Review the response to isolate essential and nonessential phrases. Essential phrases will become familiar to the examiner who has studied and practiced the scoring system. Nonessential phrases are those which are verbal "filler," often occurring in informal spoken messages. This step imposes some organization on the words and phrases competing for the scorer's attention.

3. Review all of the scoring categories for the *Miranda* item in question. This will not be necessary for the more experienced scorer, but the less experienced scorer will benefit.

4. Begin matching the response to scoring criteria and examples provided in the scoring system, starting with 2-point criteria. Attempt to discover the essential criteria within the response to be scored, but do not "read between the lines." Try to match the response to *both* the

[2]The above descriptions are general in nature and should not be used to decide on the score for a given response.

criterion statement and any of the examples provided in relation to that statement. However, the examples do not exhaust the range of possible responses; on occasion, in the absence of a matching example, one will have to decide on a score on the basis of the criterion statement alone.

5. Even if the response appears to satisfy 2-point criteria, proceed to review the response in relation to 1-point criteria. Likewise, even if it appears to meet 1-point criteria, continue to review it in relation to 0-point criteria. This process has been found to be essential in improving interscorer reliability and scoring accuracy.

6. Record the final score arrived at for the response. For some purposes, examiners may also wish to record the lettered subclass of the criterion which was used to assign the score.

7. An examinee's CMR sum score is the total of the scores obtained on the four *Miranda* items, and may range from 0 to 8.

Notes on Scoring

Experience with the CMR has revealed several points which improve interscorer reliability and general accuracy of scoring.

Training procedures in our research project indicated that scorers do not arrive at a high level of independent agreement in scores until they have scored at least 40–50 CMR protocols. Training included pairing a new scorer with a more experienced one to score together 5–10 protocols which had been selected to demonstrate a range of scoring problems. The new scorer then independently scored about 10 protocols, which were compared with an experienced scorer's independent rating of the same 10 protocols, and received intensive feedback on the source of disagreements which occurred. New scorers obtained acceptable interscorer reliability coefficients (when their scores were compared to those of experienced scorers) after another 30 practice protocols.

It is quite difficult to score CMR responses directly from tape recordings. It is necessary first to transcribe the tape-recorded responses so that they can be viewed in their entirety by scorers.

Scorers should rely only on data in the transcript. While the scorer should try to discover any evidence in the transcribed response for each essential element of the scoring criteria, it is important not to "read between the lines" when examining a CMR protocol. In addition, the scorer should avoid being biased by the quality of verbal or grammatical style in a response when deciding on a score. Very unsophisticated verbalizations are still very likely to contain a correct sense of the meanings conveyed in the *Miranda* statements. Further, highly sophisticated and intellectualized responses sometimes are found to be "empty" regarding the essential meanings to be understood.

CMR Scoring System

For each of the four *Miranda* items, criteria and examples are provided below for 2-, 1-, and 0-point credits. In most cases there are several ways to obtain the various credits, and these are presented as lettered subclasses. For example, under 2-point classification in the first *Miranda* item, a response which satisfies either Criterion A or Criterion B receives the 2-point credit.

Important: The scoring criteria below do not provide information on the scoring of responses in which examinees employ a verbatim phrase from the *Miranda* item and fail to paraphrase it. Critical phrases appear in the section on inquiry (p. 225). A response cannot be given a 2-point credit if any of these phrases appear verbatim in the response and were not paraphrased during inquiry, even if the response meets the other criteria of a 2-point response. A response can receive no more than a 1-point credit if any one critical phrase was used verbatim and was not paraphrased during inquiry. A 0-point credit must be assigned to any response which, after inquiry, contains two or more critical phrases used verbatim without having been paraphrased by the examinee.

The scoring system appears below.

I. You do not have to make a statement and have the right to remain silent.

2 Points

General: The idea that one does not have to say anything to the police, answer any question, and/or make any formal or informal statements.

A. A paraphrase regarding one's choice or implied choice of whether or not to talk, without explanation.

Examples: You do not have to say a word to police or anyone (implied choice). You do not have to say anything to anyone, but if you want to you can. You can tell them everything if you want, or just not say anything. You don't have to say anything.

B. Only the idea that one has a choice regarding whether or not to talk is essential. If a description or consequences associated with legal rights is given, it must be accurate.

Examples: You don't have to say anything, and if you don't, it will not be held against you in court. You don't have to say anything, and they can't make you if you don't want to. You don't have to answer any questions, because it can be used against you (might hurt your case, be incriminating, etc.).

1 Point

A. Choice or implied choice is present, but rationale for the right is erroneous, illogical, or inaccurate.

Examples: You don't have to talk if you don't want to, because you might not have done it (because the police might not want you to) (because your parents might get mad).

B. The idea that it is better not to say anything under any circumstances.

Examples: I think I should keep quiet. It means don't talk to the police. I would say it's best to say nothing. It means you better keep your mouth shut.

C. The idea that one can refuse not only to say anything, but also to do anything.

Examples: You don't have to do nothing you don't want to do. They can't make you do a thing. You can decide what you want to do.

0 Point

A. Stated lack of understanding

Examples: I dont' know. It doesn't mean anything at all to me.

B. The idea that you must remain silent and do not have the right or choice to talk if you want to.

Examples: You got to be quiet. It means you can't say anything. You must speak quietly.

C. The idea that you have to talk, stated generally or under certain circumstances, or that if you do not talk, it will go against you either with police or in court.

Examples: It means you don't have to talk unless you're guilty. You don't have to make statements but you have to tell them what they want to know. It means if you don't talk they lock you up.

II. Anything you say can and will be used against you in a court of law.

2 points

General: The idea that confession or any other provision of information will be repeated in court and/or can be used as evidence to convict the suspect or others whom the information might incriminate. That is, *what you say can be incriminating and/or brought up in court.*

Examples: Whatever you say can be used to try to convict you in court. If you say anything, it can hurt your case (be used as evidence) (will appear in court).

1 Point

A. The general idea that what you say may have negative consequences, but without an indication that subject understands that the consequences involve court hearing events.

Examples: I could get in trouble if I talk. If I talk it might be bad for me. I think it means it's better not to talk. What you say can hurt you (be held against you).

B. A response which would qualify as a 2-point response, except that erroneous qualifiers have been added which spoil the response or indicate only partial understanding. Included here are responses referring to consequences in settings other than the court hearing.

Examples: Since what you say can hurt you, they have told you to be silent. If you lie, that might go bad for you because they tell everything you said in court. They tell all you say in court, and you can't be found guilty if you don't confess. What you say could go badly for you in detention.

0 Point

Responses indicating lack of understanding, or responses which (whether true or not) do not focus on potential self-incrimination. Some responses in this category empasize the dangers produced by disobedience; others focus only on police as adversary.

Examples: I can't figure out what it means. Swearing at the cops will get you in trouble in court. It would hurt you to do or say anything you are not supposed to. It doesn't matter what you say, they are going to make it look like you did it and admitted it. You say you didn't do it and they say you did, it's your word against theirs. It just means you can't win.

III. You are entitled to consult with an attorney before interrogation and to have an attorney present at the time of the interrogation.

2 Points

General: The idea that one has a right to consult an attorney before and during interrogation, or that one does not have to answer questions until a lawyer is present.

Examples: I can talk to a lawyer before anything else happens and during questioning. You can have your lawyer with you before and during talking to the cops. You can get a lawyer to come talk to you now and be with you at questioning. A lawyer can come and talk to you right now and be with you when cops talk to you. They can't question you without a lawyer if you want one. You can have your lawyer there while police talk to you.

1 Point

A. Responses in which the type of person with whom one may consult is left unclear; otherwise, the response is adequate.

Examples: You can have someone working for you there when police talk to you. Before and during questioning, you are allowed to talk to someone if you want. It's a procedure to help the defendant before or during any police questioning if you want.

B. (1) The time when legal counsel is available is not specified, even after inquiry. (2) Only before interrogation is specified.

Examples: You can have a lawyer if you want. You can talk to your lawyer. Everybody gets a lawyer if they want one. You can see your lawyer before being questioned. You can have a lawyer before interrogation, but I don't know what interrogation means.

0 Point

A. Responses indicating lack of understanding of the right to attorney.

Examples: I don't understand that one. You can have someone question you about what you've done. You don't have to say anything if you don't want to. They are telling you that a lawyer is coming.

B. Responses in which legal counsel is referred to in conjunction with a legal or court procedure other than interrogation.

Examples: You can have a lawyer when it comes time to go to court (when you have a hearing). You can ask for a lawyer after you have been in detention a while. You can have a lawyer before court.

C. Responses in which who may be consulted is vague or incorrect, *and* no time is specified.

Examples: You can have someone to be with you, I don't know who. A partner can see you through and give you advice.

D. Responses in which all elements may be correct, but someone other than attorney is specified.

Example: You can talk to a social worker before the police ask you questions.

IV. If you cannot afford an attorney, one will be appointed for you.

2 Points

In all cases, it must be clear that an attorney (lawyer, public defender, legal counsel) *is being referred to. In addition, either of two conditions is sufficient to convey adequate understanding* of the statement:

A. If the response includes a clear interpretation of "cannot afford," then any of a variety of substitute terms for "appoint" may be used.

Examples: If you don't have money for a lawyer, the court will provide one for you. If you ain't got money to pay, a charity case lawyer will represent you instead. If you can't pay a lawyer, the court will get (give you) (have you represented by) (put you in touch with) (find you) a lawyer.

B. If the response does not include an interpretation of "cannot afford," then either the word "free" or an equivalent word must appear in relation to acquiring legal counsel, or the word "give" must be used where "appoint" would be appropriate.

Examples: The court will get you a lawyer free if you want a lawyer. They will give you a lawyer if you ask them to. The court will pay for a lawyer to represent you.

1 Point

A. Responses in which all above criteria are met except that an attorney is not specified and it is vague regarding who may be appointed.

Examples: You can have them get you someone to talk to for free. They will provide someone to help you if you don't have enough money to pay for help.

B. The idea that legal counsel is involved, but: (1) with neither a paraphrase of "cannot afford" nor the element of free counsel included in the response; or (2) "cannot afford" is interpreted but "appoint" is not paraphrased correctly. Often these responses will mention court assistance in locating a lawyer.

Examples: The court can get you a lawyer if you want. They will call a lawyer for you. They'll find a lawyer to take your case.

C. Legal counsel is mentioned, but reduced cost rather than free counsel is indicated.

Examples: You can get a lawyer through the court at a minimum cost. If you are poor, they will find a lawyer for you at a reduced price.

0 Point

A. Responses indicating clear lack of understanding and/or no sense of the financial benefit or court assistance extended by this right statement.

Examples: I don't understand it. A lawyer will be coming to help me. You have an attorney with you. They don't do that well anyway. Lawyers are hard to find. If you don't think you need an attorney, they'll get one anyway.

B. Response refers to someone other than an attorney.

Example: If you can't pay for a social worker, the court will get you one free.

COMPREHENSION OF *MIRANDA* RIGHTS, TRUE OR FALSE

The CMR-TF consists of twelve true-or-false items in four sets of three items. Each set corresponds to one of the four *Miranda* warnings. The purpose of the measure is to assess a subject's understanding of each *Miranda* warning by their ability to identify whether or not a particular preconstructed sentence has the same meaning as the *Miranda* warning statement. It is administered individually to subjects. It consists of a set of instructions, examples to explain the task, and the presentation of the *Miranda* warning statements and their corresponding CMR-TF items. All presentations of warnings and items are both oral and in writing on cards which are handed to the subject.

Administration

Instructions to the subject are as follows: "Now I am going to show you the sentences we talked about earlier in the session." (The *Miranda* warnings had been presented to subjects in another experimental procedure earlier in the research session.) "After I read a sentence to you, I will read three more statements. Each statement means either the same thing or not the same thing as the first sentence. I want you to tell me whether each statement is the same or different from the sentence on the card."

These instructions are followed immediately by the examples:

Here are two examples so that you know what to do. [Put example A card on table.] This sentence says "I have volunteered to be in this study." Now look at this card. [Put example item A1 card on table and read.] "I have agreed to take this test and nobody forced me to do it." Now, does that card say the same thing or something different from the first sentence? [If subject says "same," remove card A1, leave card A, and proceed to second example. If subject says "different," explain why they are the same, and go on to second example.] Here is the next card. [Put example item A2 card on table beside example A.] "I have to take this test whether I want to or not." Is that the same as the first sentence [point to example A card] or something different? (If "same," discontinue test. If "different," proceed to CMR-TF items.)

To begin the CMR-TF items, a card bearing the first *Miranda* warning is placed before the subject. The examiner then proceeds through the three related CMR-TF statements in the manner shown in the examples. After the three item statements, the examiner proceeds to the second *Miranda* warning, and so on.

CMR-TF Items

The following are the *Miranda* warnings, their corresponding CMR-TF items, and the *correct* response for each item.

Miranda I: You do not have to make a statement and have the right to remain silent.

1. It is not right to tell lies.	Different, or false
2. You should not say anything until the police ask you questions.	Different, or false
3. You do not have to say anything about what you did.	Same, or true

Miranda II: Anything you say can and will be used against you in a court of law.

4. What you say might be used to prove you are guilty.	Same, or true
5. If you won't talk to the police, then that will be used against you in court.	Different, or false
6. If you tell the police anything it can be repeated in court.	Same, or true

Miranda III: You are entitled to consult with an attorney before interrogation and to have an attorney present at the time of the interrogation.

7. You can talk to your social worker before anything happens.	Different, or false
8. A lawyer is coming to see you after the police are done with you.	Different, or false
9. You can have a lawyer now if you ask for one.	Same, or true

Miranda IV: If you cannot afford an attorney, one will be appointed for you.

10. If you don't have the money for a lawyer the court will appoint a social worker to help you.	Different, or false
11. You can get legal help even if you are poor.	Same, or true
12. The court will give you a lawyer free if you don't have the money to pay for one.	Same, or true

Scoring

One point is received for each correct answer. Therefore, CMR-TF scores range from 0 to 12. One might employ subscores (range 0–3) corresponding to each of the four *Miranda* warnings, although the present research did not make use of subscores.

COMPREHENSION OF *MIRANDA* VOCABULARY

The Comprehension of *Miranda* Vocabulary (CMV) measure is an objective method for assessing an individual's understanding of six critical words which appear in standard *Miranda* warnings. The CMV employs a format which is similar to the Wechsler Vocabulary subtest, but with a standardized "inquiry" or questioning which is employed when an examinee's original response requires clarification. It was developed as a companion measure to the Comprehension of *Miranda* Rights (CMR) measure, which requires examinees to paraphrase each of the four *Miranda* warnings.

In the project's study of juveniles' competence to waive rights, the CMV has played a secondary and diagnostic role in relation to the CMR. For example, when an examinee produces an inadequate CMR paraphrase of the *Miranda* warning "You are entitled to consult an attorney before interrogation and to have an attorney present during interrogation," the examinee's responses on the CMV to the words "attorney," "interrogation," or "entitled" may reveal whether the examinee's confusion on the CMR was due to an inadequate understanding of these specific words.

It is conceivable, however, that the CMV could be applied in its own right as an index of ability to comprehend the *Miranda* warnings from which the CMV words were taken. CMV scores are correlated substantially with CMR scores (Pearson $r = .67$), and the scoring system for the CMV is more easily employed and has produced slightly higher interscorer reliability coefficients than has the CMR.

It is recommended that administration of the CMV be tape-recorded and later transcribed for scoring. Examiners should have on hand six cards on which are printed the six words from the CMV. Instructions to the examinee are as follows:

> I am going to give you some cards which have words on them. As I give you a card, I will read the word, then I will use it in a sentence, then read it again. Then I would like you to tell me in your own way what the word means.

The examiner then performs the procedure just described for the first word (consult) and asks, "What does 'consult' mean?" The sequence of words and the sentences to be used which contain the words appear later.

In certain cases, the examiner must ask inquiry questions after the examinee's original response. The following describes the original responses of examinees after which inquiry must be made by the examiner, and the specific inquiry which must occur. In addition to these rules, it is permissible for the examiner to inquire as needed when an examinee's original response is confusing because of double negatives, grammatical confusion, slang, or disorganization (e.g., "Can you explain that a little more?").

EXAMINEE'S ORIGINAL RESPONSE TO WORD AND SENTENCE	INQUIRY
I. Consult. I want to consult him.	
A. When response refers to talking, but without the idea of aid or advice (e.g., to discuss with someone).	How do you mean "discuss?"
B. On any response which would receive 1 point by scoring system (see scoring system).	Give me an example of consulting someone.
II. Attorney. The attorney left the building.	
A. When only one of the three scoring elements is mentioned (see scoring system.)	Is there anything else you can tell me about what an attorney is or does?

III. Interrogation. The interrogation lasted quite a while.

A. When idea of investigation is conveyed, but without mention of questioning or B. When other aspects of interrogation are mentioned, but not questioning.	Please tell me more about what interrogation is.

IV. Appoint. We will appoint her to be your social worker.

A. When idea of action to get person in a position is clear, but idea of how this occurs is either nonessential or inappropriate (see 1-point answers in scoring system).	Please tell me more about what appoint means.

V. Entitled. He is entitled to the money.

A. When the following specific answers are given without any addition: —he has it —he will get it —he can have it	Can you tell me more about that? or How do you mean _____ _____ _____?

VI. Right. You have the right to vote.

A. When the idea that one is allowed to vote is clear, but without the notion that the privilege to lay claim to the right is protected.	Can you tell me more about what right means? or How do you mean _____ _____ _____?

Scoring of the CMV is quite similar to the process involved in scoring the Wechsler Vocabulary, in that it employs 2-, 1-, and 0-point credits. The scoring system presented here provides criteria and examples.

I. Consult (I want to consult him.)

2 Points

Conveys idea that information or advice is provided or sought pursuant to a decision.

Examples: To ask for (give) advice about something. To make plans with someone. To help to decide. Talk to make plans. To talk over problems.

1 Point

Usually, recognition that discourse is involved, but without notion of aid, advice, or recognition of directed use of the discourse.

Examples: To discuss. To talk over. To talk confidentially. To talk to. To tell someone something. To ask a question. To help someone. To get information from someone (no improvement after inquiry).

0 Point

States only the objective. Also, inaccurate meaning.

Examples: To insult. To decide. To plan something. To discover or find out.

II. Attorney (The attorney left the building.)

Three elements are described here, with scoring criteria appearing below.

1. Someone who is empowered to act for (and in the interest of) another person in legal proceedings.

   Examples: The attorney is someone who's on your side. Someone who defends you. Who stands for your rights. He fights for you in court. Someone in your favor. Helps to get you out of trouble. Makes sure you get a fair deal.

2. Someone especially trained in law and legal processes.

   Examples: Somebody who knows everything about courts. He knows all about the law. He knows what your rights are. Someone who can interpret laws, knows what they mean.

3. An accurate synonym.

   Examples: Lawyer, public defender, counselor, legal counsel, legal consultant or advisor.

2 Points

Any response satisfying at least two of the elements listed above.

1 Point

A response including only one of the three elements above.

0 Point

A response including none of the above three elements.

Examples: An important person. A person who decides whether you are guilty or innocent. Someone who makes laws. A sort of policeman. A social worker.

III. Interrogation (The interrogation lasted quite a while.)
Formal Definition: to ask questions formally; to examine by questioning.

2 Points

Idea of being questioned.

Examples: Questioning someone. When police ask you questions. When they ask you about whether or not you did the crime. When they put the lights on you and ask you to confess.

1 Point

Idea of investigation without mention of questioning, or mention of other aspects which could be part of an interrogation.

Examples: an investigation of a crime. When they examine the evidence. When they tell you they think you did or didn't do the crime. When they brief (tell) you about what might happen to you if you did the crime.

0 Point

Other legal processes, or clearly incorrect responses.

Examples: A hearing. Court day. When you go to court. Your trial. Being put in detention. I don't know what it means.

IV. Appoint (We will appoint her to be your social worker.)
Formal Definition: to ordain, prescribe; to name or select for an office or position.

2 Points

The idea that a person is named, selected, assigned, told, or designated to do a job or fill a position.

Examples: To put someone on the case. To give someone the job. To get a person to do the job. To assign someone to the duty. To pick someone. To tell someone to do it. To name someone to do it.

1 Point

The idea of action to get a person into a position, but with notions which are nonessential (and often too specific) regarding idea of designation.

Examples: To recommend someone. To offer them money to do the job. To pass a law to put someone in a position. To examine someone to see if they can do the job. To elect someone to do it.

0 Point

Examples: To point to someone. To help someone do something.

V. Entitled (He is entitled to it.)
Formal Definition: given a claim or legal title to; qualified (to do something).

2 Points

Notion of being qualified or deserving to do or receive something.

Examples: Has a right to it. Deserves it. Should have (or get) it. Has it coming to him. It is owed to him. He is allowed to (do, get, have) it. No one is allowed to take it away from him. He owns it, it belongs to him. It is his.

1 Point

Idea of possession, receipt, or action without notion of qualification or deservingness.

Examples: He has it. He will get (do) it. He can have it.

0 Point

Examples: What something is called. The title of something. To be attached to something. To want to have (do) something.

VI. Right (You have the right to vote.)
Formal Definition: that to which a person has a just claim; a power, privilege, etc. that belongs to a person by law, nature, or tradition.

2 Points

An action or condition which is allowed to a person, as well as the notion that this privilege is protected, "inalienable," or not able to be denied arbitrarily by others.

Examples: It means you can do something no matter what. By law, if you qualify, you can do it if you want. You can legally do it even if someone else doesn't like it. You can do it because you were born here. You are entitled to it.

1 Point

The idea of being allowed to do something, without the notion of protection of one's privilege to lay claim to that allowance.

Examples: You can do it. You're allowed to do that. You can if you want to. You can do it without asking. It's your decision. It's your privilege.

0 Point

No recognition of allowance or privilege.

Examples: Your right hand. Left, right. Like you should vote, it's important to do that. Means something is the right thing to do.

Although examinee's response may include both his or her original response and a response following the examiner's inquiry, the total response is to receive only one score. It is important not to allow oneself to be biased by the quality of verbal or grammatical style in the response. Very unsophisticated verbalizations, lacking in grammatical or structural clarity, are still very likely to contain a correct sense of the meaning of a vocabulary word. Conversely, highly sophisticated and intellectualized responses sometimes can turn out to be "empty" regarding the essential meanings to be understood.

It will be important to rely only on the data offered in the transcript when assessing the degree of understanding of the examinee. The scorer should try to discover evidence in the response for the meaning of the word in question, but at the same time one must endeavor not to "read between the lines."

The following general procedure should be used in scoring CMV responses:

1. Read through the whole response before attempting to match it to scoring criteria.

2. Review all of the scoring categories for the word in question. This will not be necessary for the experienced scorer, but the less experienced scorer should quickly review the categories available.

3. Begin matching the response to scoring criteria and examples, starting with 2-point criteria. Try to match a given response to both the criterion statement and one of the examples provided before deciding on its score. However, the examples provided do not exhaust the range of possible responses and on occasion one will have to decide on a score on the basis of the criterion statement alone.

4. If the response does appear to satisfy 2-point criteria, proceed anyway to review the response in light of 1-point criteria. Likewise, if a response appears to meet 1-point criteria, proceed to review it in light of 0-point criteria and examples. This process has been found to be essential in improving interscorer reliability.

5. Record the final score arrived at for the response, and make the assignment of a summary score when all six vocabulary words have been scored. The summary score is the sum of the examinee's scores on all six words.

INTERSCORER RELIABILITY FOR CMR AND CMV

Training of research assistants to score the CMR and CMV involved from one to two months of individual and group instruction, meeting for two 2-hour sessions per week with practice scoring on other days. It required the scoring of about 60–80 protocols, with group discussion of discrepancies in scoring between trainees and the principal investigator, in order to arrive at the degrees of scorer agreement presented below.

The correlations to be reported were between pairs of raters at two times in the course of the study. The first set of correlations is between three pairs of scorers who were three research assistants each of whom independently scored all of the first 76 protocols obtained in the study in Chapter 4. The second set of correlations is between two of these scorers, who independently scored the last 90 protocols in the Chapter 4 study. By this scoring time, they had accumulated about 8 months of scoring experience with about 300 protocols. Finally, a new trainee independently scored the same 90 protocols and was compared to one of the more experienced assistants. Correlations for all of these pairs of scorers appear in Tables B-1 and B-2.

Finally, we examined the percentage of scoring events in which pairs of scorers were in perfect agreement on the first 76 protocols. The total number of scoring events was 912, which is 76 protocols multiplied by four *Miranda* responses per protocol, and that figure multiplied by the three pairs of scores for each *Miranda* response. Of these 912 scoring events on the CMR, 90.12% involved agreement (both scorers gave a 2, both gave a 1, or both gave a 0). In only 0.32% of the cases did one scorer

Table B-1. CMR Reliability

	CMR items				
Scorer pairs	I	II	III	IV	Total score
On first 76 protocols					
A/B	.95	.90	.82	.86	.92
B/C	.93	.92	.86	.79	.95
A/C	.97	.92	.91	.75	.94
On last 90 protocols (B/C)	1.00	.91	.94	.89	.96
Between experienced and inexperienced scorers (B/D)	.89	.85	.90	.87	.89

Table B-2. CMV Reliability

	CMV items						
Scorer pairs	I	II	III	IV	V	VI	Total score
On first 76 protocols							
A/B	.96	.87	.90	.89	.98	.94	.98
B/C	.91	.91	.95	.73	.99	.93	.97
A/C	.94	.96	.95	.88	.99	.97	.97
On last 90 protocols (B/C)	.92	.91	.94	.85	.98	.94	.98
Between experienced and inexperienced scorers (B/D)	.88	.94	.90	.88	1.00	1.00	.98

give 2 and other 0. The corresponding percentage of events with perfect agreement on the CMV was 95.25%, with 0.42% of the cases involving 2 and 0 scores from different scorers on the same protocol.

Overall, the results indicate a very high degree of scorer reliability for both of the *Miranda* measures. This is achieved, however, only after a considerable period of training and rigid adherence to the criteria in the scoring manuals.

Appendix C

Data Supplementing Chapter 4

Table C-1. Three-Month Detention Cohort (Percentages)

Variable	Tested (N=105)	Felony prohibited (N=181)	Brief stay prohibited (N=191)	3-month detention population (N=477)	11-month study sample (N=431)
Age					
10–13	11.5	11.4	14.5	12.7	13.0
14	23.8	25.8	21.5	23.6	25.8
15	31.4	30.2	28.8	29.9	28.3
16	33.3	32.4	35.1	33.7	26.9
Sex					
Male	49.5	80.2	59.7	65.3	59.4
Female	50.5	19.8	40.3	34.7	40.6
Race					
White	76.2	65.4	60.2	65.7	73.3
Black	23.8	34.6	39.8	34.3	26.7
SES					
Middle (upper)	16.2	15.5	6.8	12.2	15.8
Middle	36.9	38.6	31.4	35.2	32.7
Middle (lower)	21.0	25.4	31.9	26.8	23.0
Low	5.0	5.5	13.6	8.7	7.2
Unclassified	21.0	15.0	16.2	17.0	21.3
No. prior felonies					
0	63.8	52.2	76.4	64.4	67.3
1–2	26.6	27.4	17.1	23.2	25.3
3+	9.5	20.6	6.3	12.3	7.4
No. prior detentions					
0	24.8	36.8	56.0	41.8	30.9
1–2	27.6	34.6	26.7	30.0	38.3
3+	47.6	28.6	17.2	28.2	30.5
No. prior referrals					
0	16.2	14.8	36.6	23.8	18.6
1–2	17.1	26.3	29.3	25.5	32.2
3+	66.6	58.8	34.1	50.7	49.2

TABLE C-2. CORRELATIONS BETWEEN CMR/CMV ITEMS AND TOTAL SCORES

CMR items	I	II	III	IV
II	.31			
III	.24	.22		
IV	.32	.26	.12	
CMR total	.65	.73	.67	.55

CMV items	I	II	III	IV	V	VI
II	.26					
III	.37	.27				
IV	.23	.14	.36			
V	.47	.18	.28	.19		
VI	.26	.17	.30	.25	.24	
CMV total	.72	.51	.66	.54	.71	.55

TABLE C-3. MULTIPLE REGRESSION ANALYSIS FOR CMR SCORES

Variable	Multiple *R*	Cumulative % of variance	% of variance change
IQ	.498	.248	.248
Age	.541	.292	.044
Race	.558	.311	.018
SES (middle)	.563	.317	.006
Prior misdemeanors	.566	.321	.003
(Remaining variables)	(.575)	(.330)	(.008)

TABLE C-4. MULTIPLE REGRESSION ANALYSIS FOR CMV SCORES

Variable	Multiple *R*	Cumulative % of variance	% of variance change
IQ	.613	.376	.376
Age	.714	.510	.134
Race	.723	.523	.013
Sex	.726	.527	.003
SES	.728	.530	.002
(Remaining variables)	(.733)	(.537)	(.007)

Appendix D

Function of Rights in Interrogation

INTRODUCTION

The FRI was developed as a method to assess juveniles' understanding regarding the significance of *Miranda* rights in the context of interrogation. Other measures in this project would indicate whether a juvenile understands that he or she has "a right to talk to a lawyer before and during questioning by police." But an understanding of the significance of this right requires at least an understanding of the role of the lawyer as an advocate, and a sense of the types of question which police might ask. The FRI is designed to assess this functional type of understanding, as differentiated from an understanding of single words and of *Miranda* phrases.

General Criteria for Understanding the FRI

A panel of lawyers and psychologists arrived at three areas of understanding which were viewed as important regarding the function and significance of rights in interrogation. These included an understanding of the nature of police interrogation, the function and significance of legal counsel, and the function of the right to silence. These three content areas have been described in detail in Chapters 3 and 6. The structured interview format of the FRI assesses each of these three areas of understanding by a different set of five questions. A scoring system is provided for designating the quality of each response. In addition to the total score, three subscores are derived which indicate the adequacy of responding in each of the three FRI areas of understanding. These subscores are referred to as NI (nature of interrogation), RC (right to counsel), and RS (right to silence).

Structure of the FRI

The FRI was first conceptualized as a sentence completion task. It was converted to a "structured interview" format when it was found that the requirement of written responses restricted its usefulness with a delinquent population and that clarification of responses often would be necessary in order to ensure that the youth had demonstrated his/her level of understanding. The interview questions occur in the context of visual stimuli (to enhance contextual set and subsequent responding). The stimuli are four standard drawings depicting relevant police, legal, and court procedures. Each is accompanied by a brief verbal "story" provided by the examiner in order to establish a contextual set for responding. Stimulus cards employed with various items are as follows:

Card A: "Joe's Interrogation," a scene of a boy sitting at a table across from two police officers. Items NI-1 through NI-5, all related to understanding of the nature of interrogation, are asked in reference to this scene.

Card B: "Tim and His Lawyer," depicting a boy and a lawyer in consultation in a room. Questions are items RC-1 through RC-4, all related to the understanding of the function and significance of the right to counsel.

Card C: "Greg's Interrogation," depicting a boy entering an interrogation room accompanied by two police officers. The questions are items RS-1 through RS-3, regarding the function and significance of the right to silence.

Card D: "Greg's Court Hearing," depicting a courtroom hearing with judge, police officers, parents, the youth's lawyer, and the youth. Items RS-4 and RS-5 regarding the function of the right to silence and RC-5 regarding the function of the right to counsel, are asked in this context.

ADMINISTRATION PROCEDURE

The FRI procedure is presented as a structured interview with visual stimuli to enhance response. A visual stimulus is presented, followed by a paragraph to produce a context in which the subject is to respond. This is then followed by a series of questions for each stimulus.

After each question, the interviewer must often employ "clarification questions," depending on the ambiguity of the subject's original response. The procedure below describes when clarification is necessary, and how it is to be sought. In most instances it is necessary for the interviewer to have a working knowledge of the scoring criteria in order to follow the instructions for seeking clarification. Following each question are examples of types of responses which require clarification. Each of these response types is followed immediately by the allowable clarification questions one can ask the subject. In addition, any time a subject seems reluctant (due to lack of confidence) or overly vague, encouragement and slight rewording of the original question is allowable.

General Instruction

"I am going to show you several pictures of people doing things. After I tell you something about a picture, I will be asking you questions about what you think the people in the picture could be doing and thinking and feeling. With these questions, it's best if you just give me a short answer."

I. Show Card A: Joe's Interrogation

Give subject the card and say: "This is a picture about a boy named Joe. The policemen in the picture have brought Joe into detention. There has been a crime. The policemen want to talk to Joe. Remember that Joe is in detention and the policemen want to talk to him."

NI-1 "What is it that the policemen will want Joe to do?"
- a. *Talk Only* (talk, answer questions, etc., without indication of topic), "About what?"
- b. *No Talk* (when there is no mention of questions or talking), "What important thing might they ask Joe to do?"

NI-2 "Finish this sentence. The police think that Joe ______."

NI-3 "What is the most important thing the police might want Joe to tell them?"
- a. *Not Incriminating* (when nothing is said about potentially incriminating information), "What other important thing?"
- b. *The Truth,* "About what?"

NI-4 "How are the policemen probably feeling?"
- a. *For All Responses,* "Why are they feeling that way?"

NI-5 "How is Joe probably feeling?"
  a. *For All Responses,* "Why is he feeling that way?"
  b. *No Affect* (if response does not refer to affect), "How is he feeling about what is happening now?"

II. Show Card B: Tim's Lawyer

"This is Tim. He is in detention, too, because the police think he broke into a house. The police have not questioned him yet. Here Tim is meeting with his lawyer. The lawyer is asking Tim some things before Tim goes to be talked to by the police. Tell me what you think might really happen here."

RC-1 "What is the main job of the lawyer?"
  a. *Talk, No Benefit* (when asking questions and discovering information are mentioned, but with no indication whether this is to provide benefit to Tim), "Why does the lawyer do that?", "Can you tell me more?"
  b. *Benefit Innocent* (when response suggests that lawyer helps only the innocent), "And what is his job if Tim is not innocent?"

RC-2 "While he is with his lawyer, what is Tim supposed to do?"
  a. *Talk Only* (when only talking is mentioned), "Can you tell me more?", "Talk about what?"
  b. *Compliance Only* (when mere compliance mentioned), "Can you tell me more about what he's supposed to do?"

RC-3 "What is the main thing Tim's lawyer will be talking to Tim about?"

RC-4 "Imagine that Tim's lawyer is saying, "I want you to tell me exactly what you did and tell me the truth about what happened." Then Tim tells him that he did the crime. Why would Tim's lawyer want to know that?"
  a. *Information Only* (mentions getting information, but not assistance), "Why would he want to know that?"
  b. *No Assistance* (when not clear that lawyer's actions are to assist Tim), "Why would he want to do that?"

III. Show Card C: Greg's Interrogation

"This is Greg. The police have taken him to detention because they want to talk to him. Greg stole some money from a store, but the police are not sure he did it because nobody saw Greg do it. They are getting ready to ask him questions. Greg knows he doesn't have to talk if he doesn't want to, and he is trying to decide whether or not to talk."

RS-1 "Finish this sentence. If Greg decides to tell the police about what he did, then the things he says ______."

a. *Trouble Only* (can cause him trouble, can be held against him, with no reference to court), "Can you tell me more?", "In what way?"

RS-2 "If Greg decides not to talk, what is the most important thing the police are supposed to do?"

a. *Detained Only* (mention only of detainment), "What other important thing?"

RS-3 "Finish this sentence. If the police tell Greg he has to talk even if he has said he doesn't want to, then ______."

a. *Won't Talk* (he won't/shouldn't/won't want to talk—negative decision, no further elaboration), "Why won't/shouldn't he talk?"

b. *Will Talk* (he will/should/might or might not talk—positive or ambivalent decision, no mention of the conflict with rights, no statement of why he will talk), "Can you tell me more?"; (for ambivalent responses), "What should Greg do, and why should he do it?"

c. *Will Subvert* (will tell a lie, try to kill himself—attempts to subvert police demands, other than asserting rights), "Can you tell me more about that?"

d. *Detained* (lock him up, with no elaboration), "Why?"

IV. Show Card D: Greg's Court Hearing

"This is Greg three weeks later. He is at his court hearing. The judge is here, and the policemen who arrested and questioned Greg are here. Greg's lawyer and his parents are sitting near him."

RC-5 "If Greg's lawyer did just what he is supposed to do here in court, how would Greg be feeling?"

a. *Negative Affect or Outcome* (no mention of lawyer's role), "How does Greg feel about what the *lawyer* is doing?"

b. *All Responses*, "Why would he feel that way?"

RS-4 "What is supposed to happen when the judge is told that Greg would not talk to the police?"

a. *Judge Asks* (responses in which judge inquires), "What if Greg still will say nothing?"

RS-5 "Greg did not tell the police anything about what he did. Here in court, if he were told to talk about what he did that was wrong, will he have to talk about it?"
a. *All Responses,* "Why?"

SCORING PROCEDURES

For each of the FRI statements, each subject is to receive 2-, 1-, or 0-point credit for his or her response. Criteria for scoring the responses (including examples) are presented below. The examples provided do not exhaust the possible responses within a scoring category, but are presented to give a feel for the more formal criteria to which the scorer must ultimately refer.

Generally, 2-point responses meet the criteria for understanding the function or significance of the element in question. Vague or partial responses which cannot be clearly viewed as correct or incorrect are given 1 point. Those responses which demonstrate lack of understanding of the function or significance of the element in question receive 0-point credit.

In many cases, the scorer will find that a subject originally gave an inferior response to the question, but provided a more satisfactory response after being asked a "clarification question" by the examiner. If a subject's original response meets 1-point criteria, but his or her response to the examiner's clarification question would receive a 2-point credit, the subject is given 2 points for the total response.

In other instances, an original 1-point response may be clarified by a subject in a manner which indicated that the subject does not understand the essential function or significance of a given element (0-point response). In such cases, 0 is the correct score assignment for the total response. However, when a subject's first response receives a 2-point credit, it is very rare that the addition of more information would reduce the response to 0-point credit, even when the additional information weakens the adequacy of the original response.

Scoring Criteria

•NI-1 "What is it that the police will want Joe to do?"

2 Points: Clear indication that the police desire a confession, or to acquire information about Joe's actions at time of crime.

Examples: Tell them where he was at time of the crime. To tell why he did it. To tell who he was with when he stole the stuff. Confess. Say he did something. Nark on people. Tell where he was at a certain time. Tell them what happened.

1 Point: Statement that police want suspect to talk, but without clear mention of the nature of the information sought.

Examples: Talk about something. Tell them something. Talk, but he won't answer some questions. Give some information. Make a statement. Tell the truth.

0 Point: Reserved for responses which include no mention of talking, confession, or providing information specific to the question of one's alleged criminal/delinquent involvement.

Examples: Act with good manners. Stay in detention for a while. Sign some papers so they will know who Joe is. Behave himself. Never get in trouble again. Listen.

•NI-2 "Finish this sentence. The policemen think that Joe ______."

2 Points: Responses may be of three types, signifying adversary conditions (all types are simply scored 2, and are not scored or designated A, B, or C).

A. Police see Joe as probably guilty of alleged criminal act, or probably involved in such a way that he has knowledge of alleged act.

Examples: Committed a crime. Had something to do with a crime. Did a bad thing. Stole a TV from a house. Is a criminal. Is guilty. Is part of a gang

B. Police see Joe as noncooperative, as withholding information, or as not trustworthy.

Examples: Is telling a lie. Is holding back information. Can't be trusted.

C. Police perception of Joe as untrustworthy or involved in criminal act is implied, but not clearly stated.

Examples: Belongs in detention. Did something. Got too involved in something.

1 Point: Police see youth as probably guilty, but not fully responsible for his actions (thus reducing adversary conditions).

Examples: Is crazy. Is sick. Has just fallen in with bad company. Needs a psychiatrist.

0 Point: Police are sympathetic with suspect, or do not see him as guilty.

Examples: Is not really bad. Is okay. Is not guilty. Needs their help and they can help him.

If subject obtained 2-point credit on NI-1, skip this item and give automatic 2-point credit for NI-3.

•NI-3 "What is the most important thing the police might want Joe to tell them?"

2 Points: About Joe's involvement in or knowledge of a crime.

Examples: Whether he did it or not. About what he was doing before they picked him up. Whether he knows who did the crime. Whether there were friends involved with him.

1 Point: The truth.

0 Point: Moralistic or relatively nonincriminating information.

Examples: Why he's so bad. Where he lives. What his name is. Whether or not he wants to go home.

•NI-4 "How are the police probably feeling?"

2 Points: Affect/reasoning of the subject's response reflects police intentions to deal with the youth as adversary.

A. Angry.

Examples: Angry cause Joe won't talk. Mad. Aggravated. Upset cause they have to go through all this.

B. Good, self-satisfied.

Examples: Happy. Good. Proud. Happy cause they caught somebody doing wrong. Like they are really something. Superior.

C. Justified.

Examples: That he did it. That he's guilty. That he ought to be put in jail.

D. Frustrated.

Examples: That he's not cooperating. That he is lying. That he won't tell the truth. Like they want to smack him.

1 Point: Not applicable.

0 Point: Emotions which are inconsistent with adversary quality of interrogation, or don't know, or mixed responses.

Examples: I don't have any idea. Embarrassed. Sorry for him. Sad about the boy. Sorry. Joe needs help very bad. Real bad about it, cause they didn't want to upset him. Mad, because they don't want to have to do this to Joe. If he did it, they feel mad at him, but if they framed him, they feel bad and are going to help him out.

•NI-5 "How is Joe probably feeling?"

2 Points: Negative emotions appropriate for the accused in an adversary situation.

Examples: very mad. Bad. Sad. Like a criminal. Low down. Scared. Miserable. Dumb. Like a chump. Like he shouldn't have done what he did. That his parents are going to be upset. Sorry.

1 Point: Not applicable.

0 Point: Feelings not reflecting the adversary process.

Examples: Pleased. Good. All right. Like everything is okay.

•RC-1 "What is the main job of the lawyer?"

2 Points: Any response indicating clearly that the lawyer is to assist or work in the interests of the client.

Examples: Help Tim. Protect Tim's rights. Defend Tim. Help Tim get out. Get Tim off the hook. To get everyone to believe Tim. To help Tim understand what is going on and to help him through it. To help him get out of detention. Give him some clues that can help Tim get out of trouble.

1 Point: Responses referring to some portion of the process by which the lawyer works on behalf of a client, but the idea of helpfulness or assistance is not clearly conveyed (response could also apply to interrogator).

Examples: Find out as much as he can. Find out what happened. Find out if Tim did it. Talk to Tim. Get Tim to trust him. Find out the truth from Tim.

0 Point: Responses placing the lawyer in a role contrary to an advocate for the client (response implies lawyer as adversary.)

Example: Decide whether or not Tim should be found guilty. Decide whether Tim should be sent home or to jail. Get Tim to confess. To see what the judge should do to Tim. He protects him if he's innocent.

•RC-2 "While he is with his lawyer, what is Tim supposed to do?"

2 Points: Responses clearly indicating a helping and trustful relationship. Responses which imply mere compliance are not given 2 points, but are scored 1 or 0 (unless elaboration by subject places the response in the 2-point category).

Examples: To help the lawyer. To tell the lawyer the truth about everything. Trust him and do what the lawyer thinks is best. Do what he says because he's on Tim's side. Tell him what he did and why. Cooperate with him. Answer his questions.

1 Point: Responses may be of two types.

A. Responses stating mere passive compliance.

Examples: Do what the lawyer says. Listen to instructions. Listen to what the lawyer's saying.

B. References simply to verbalization.

Examples: Talk to him. Discuss things. Ask him questions about what's happening.

0 Point: Responses indicating the need for silence, caution, mistrust, or strong inhibition of one's own behavior.

Examples: Speak only when spoken to. Don't run away. Keep quiet about what he did. Don't confess to anything. Keep his mouth shut. Plead the fifth. Behave himself.

•RC-3 "What is the main thing Tim's lawyer will be talking to Tim about?"

2 Points: Two types of responses.

A. Providing information or advice regarding future events in interrogation or other court-related processes.

Examples: What is going to happen. What to say. What he can do to help him. What to do, when to do it, and how.

B. Emphasis on obtaining Tim's view of the alleged offenses.

Examples: If he really did it or not. How the crime happened. What it was that he did. Why he did it.

1 Point: Moralistic questioning, or less important but still relevant topics.

Examples: Why what he did was wrong. When the hearing date will be. How long he'll be in detention.

0 Point: Accusatory statement by lawyer; also, information or discussion that is not directly related to alleged offense or to police or court procedures.

Examples: He shouldn't have done it and he will pay for it. That he should try to do better in school. That he's a failure. About his problems at home (or other counseling topics).

•RC-4 "Imagine that Tim's lawyer is saying 'I want you to tell me exactly what you did and tell me the truth about what happened.' Then Tim tells him that he did the crime. Why would the lawyer want to know that?"

2 Points: Lawyer is seeking information to assist him in Tim's defense.

Examples: So he can help Tim out better. So he can build a good case. So he can help Tim beat the rap. To get Tim's side of the story and help him better.

1 Point: To get truthful information, but no mention of assistance nor of judgment.

Examples: To get the facts. To find out if Tim did it. To get all the information he can.

0 Point: To make judgments which are contrary to the role of an advocate, or to assist the court in learning of Tim's guilt.

Examples: To tell the judge about it. To decide whether Tim should go to a jail or someplace. To decide whether Tim should be found guilty. So he can get him to give himself up.

•RS-1 "Finish this sentence. If Greg decides to tell the police about what he did, then the things that Greg says ______."

2 Points: A relationship is made between what is said and later court hearing or record.

Examples: Can be used against him in court. Will get him into trouble at court time. Can turn against him later in court. Will be told to the judge later on. Will go into his record. Will get him into detention and they will set a court date.

1 Point: Idea that what he says can cause him trouble, but without specification of how or when.

Examples: Will be held against him. Can get him into trouble. Will get him into detention.

0 Point: Responses irrelevant to the essential issues of later use of confession; also, failure to recognize importance of confession.

Examples: Will be true. Won't matter anyway. He will tell the policemen.

•RS-2 "If Greg decides not to talk, what is the most important thing the police are supposed to do?"

2 Points: Any action that is not coercive, and represents a legally-sanctioned and probable response by police involving no further questioning.

Examples: Do nothing. Leave him be. Don't question him. Get him a lawyer. Phone his mother. Let him go.

1 Point: Responses which are not clearly coercive, but which emphasize detainment.

Examples: Hold him until his court hearing. Take him to detention.

0 Point: Further questioning; also, don't know.

Examples: Remind him of his rights. Try to make him talk without forcing him. Tell him the trouble he can get into for hiding the truth. Ask him why he won't talk.

•RS-3 "If Greg says he doesn't want to talk, but the police tell him he *has* to talk, what should happen then?"

2 Points: Responses may be of two types.

A. Recognition of the illegality of the police action, or the falseness of their claim. Decision to talk or not talk is not relevant to scoring 2 points.

Examples: They will be lying cause he don't have to. They would be going against his rights. It still doesn't mean he has to talk. Greg can tell them he doesn't have to talk. They are wrong. He'll know that he doesn't have to really. He'll talk even though he knows he doesn't have to. They shouldn't be saying that. They will have to let him go. Stop asking him questions and put him back in detention. Nothing should happen, but they will probably beat him up. He doesn't have to talk until he gets to court.

B. Seeking intervention by anyone who could potentially be an advocate.

Examples: Greg should ask to talk to his lawyer. He'll ask to see his social worker first. He will tell them he wants to talk to his parents now.

1 Point: Responses primarily refer to Greg's decision, without offering either a reason for the decision, or recognition of illegality of police action.

A. Responses indicating that the youth will not or should not talk, but without recognition of impropriety of the police statement.

Examples: Greg still won't talk. He shouldn't if he's smart.

B. Responses indicating simply that Greg will talk, or that he may or may not talk (ambivalent responses).

Examples: Greg will tell them the truth. He would talk and get himself messed up. He will get scared and talk. He might talk. He will rebel or he might tell everything. He'll have to talk.

C. Responses which could represent attempts to subvert police demands.

Examples: Then Greg will probably tell the police a lie. He will make up something. He would tell them something but not much. He would go in the bathroom and eat soap.

D. Lock him up (without further explanation).

0 Point: Responses may be of two types.

A. Responses in which youth does or does not decide to talk solely on the basis of the importance of avoiding future negative consequences, without any sign of recognition of the inappropriateness of the police demand.

Examples: Greg will talk because he doesn't want to get beat. He still won't talk because it would get his friends in trouble. He'll talk so he can get out of going to detention.

B. Other responses showing no recognition of impropriety of the police demands.

Examples: Greg will wish he had never stole the money. Greg will be sad. The police will start asking him questions.

•RC-5 "If Greg's lawyer did just what he is supposed to do here in court, how would Greg be feeling?"

2 Points: Affect or attitude reflecting knowledge of lawyer's intended role as advocate; generally positive affect or "mixed" responses.

Examples: Good, because he's going to get out. Relieved. Good. Better. Like there is some hope. Like things are okay. Like the lawyer is doing the best he can. Satisfied. Like he got a fair deal. Good because he's trying to help, bad because some things he's saying could hurt. Happy if the lawyer says good things, but bad cause some things might not be right.

1 Point: Bad or negative outcome, without reference to the lawyer's role.

Examples: Probably feeling bad, because they might not let him go. Worried, the judge might go hard on him. Guess he's feeling bad, with all those people around him asking questions.

0 Point: Generally negative affect.

Examples: Mad. Like a criminal. Scared. Miserable. Like there is no hope. Guilty. Sad because some of what lawyer said was bad. Upset cause the lawyer told what he had done.

•RS-4 "If the judge finds out that Greg wouldn't talk to the police, then what should happen?"

2 Points: Any response that does not constitute a penalty for assuming one's right to silence, nor suggests prejudice against youth because of it.

Examples: Nothing bad will happen. Go on with the hearing. The judge will just listen to what everybody else has to say. Greg can always talk to his lawyer. The judge will have to let him go.

1 Point: Inquiry regarding silence itself.

Examples: Ask Greg why he wouldn't talk. The judge might ask Greg if he still wishes to say nothing.

0 Point: Any response indicating prejudice regarding motive for maintaining silence, increased penalty, reflection on probable guilt, or asking youth to give information about the alleged offense.

Examples: Make punishment worse. Judge will say if he wasn't guilty he should have nothing to hide. Think he's guilty. Think that something is wrong. Make him talk now. Judge will ask Greg what did happen. Judge will send him back to detention. Judge will send him somewhere.

•RS-5 "Greg did not tell the police anything about what he did. Here in court, if he is asked to talk about what he did that was wrong, will he have to talk?"

2 Points: No.

1 Point: Yes, if his lawyer says it's best to.

0 Point: Yes. I don't know. Only if the judge tells him to.

Appendix E
Waiver Expectancy Interview

INSTRUCTIONS TO SUBJECT

What I'll be doing is reading you some very short stories one at a time. Each time the story will be about a guy/girl who gets in some kind of trouble and gets picked up by the police. Also, in each one the police want to ask the guy/girl some questions about what they think the guy/girl did. So the guy/girl in the story is going to have to make some decisions, like what to say or not say to the police and things of that sort.

At the end of a story, I'll be asking you about what you think the guy/girl had better do. You are sort of giving them advice. Then we'll talk about why they had better decide to do that. Now, there aren't any right or wrong answers to these questions, and so there are no scores. It's all a matter of opinion, and everybody has their own opinions.

Do you have any questions about this? O.K. let me read the first story; listen carefully, and then if you want me to repeat any of it, I will.

SITUATION A

Story. Joe is 15 years old. One day he broke into a house when no one was home and took some money. Somehow the police figured out that *it might have been* Joe who broke into the house. So a day later the police got Joe at school and took him to the juvenile detention center to ask him some questions about whether or not he did the crime. When they got to the detention center, they took Joe into a room where a detention officer and Joe's parents were waiting. The detention officer explained to Joe that he has a right to remain silent and does not have to say anything if he does not want to.

Now Joe is being asked what he is going to do. They are sitting in the room, and the police and Joe's parents are waiting for him to decide.

Questions. (Questions to subjects are in Roman type. Notes to the interviewer are in Italic type.)

1. There are several things that a person could do in this situation. What are Joe's choices? What are all the things he could do? (*Not what he would do.*) *Question until subject can think of no more options.*

2. Okay, those are the things Joe could do (*summarize them for subject*). What would you tell Joe to do? What would you suggest for him to do? *If subject says talk to police:* What do you think he should say?

3. What do you think will happen if he (*restate option chosen by subject in Question* 2)?

4. *Inquire about why the subject did not choose* two of the options below in *Question 2 above.*

a. Talk and admit to the offense.
b. Talk and deny involvement in the offense.
c. Tell the police he refuses to talk.

5. *For both options, ask:* What would happen if he (*insert one of the two nonchoices here, then ask question again for other nonchoice*)

6. So thinking about all those things we have talked about so far, would you still tell Joe to (*restate choice from Question* 2)?

7. *If lawyer not mentioned by subject to this point:* When a person is arrested by the police, the person is told that he can talk to a lawyer right now if he wants. Would you tell Joe to get a lawyer or not to get a lawyer?

8. Why would you tell him to do that?

9. Let's go to the story for a minute and change it a bit. You remember that Joe stole some money from a house, and the police picked him up because they think he might have done it. Let's say that on their way to the detention center, Joe hears one policeman say to the other that he already has some proof that Joe broke into the house. Would you tell Joe to answer the policemen's questions or to keep silent and not answer their questions?

10. Why would you tell him to do that?

Situation B

Story. Now here is another story. Frank is 14 years old. One night he stole a neighbor's car, hotwired it, and started off toward his part of town. When he was part-way there he ran out of gas, so he got out of the car and stood there thumbing a ride—hitch-hiking. Soon the police came by and saw him standing a little ways from the car. They took Frank to the detention center to ask him about the car and what he was doing there.

Before the policemen questioned him, a detention officer explained to Frank that he could remain silent if he wanted to. Also, he could get a lawyer to be with him right now if he wanted. And if he does not have enough money for a lawyer, they will get him a lawyer free if he wants, a lawyer that is hired by the court to be his lawyer.

Now Frank is wondering whether or not to talk and whether or not he ought to ask the officer to give him a lawyer right now. The policemen are waiting for him to decide.

Questions. (Questions to subjects are in Roman type. Notes to the interviewer are in Italic type.)

1. What would you tell Frank to do? What would you suggest for him to do? *If subject says "talk to police"*: What do you think he should say?

2. What do you think will happen if he (*restate option chosen by subject in Question 1*)?

3. *Inquire about why the subject did not choose two of the options below in question 1 above.*

a. *Talk and admit to offense.*
b. *Talk and deny involvement.*
c. *Refuse to talk, with or without mention of lawyer.*

4. *For both options, ask:* What would happen if he (*insert one of the two nonchoices here, then ask question again for other nonchoice*)?

5. So thinking about all those things we've talked about here, would you still tell Frank to (*restate choice from Question 1*)?

Skip 6–8 if choice in Question 1 was to get a lawyer.

6. Would you tell Frank to get a lawyer to be there when he talks to the police, or not to get a lawyer now?

7. If Frank did ask for a lawyer, what do you think would happen when the lawyer got there?

8. Are there any other reasons why Frank should/shouldn't (*depending on above choice*) get a lawyer now?

9. If Frank were to try to get a lawyer to be with him now, would it make any difference if he got one that his parents paid for or if he got one free, one appointed by the court?

10. *If answer to 9 is yes:* What difference would there be? *If answer to 9 is no:* Does that mean that they would both do a good job, or both would not help much? Why?

11. Now I want you to imagine that Frank really did not steal that car. He was hitch-hiking home, the car was just sitting by the road when he happened to walk by, and the police saw him just as he walked by it. Would you suggest to Frank that he ask for a lawyer to be there when the police ask him questions, or not to ask for a lawyer?

12. Why would you suggest that?

Situation C

Story. The police think that Charles might be the person who shot a storekeeper during a robbery the night before. Charles is 15, has been in trouble with the police before, and did do the robbery and shooting. The police pick him up and take him to a police station to ask him questions. There he is told that he can remain silent if he wants, and that he can have a lawyer free to be there if he wants one.

Questions. (Questions to subjects are in Roman type. Notes to the interviewer are in Italic type.)

1. What would you tell Charles to do in this case? What would you suggest for him to do? *If subject says "talk to police"*: What do you think he should say?

2. (A) What do you think will happen if he (*choice from question 1*)? (B) What do you think the police would do if he (*choice from question 1*)? (C) Later when Charles is in court, what do you think the judge would do if he (*choice from question 1*)?

3. *Inquire about any two options below that subject did not choose in response to question 1 above.*

a. Talk and admit to offense.

b. Talk and deny involvement.
c. Refuse to talk, with or without mention of lawyer.

4. *For both nonchoice options, ask Questions* (a), (b), and (c) *from question 2, first inserting one of the nonchoices for all three questions, then inserting the other nonchoice option for all three.*

5. So thinking about all those things, would you still tell Charles to (*restate choice from question 1*)?

Skip 6–7 if choice in question 1 was to get a lawyer.

6. Do you think that in this case you would tell Charles to get a lawyer right now, or would you tell him not to?

7. Why would you tell him that?

8. Imagine that Charles really did *not* do the shooting or robbery. Would you still suggest to Charles to (restate choice *from question 1*)?

9. Why would you suggest that?

Inquiry about Research Relationship

Subject Instructions. Okay, that is all of those types of questions. Before we are finished, though, I'd like to ask you just a few questions about this thing we just did together. You remember I said I would not be telling any of your answers to the court, and that is the truth—I won't be. But I sometimes wonder if, when guys or girls answer these questions for me, they might not be sure about who I am or what I'm doing.

Questions. (Questions to subjects are in Roman type. Notes to the interviewer are in Italic type.)

1. Do you remember who it is I work for? *If yes:* Who? *If no, explain that you are from St. Louis University and working on research there, and that you have no connection with the Court.*

2. I wonder, do you think that most guys or girls would believe me when I tell them that, or might they think I am working for the court?

3. While you were answering these questions, did it ever cross your mind that I might be working for the court or might tell your answers to the court? *If no, end interview. If yes, proceed.*

4. Did it just cross your mind, or did you think about it often—think it might really be true? *If just crossed subject's mind, end interview. If often or really might be true, proceed.*

5. Do you think your answers might possibly have been different if you had been really sure I was from St. Louis University and was going to say absolutely nothing to anyone in the court?

End interview with thanks and answering reasonable questions about purpose of the study.

TABLE E-1. DEFINITIONS OF CONSEQUENCE CONTENT CATEGORIES

1. *Anger produced/avoided*
   Physical, hostile retaliation or angry response from others (or mention of absence of same).

   Examples: They'll get angry. They'll beat him up. He won't get punished. Judge will be mad.

2. *Questioning pursued/curtailed*
   Continued verbal pressure to provide information (or mention of absence of same).

   Examples: Ask more questions. Force him to talk. Put him through more. Won't get hasseled. They'd get it out of him.

3. *Freedom/temporary detainment*
   Placement in jail or detention for "holding," versus immediate release from physical custody.

   Examples: Let him go. Can't do anything. Send him home. Taken into custody. He'll be out for awhile. He'll be off the hook. Put in detention. Hold him till trial. Lock him up.

4. *Assumption of innocence/guilt*
   Assumption by others that the suspect is or is not guilty of the alleged crime.

   Examples: Everybody knows he did it. They'll believe him. They'll think he's telling truth. They'll be suspicious. They'll think he's lying. They'll think he must be guilty.

5. *Leniency/harshness*
   Responses which focus generally on "easier" or "harder" outcomes, but where the nature of the outcome (e.g., detention, disposition) is not mentioned.

   Examples: Go easier on him. Less trouble for him. Shorter sentence. Go harder on him. Give him more time. Longer sentence. More time to do.

6. *Counsel provided/withheld*
   Police or others present will or will not take steps to provide the juvenile with an advocate (whether lawyer, parent, social worker, etc.).

   Examples: They'll call his parents. They'll call a lawyer. Lawyer will come to assist him.

7. *Investigative action pursued/avoided*
   Police or others do or do not take steps to seek out evidence of the juvenile's involvement in a crime (apart from continued questioning of the juvenile).

(*continued*)

TABLE E-1 (*continued*)

Examples: They'll look for evidence. Just go on the evidence. They might have some proof he did it. He'd end up telling someone. They'll hold a lineup. They'll find out other ways.

8. *Disposition*
   Favorable or unfavorable judicial decisions, ranging from adjudication decisions to decisions about continued custody or placement.

   Examples: He'll lose the case. He'll get out of it (long term). Put on probation. Sentence him. Send him up. They'll find him guilty.

9. *Court proceedings initiated/avoided*
   Any police or court procedure (or mention of absence of same) which formally moves the case to higher stages in the judicial process.

   Examples: They'll set up court date. He'll get a record. He'll be written up for report. He'll get busted. He'll go to court, hearing, etc. They'll drop charges. They'll postpone hearing until more evidence.

10. *Other*
    Any consequences not meeting criteria for 1–9. Often idiosyncratic.

TABLE E-2. VALUES OF CONSEQUENCES

Strategy	Positive consequence	Negative consequence
Talk/admit	Let go	Put in detention
	Less trouble	Hold for trial
	Go easier	Get sent up
	Put on probation	Get a record
	Shorter sentence	Beat up
Talk/deny	Let go	Get angry
	Go on the evidence	Beat up
	Believe him	Go harder
	Get out of it	Not believe
		Say too much
		Look for the evidence
		Get in trouble
		Get caught
		Might have some proof he did it
Don't talk	Send home	Get angry
	Go on the evidence	Beat up
	Can't do anything	Put in detention

(*continued*)

Table E-2 (*continued*)

Strategy	Positive consequence	Negative consequence
	Call lawyer	Go harder
	Call parents	Think guilty
		Force him
		Get sent up
		Try to get parents to make talk
		Go to court
Ask for a lawyer	Go home	Implies guilt
	Get off	Prove guilty—his job
	Get off for awhile	Set a court date
	Lighter sentence	Set hearing
	Won't incriminate self	Charge against you
	Follow court decision	

Note. Negative consequence has harmful or unpleasant implications. Positive consequence has relatively more favorable, more promising or more pleasant implications.

Table E-3. Short- and Long-Range Consequences

Short-range examples	Long-range examples
Be angry	Sent up
Beat up	Put in training school
Put in detention	Held for trial
Think he's guilty	Get a record
Not believe him	Go easier in court
Ask more questions	Put on probation
Look for evidence—find out; might have some proof	Go harder in court
Think he's lying	Call lawyer, lawyer will help him
Say too much	Nothing they can do
Let go	Put away
Send home	Take lot longer
Charge you	Set up court date
Get in trouble	Set up hearing
Call parents	Get out of it (in relation to court judge)
Out for awhile	
Written up for report	
Get caught	
Get out of it easier (unless mentions judge)	

Note. Long range consequences generally deal with post-interrogation consequences such as the disposition of the case or court-related events or possible legal protection. Short range consequences refer to the immediate interrogation situation and the reactions of police or to the immediate consequences of the situation.

Appendix F

Data Supplementing Chapter 8

TABLE F-1. MEANS ON FOUR CRITICAL ITEMS, FOR AGE AND DELINQUENCY INSTRUCTIONAL CONDITIONS[a]

	Age		Status	
Sample	10–13	15–17	Nondelinquent	Delinquent
Should be allowed to withhold information from police.				
I	2.59	2.86	2.84	2.60
II	2.56	2.70	2.63	2.64
Should not have to provide information to court about own involvement in crime.				
I	2.44	2.66	2.74	2.35[b]
II	2.32	2.72[c]	2.53	2.51
Should have right to decide whether needs lawyer.				
I	3.15	3.64[c]	3.42	3.36
II	3.33	3.47	3.32	3.48
Should have same rights as adults in court.				
I	4.69	4.78	4.79	4.67
II	4.88	5.14	5.22	4.80[d]

[a] Higher means = more favorable attitude toward juveniles' rights. Scores range from 1 to 6.
[b] Nondelinquent vs. delinquent, $p < .02$.
[c] Younger vs. older, $p < .03$.
[d] Nondelinquent vs. delinquent, $p < .003$.

TABLE F-2. CRA SCALE MEANS AND MEAN RATINGS ON CRITICAL ITEMS, BY TYPE OF ADVICE IN HYPOTHETICAL SITUATION

CRA variable and sample	Confess/make statement	Remain silent and/or get lawyer	F
LN			
Sample I	47.75	49.35	5.36[a]
Sample II	47.63	49.62	8.89[a]
LS			
Sample I	19.78	23.24	19.76[b]
Sample II	21.18	22.90	3.50[c]
ES			
Sample I	22.57	23.29	0.99
Sample II	23.24	25.19	4.73[d]
Right to silence, police			
Sample I	2.21	3.03	17.70[b]
Sample II	2.25	2.80	6.35[a]
Right to silence, court			
Sample I	1.82	2.88	30.66[b]
Sample II	1.87	2.75	18.54[b]

[a] $p < .025$.
[b] $p < .001$.
[c] $p < .10$.
[d] $p < .05$.

Appendix G

Research Ethics Procedures

Very careful attention was given to ethical considerations in the conduct of our research with juvenile subjects. Here we describe the procedures which were designed to provide the necessary safeguards and protections for the subjects. Our purpose in this description is not merely archival. Researchers should be held no less accountable for their attention to ethical research procedures than for the integrity of their research design. Further, future researchers might benefit by our description of the way in which we resolved some very difficult issues in research with children whose freedoms are restricted.

The project's ethics procedures were the product of several months of deliberation involving three review groups (in addition to the grant agency). One group, of course, was the St. Louis University Internal Review Board, whose responsibility it was to assure that the research plans met the requirements of HEW guidelines at the outset of the project. Another important reviewing group was the St. Louis County Juvenile Court, which had custody of the juvenile subjects at the time of the study. The court's judiciary, legal staff, public defender, social service chiefs, and detention center supervisor all were involved in formulating procedures which would meet legal and ethical requirements. Finally, a local working panel was formed by the project director specifically to review and monitor the procedures. This panel consisted of a juvenile court attorney, a youth advocate attorney with no prior involvement in the project, and a clinical-research psychologist with no prior involvement or personal relationship with the investigators.

RISKS AND BENEFITS

In general, children whose freedom is being restricted (as in detention) are considered to be a high risk group, and their use as research subjects requires a compelling argument concerning the potential benefits of the research to the subjects or to society. The present study offered little or not direct benefit to the juvenile subjects themselves. On the other hand, the potential benefits of the results in protecting the rights of juveniles in the future was considerable. Further, the use of any sample of juveniles other than those who were in contact with police and the juvenile justice system was likely to lead to equivocal conclusions when attempting to generalize to delinquent populations. Finally, the experimental procedures themselves were considered very unlikely to produce stressful reactions or in any way to negatively effect the juvenile subjects, especially considering the extent of the procedural protections to be described below. Given all of these factors, then, the decision to employ a juvenile sample in a detention center and other restrictive settings was considered justifiable.

CONSENT OF PARENTS

We obtained the consent of the parents of all juveniles who eventually constituted the samples from the boys town and the boys school. Parents received a letter describing the research procedure and identifying it as approved by, but not promoted by, the administration of the boys town or boys school. Mailing was performed by the facilities themselves, thus avoiding the need to reveal parents' names and addresses to the research staff.

Parental consent was not obtained, however, for juveniles who eventually constituted the sample from the detention center. This deviation from the usual ethical policy was approved by the various review boards only after the project had demonstrated a clear justification for the procedure, documented why parental consent could not even be sought, and provided alternative protections. That documentation is summarized as follows.

State law did not require parental consent for the interview or testing of juveniles in detention. Because the juveniles were temporary wards of the court, the law placed authority for such matters in the juvenile court judge or a juvenile officer to whom the judge delegates the authority.

For ethical reasons, however, we wished to obtain parental consent even though the law did not require it. To do so, parents would have had to have been contacted within 24 hours after a juvenile's admission to detention. The reason for this requirement was that the great majority of juveniles did not remain in detention longer than three days. Thus, we would need to test juveniles during the second day of their detention in order to achieve a sample which was representative of the population of detained juveniles. (Testing during the first detention day was ruled out in order to allow juveniles some time to adapt to the detention setting without requests for testing.)

A series of investigations demonstrated to us that we would almost never be able to contact parents to obtain their consent during the first 24–36 hours of juveniles' detention. For example, only 13% of the juveniles remaining in detention beyond 18 hours received a visit from their parents at *any time* during the first 72 hours of their detention stay. Parents who were approached at detention in relation to another research study often confused the research request with the many other demands and questions posed to them by detention officers at the time of their visit. Traveling to parents' homes to request consent also interfered with court procedures; very often probation officers were visiting parents at the same time, in attempts to persuade parents to "take back" their children who were in detention. Finally, phoning the parents would have meant that our sample would have consisted only of juveniles whose parents had phones, and this probably would have reduced the heterogeneity of the sample. Also in regard to a phone procedure, we could not verify the identity of the other party (thus providing a risk of breach of confidentiality and violation of law which protects the anonymity of arrested juveniles), nor could parents have verified our identity.

Given these circumstances, the review boards concluded that juveniles could be approached to volunteer as research subjects without parental consent under certain conditions: (1) the approval of the court, as guardian; (2) the development of a method for screening each individual prospective subject to avoid emotional reactions to testing by certain juveniles; (3) testing no earlier than 24 hours after admission to detention; and (4) an adequate plan for obtaining the informed consent of juveniles, and for assuring confidentiality. The following sections describe these conditions, which eventually were approved by the review boards.

SCREENING AND COURT APPROVAL

The court approved in principle the participation of detained juveniles in this study. In addition, the court assigned a detention staff member, a social worker who supervised other workers in the detention center, to screen juveniles for potential participation in the research study. This was done in the normal course of the social worker's duties, which involved contact with each juvenile during the first day of detention. This person ruled out research participation for any juvenile displaying unusual emotional behavior during the first 24 hours of detention. The screening procedure, in addition to refusal by juveniles themselves, eliminated about one in every twelve juveniles in detention from research participation.

JUVENILES' INFORMED CONSENT

Each potential juvenile subject was approached by a research assistant in the juvenile's detention unit. Juveniles had already been informed by the social worker that they would be approached by university researchers and that they did not have to agree to participate in tbe research.

The research assistant carefully explained who he or she was and that he or she worked for a university and had no association with the court. Juveniles were told that they would be asked questions about "police and courts," but would not be asked to give any personal information about their own experiences. They were told that the questions were only a university study, that the information was not being collected by the court, and that the court would be told nothing about their answers or even whether or not they had participated. They were told the approximate time length of a session, and were assured that if they began the session they could stop at any time they wished. If a juvenile agreed to participate, a consent form was then signed. A juvenile's refusal was not questioned, but was met with reassurance that the refusal was of no consequence.

The monitoring of these procedures was the responsibility of a full-time employee of the research project, a psychologist who was provided a private research office in the detention center (hereafter referred to as the On-Site Project Supervisor).

In the study reported in Chapter 7, a procedure was employed for assessing juveniles' understanding of the information provided to them by research assistants in the informed consent procedure. This assessment occurred at the end of the experimental session. If a juvenile did not meet a certain criterion for understanding, the juvenile was not included in the study sample, on the assumption that the juvenile's responses might have been influenced by a misperception of the researcher's role or the use of the data.

The assessment simply involved five questions: (1) Did the juvenile remember who the research assistant worked for? (2) Did the juvenile think that other juveniles in detention would believe that the assistant worked for a university and not the court? (3) During the session, was the juvenile aware at any time of thinking that the assistant might be working for the court or might report the answers to someone at the court? (4) If so, did it just (a) "cross your mind," or did the juvenile (b) "think about it often"? (5) If the juvenile thought about it often, did the juvenile believe that his or her answers would have been different if this had not been so? A positive answer to question 4b ruled out the inclusion of the juvenile in the research sample.

The final sample of 183 juveniles in the interview study were those out of 192 tested who met the aforementioned requirements for inclusion of their data in the study. The responses of the 192 juveniles who were tested were as follows. Only 54.3% remembered at the end of the session that the experimenter represented a university research group. (Subjects who did not remember were once again informed of the experimenter's identity and associations.) When asked whether most juveniles would believe the experimenter's claim that he or she was not working for the court, 39.1% said that most juveniles probably would not believe this. On the other hand, only 21.8% said that while they were participating in the session, it occurred to them that we might report their answers to the court. Of this last group (42 juveniles), 78.5% said that it had merely crossed their mind and they had decided it was probably not true; the remaining 21.4% (9 juveniles, 4.6% of the 192 tested) said they had thought about it often during the session. These were the juveniles whose data were excluded from the study, even though all nine went on to state that their answers would have been no different if they had believed the sessions were truly confidential.

CONFIDENTIALITY

Raw data forms from each experimental session were taken immediately by assistants to the private detention office of the full-time On-Site Project Supervisor (OPS) for locked filing in the OPS office, with access only to the OPS. Within 48 hours of a session, the OPS obtained necessary demographic information on the juvenile subject from the court's computer records. Demographic information was placed on the raw data form, the juvenile's name was removed, and the form was free of address, code number, or any other device which might allow the data to be identified with the juvenile. This completed, the anonymous data form was then transferred to the university research office. The only record of a juvenile's participation which remained at the detention center was the juvenile's signed (uncoded) consent form. These were stored in a locked file in the OPS office.

MONITORING

Throughout the two years of data collection at the detention center, all of the foregoing procedures were continuously monitored in weekly meetings of the research staff and research assistants and in twice-monthly visits to the detention center by the principal investigator. During the two years, there were no signs of negative effects on any of the juvenile participants, nor were there any complaints or criticisms of our procedures by the court, juveniles, or parents.

References

Aries, P. *Centuries of childhood.* New York: Knopf, 1962.

Asch, S. Studies of independence and conformity: A minority of one against a unanimous majority. *Psychological Monographs,* 1956, *70* (9, Whole No. 416).

Barthel, J. *A death in Canaan.* New York: Dell, 1977.

Bittner, E. *The functions of the police in modern society.* Chevy Chase, Md.: NIMH, Center for Studies of Crime and Delinquency, 1970.

Catton, K., & Erickson, P. *The juvenile's perception of the role of defense counsel in juvenile court.* Unpublished manuscript, Center for Criminology, University of Toronto, Canada, 1975.

Chafee, Z., Pollak, W., & Stern, C. *The third degree.* Washington, D.C.: National Commission on Law Observance and Enforcement, 1931.

Cicourel, A. *The social organization of juvenile justice.* New York: John Wiley, 1968.

Comment. Interrogation of juveniles: The right to a parent's presence. *Dickenson Law Review,* 1972–73, *77,* 543–560.

Connor, W. *The juvenile court: Its impact on children adjudged to be delinquent.* Unpublished Master's Thesis, Center of Criminology, University of Toronto, Canada, 1972.

Copple, C., & Succi, G. The comparative ease of processing standard English and Black nonstandard English by lower-class black children. *Child Development,* 1974, *45,* 1048–1053.

Corbett, J., & Vereb, T. *Juvenile court statistics, 1974.* Washington, D.C.: National Institute for Juvenile Justice and Delinquency Prevention (undated).

Corotto, L. The relation of performance and verbal IQ in acting-out juveniles. *Journal of Psychological Studies,* 1961, *12,* 162–166.

Costanza, P., & Shaw, M. Conformity as a function of age level. *Child Development*, 1966, *37*, 967–975.

Cressey, D., & McDermott, R. *Diversion from the juvenile justice system.* Ann Arbor, Mich.: National Assessment of Juvenile Corrections, 1973.

Davis, S. *Rights of juveniles: The juvenile justice system.* New York: Clark Boardman, 1974.

Davis, W., & Phares, E. Internal-external control as a determinant of information-seeking in a social-influence situation. *Journal of Personality*, 1967, *35*, 547–561.

Driver, E. Confessions and the social psychology of coercion. *Harvard Law Review*, 1968, *82*, 42–61.

D'Zurilla, T., & Goldfried, M. Problem-solving and behavior modification. *Journal of Abnormal Psychology*, 1971, *78*, 107–126.

Ebel, R. *Essentials of educational measurement.* Englewood Cliffs, N.J.: Prentice-Hall, 1972.

Emerson, R. *Judging delinquents: Context and process in juvenile court.* Chicago: Aldine, 1969.

Empey, L. The social construction of childhood, delinquency and social reform. In M. Klein (Ed.), *The juvenile justice system.* Beverly Hills, Cal.: Sage, 1976.

Entwhisle, D. Subcultural differences in children's language development. *International Journal of Psychology*, 1968, *3*, 13–22.

Ferguson, A., & Douglas, A. A study of juvenile waiver. *San Diego Law Review*, 1970, *7*, 39–54.

Ferster, E., & Courtless, T. The beginning of juvenile justice, police practices, and the juvenile offender. *Vanderbilt Law Review*, 1969, *22*, 567–608.

Ferster, E., Courtless, T., & Snethen, E. The juvenile justice system: In search of the role of counsel. *Fordham Law Review*, 1970–71, *39*, 375–412.

Friedman, L. The idea of right as a social and legal concept. *Journal of Social Issues*, 1971, *27*, 189–197.

Galtung, J. *Theory and methods in social research.* New York: Columbia University Press, 1967.

Genden, J. Separate legal representation for children: Protecting the rights and interests of minors in judicial proceedings. *Harvard Civil Rights–Civil Liberties Law Review*, 1976, *11*, 565–595.

Gomolak, N. *Juvenile investigation procedures and interviewing and interrogating juveniles.* Columbia, Mo.: Missouri Law Enforcement Assistance Council, 1973.

Gomolak, N. *Missouri police juvenile officer's manual guide.* Columbia, Mo.: Missouri Council of Criminal Justice, 1975.

Gordon, R. Prevalence: The rare datum in delinquency measurement and its implications for the theory of delinquency. In M. Klein (Ed.), *The juvenile justice system*. Beverly Hills, Cal.: Sage, 1976. Pp. 201–284.

Grambs, J. The self-concept: Basis for re-education of Negro youth. In W. Kvaraceus (Ed.), *Negro self-concept: Implications for school and citizenship*. New York: McGraw-Hill, 1964. Pp. 11–34.

Grisso, T., & Pomicter, C. Interrogation of juveniles: An empirical study of procedures, safeguards, and rights waiver. *Law and Human Behavior*, 1977, *1*, 321–342.

Grisso, T., & Vierling, L. Minors' consent to treatment: A developmental perspective. *Professional Psychology*, 1978, *9*, 412–427.

Gronlund, N. *Readings in measurement and evaluation*. New York: MacMillan, 1968.

Grunder, T. Two formulas for determining the readability of subject consent forms. *American Psychologist*, 1978, *33*, 773–775.

Hathaway, S., & Monachesi, E. *Adolescent personality and behavior: MMPI patterns of normal, delinquent, dropout, and other outcomes*. Minneapolis: University of Minnesota Press, 1963.

Havighurst, R., Bowman, P., Liddle, G., Matthews, C., & Pierce, J. *Growing up in River City*. New York: Wiley, 1962.

Inbau, F., & Reid, J. *Criminal interrogation and confessions*. Baltimore: Williams and Wilkins, 1967.

Institute of Judicial Administration–American Bar Association. *Juvenile justice standards project: Standards relating to pretrial court proceedings*. Cambridge, Mass.: Ballinger, 1977.

Jennings, K. People versus object orientation, social behavior, and intellectual abilities in preschool children. *Developmental Psychology*, 1975, *11*, 511–519.

Jones, H., & Conrad, H. The growth and decline of intelligence. *Genetic Psychology Monographs*, 1933, *13*, 223–298.

Kahn, R., & Connell, C. *The dynamics of interviewing*. New York: Wiley, 1957.

Kardiner, A., & Ovesey, L. *The mark of oppression*. New York: World, 1962.

Katz, I. Negro performance in interracial situations. In P. Watson (Ed.), *Psychology and race*. Chicago: Aldine, 1973. Pp. 256–266.

Kay, R., & Segal, D. The role of the attorney in juvenile court proceedings: A non-polar approach. *Georgetown Law Journal*, 1972–73, *61*, 1401–1424.

Keasey, C., & Sales, B. Children's conception of intentionality and the criminal law. In B. D. Sales (Ed.), *Psychology in the legal process*. New York: Spectrum, 1977, Pp. 127–146.

Keefe, R. Confessions, admissions and the recent curtailment of the fifth amendment protection. *Connecticut Bar Journal,* 1977, *51,* 266.

Kennedy, W., & Vega, M. Negro children's performance on a discrimination task as a function of examiner race and verbal incentive. *Journal of Personality and Social Psychology,* 1965, *2,* 839–843.

Kenney, J., & Pursuit, D. *Police work with juveniles and the administration of juvenile justice.* Springfield, Ill.: C. C. Thomas, 1970.

Kerlinger, F. *Foundations of behavioral research.* New York: Holt, Rinehart, and Winston, 1973.

Kobetz, R. *The police role and juvenile delinquency.* Gaithersburg, Md.: International Association of Chiefs of Police, 1971.

Kohlberg, L. Moral development and identification. In E. Stevenson (Ed.), *Child psychology, 62nd yearbook National Study for Study of Education.* Chicago: University of Chicago Press, 1963. Pp. 277–332.

Kohlberg, L. Development of moral character and moral ideology. In M. L. Hoffman & L. W. Hoffman (Eds.), *Review of child development research* (Vol. I). New York: Russell Sage, 1964.

Kohlberg, L. Stage and sequence: The cognitive-developmental approach to socialization. In D. Goslin (Ed.), *Handbook of socialization theory and research.* Chicago: Rand McNally, 1969. Pp. 347–480.

Labov, W. The logic of nonstandard English. In F. Williams (Ed.), *Language and poverty.* Chicago: Markham, 1970.

Landsman, K., & Minow, M. Lawyering for the child: Principles of representation in custody and visitation disputes arising from divorce. *Yale Law Journal,* 1978, *87,* 1125–1190.

Lefcourt, H., & Wine, J. Internal versus external control of reinforcement and the deployment of attention in experimental situations. *Canadian Journal of Behavioral Science,* 1969, *1,* 167–181.

Lemert, E. *Instead of court: Diversion in juvenile justice.* Chevy Chase, Md.: NIMH, Center for Studies of Crime and Delinquency, 1971.

Loevinger, J. *Ego development: Concepts and theories.* San Francisco: Josey-Bass, 1976.

Manoogian, S. Factors affecting juveniles' comprehension of *Miranda* rights. Unpublished doctoral dissertation, St. Louis University, 1978.

McMillian, T., & McMurtry, D. The role of the defense lawyer in the juvenile court: Advocate or social worker? *St. Louis University Law Review,* 1969–70, *14,* 561–603.

Melton, G. Children's rights: Children's own concepts and attitudes. Paper presented at the meeting of the American Psychological Association, New York City, September, 1979.

Merton, R., Fisk, M., & Kendall, P. *The focused interview.* Glencoe, Ill.: Free Press, 1956.

Milgram, S. Behavioral study of obedience. *Journal of Abnormal and Social Psychology*, 1963, *67*, 371–378.

Miller, G. Some preliminaries to psycholinguistics. *American Psychologist*, 1965, *20*, 15–20.

Muuss, R. The relationship between causal orientation, anxiety, and insecurity in elementary school children. *Journal of Educational Psychology*, 1960, *51*, 122–129.

National Advisory Commission on Criminal Justice Standards and Goals. *A national strategy to reduce crimes*. Washington, D.C.: U.S. Government Printing Office, 1973.

Nejelski, P. Diversion: Unleashing the hound of heaven. In M. Rosenheim (Ed.), *Pursuing justice for the child*. Chicago: University of Chicago Press, 1976. Pp. 94–118.

Palermo, D. Racial comparisons and additional normative data on the Children's Manifest Anxiety Scale. *Child Development*, 1959, *30*, 53–57.

Patel, A., & Gordon, J. Some personal and situational determinants of yielding to influence. *Journal of Abnormal and Social Psychology*, 1960, *61*, 411–418.

Paulsen, M., & Whitebread, C. *Juvenile law and procedure*. Reno, Nev.: National Council of Juvenile Court Judges, 1974.

Piersma, P., Ganousis, J., & Kramer, P. The juvenile court: Current problems, legislative proposals, and a model act. *St. Louis University Law Journal*, 1975, *20*, 1–99. Reprinted as monograph by *St. Louis University Law Journal*, 1976.

Piersma, P., Ganousis, J., Volenik, A., Swanger, H., & Connell, P. *Law and tactics in juvenile cases*. Philadelphia: American Law Institute–American Bar Association, 1977.

Piliavin, I., & Briar, S. Police encounters with juveniles. *American Journal of Sociology*, 1964, *70*, 206–214.

Platt, A. *The child savers*. Chicago: University of Chicago Press, 1969.

Platt, J., Spivack, G., Altman, N., Altman, D., & Peizer, S. Adolescent problem-solving thinking. *Journal of Consulting and Clinical Psychology*, 1974, *42*, 787–793.

President's Commission on Law Enforcement and Administration of Justice. *Task force report: Juvenile delinquency and youth crime*. Washington, D.C.: U.S. Government Printing Office, 1967.

Quay, L. Language dialect, reinforcement, and the intelligence test performance of Negro children. *Child Development*, 1971, *42*, 5–15.

Quay, L. Language, dialect, and intelligence test performance in disadvantaged black children. *Child Development*, 1974, *45*, 463–468.

Rafkey, D., & Sealey, R. The adolescent and the law: A survey. *Crime and Delinquency*, 1975, *21*, 131–138.

Rogers, C., & Wrightsman, L. Attitudes toward children's rights: Nurturance or self-determination? *Journal of Social Issues*, 1978, *34*, 59–68.

Rogers, P., & Rogers, C. Children's rights: Attitudes as a function of intrinsic developmental perspective. Paper presented at the meeting of the American Psychological Association, New York, September, 1979.

Ross, J. The middle-class in urban Italy, fourteenth to early sixteenth century. In L. de Mause (Ed.), *The history of childhood*. New York: Psychohistory Press, 1974.

Roth, L., Meisel, J., & Lidz, C. Tests of competency to consent to treatment. *American Journal of Psychiatry*, 1977, *134*, 279–283.

Rotter, J. *Social learning and clinical psychology*, Englewood Cliffs, N.J.: Prentice-Hall, 1954.

Rotter, J., Chance, J., & Phares, E. *Application of a social learning theory in personality*. New York: Holt, Rinehart, and Winston, 1972.

Rules of practice and procedure in juvenile courts. Columbia, Mo.: Supreme Court of Missouri, reprinted by Institute of Public Safety, College of Public and Community Services, University of Missouri, Vol. 2, No. 2, April, 1976.

Sarason, I. Empirical findings and theoretical problems in the use of anxiety scales. *Psychological Bulletin*, 1960, *57*, 403–415.

Schlossman, S. *Love and the American delinquent: The theory and practice of "progressive" juvenile justice, 1825–1920*. Chicago: University of Chicago Press, 1977.

Schontz, F. *Research methods in personality*. New York: Appleton-Century-Crofts, 1965.

Seeburger, R., & Wettick, R. *Miranda* in Pittsburgh: A statistical study. *University of Pittsburgh Law Review*, 1967, *29*, 1–26.

Seeman, M., & Evans, J. Alienation and learning in a hospital setting. *American Sociological Review*, 1962, *27*, 772–783.

Selltiz, C., Wrightsman, L., & Cook, S. *Research methods in social relations*. New York: Holt, Rinehart, and Winston, 1976.

Selman, R., & Damon, W. The necessity (but insufficiency) of social perspective taking for conceptions of justice at three early levels. In D. J. DePalma & J. M. Foley (Eds.), *Moral development: Current theory and research*. Hillsdale, N.J.: Lawrence Erlbaum, 1975.

Shantz, C. The development of social cognition. In E. M. Hetherington (Ed.), *Review of child development research* (Vol. 5.) Chicago: University of Chicago Press, 1975.

Shure, M., & Spivack, G. *A mental health program for mothers of young children: An interpersonal problem-solving approach toward social adjust-*

ment. (Report of research and training, MH-20372.) Washington, D.C.: National Institute of Mental Health, 1975.

Silberman, C. *Criminal violence, criminal justice.* New York: Random House, 1978.

Spence, J., & Spence, K. The motivational components of manifest anxiety: Drive and drive stimuli. In C. Speilberger (Ed.), *Anxiety and behavior.* New York: Academic Press, 1966. Pp. 291–326.

Spivack, G., & Shure, M. *Social adjustment of young children: A cognitive approach to solving real-life problems.* San Francisco: Jossey-Bass, 1974.

Spivack, G., & Swift, M. The Devereux Elementary School Behavior Rating Scale: A study of the nature and organization of achievement related disturbed classroom behavior. *Journal of Special Education,* 1966, *1,* 71–90.

Spivack, G., Platt, J., & Shure, M. *The problem-solving approach to adjustment.* San Francisco: Jossey-Bass, 1976.

Stapleton, W., & Teitelbaum, L. *In defense of youth.* New York: Russel Sage, 1972.

Tapp, J. Psychology and the law: An overture. In M. Rosenzweig & L. Porter (Eds.), *Annual review of psychology.* Palo Alto, Cal.: Annual Reviews, 1976. Pp. 258–404.

Tapp, J., & Kohlberg, L. Developing senses of law and legal justice. *Journal of Social Issues,* 1971, *27,* 65–91.

Tapp, J., & Levine, F. Legal socialization: Strategies for an ethical legality. *Stanford Law Review,* 1974, *27,* 1–72.

Tapp, J., & Levine, F. Epilogue for psychology and law. In J. Tapp & F. Levine (Eds.), *Law, justice, and the individual in society.* New York: Holt, Rinehart, and Winston, 1977. Pp. 363–368.

Teitelbaum, L., & Ellis, J. The liberty interest of children: Due process rights and their application. *Mental Disability Law Reporter,* 1978, *2,* 582–603.

Torney, J. Socialization of attitudes toward the legal system. In J. Tapp & F. Levine (Eds.), *Law, justice, and the individual in society.* New York: Holt, Rinehart, and Winston, 1977. Pp. 134–144.

Turnure, C. Cognitive development and role-taking ability in boys and girls from 7 to 12. *Developmental Psychology,* 1975, *11,* 202–209.

Veillard-Cybulska, H. Interviewers, interviewees, and procedures: The human and material aspects of the questioning of children and adolescents. *International Child Welfare Review,* 1976, *30–31,* 69–83.

Verenberg, E., & Verenberg, J. Early diversion from the criminal justice system: Practice in search of a theory. In L. Ohlin (Ed.), *Prisoners in America.* Englewood Cliffs, N.J.: Prentice-Hall, 1973. Pp. 151–183.

Walker, S. The lawyer–child relationship: A statistical analysis. *Duquesne Law Review*, 1971, *9*, 627–650.

Wechsler, D. *The measurement and appraisal of adult intelligence*. Baltimore: Williams and Wilkins, 1955.

Wechsler, D. *Manual for the Wechsler Intelligence Scale for Children—Revised*. New York: Psychological Corporation, 1974.

Weins, A., Matarazzo, J., & Gaver, K. Performance and verbal IQ in a group of sociopaths. *Journal of Clinical Psychology*, 1959, *15*, 191–193.

Weinstein, E. The development of interpersonal competence. In D. A. Goslin (Ed.), *Handbook of socialization theory and research*. Chicago: McNally, 1969.

Weiss, C. Interviewing in evaluation research. In E. Struening & M. Guttentag (Eds.), *Handbook of evaluation research*. Beverly Hills, Cal.: Sage, 1975, Pp. 355–395.

Williams, R., & Rivers, W. The effects of language on the test performance of black children. In G. Koocher (Ed.), *Children's rights and the mental health professions*. New York: John Wiley, 1976. Pp. 205–218.

Wilson, J. *Varieties of police behavior*. Cambridge, Mass.: Harvard University Press, 1969.

Wolfgang, M., Figlio, R., & Sellin, T. *Delinquency in a birth cohort*. Chicago: University of Chicago Press, 1972.

Wrightsman, L., Rogers, C., & Percy, J. *Conceptualization and measurement of attitudes toward children's rights*. Nashville, Tenn.: George Peabody College, 1976. (ERIC Document Reproduction Service No. ED-118-262).

Zimring, F. Measuring the impact of pretrial diversion from the criminal justice system. *University of Chicago Law Review*, 1974, *41*, 224–241.

Index

MIX
Papier aus verantwortungsvollen Quellen
Paper from responsible sources
FSC® C105338

If you have any concerns about our products,
you can contact us on
ProductSafety@springernature.com

In case Publisher is established outside the EU,
the EU authorized representative is:
Springer Nature Customer Service Center GmbH
Europaplatz 3, 69115 Heidelberg, Germany

Printed by Libri Plureos GmbH
in Hamburg, Germany